Bat, Ball & Bible

Related Titles from Potomac Books

The Most Famous Woman in Baseball: Effa Manley
and the Negro Leagues
—Bob Luke

Pull Up a Chair: The Vin Scully Story
—Curt Smith

A Tale of Three Cities: The 1962 Baseball Season
in New York, Los Angeles, and San Francisco
—Steven Travers

Heroes & Ballyhoo: How the Golden Age of the 1920s
Transformed American Sports
—Michael K. Bohn

Bat, Ball & Bible

Baseball and Sunday Observance in New York

CHARLES DEMOTTE

Potomac Books
Washington, D.C.

Library of Congress Cataloging-in-Publication Data
DeMotte, Charles, 1943–
    Bat, ball & bible : baseball and Sunday observance in New York / Charles DeMotte.
        p. cm.
    Includes bibliographical references and index.
    ISBN 978-1-59797-947-4 (hardcover : alk. paper)
    ISBN 978-1-59797-948-1 (electronic)
    1. Baseball—New York (State)—History. 2. Baseball—Religious aspects—Christianity. 3. Sunday legislation—New York (State)—History. 4. New York (State)—Politics and government. 5. New York (State)—Religious life and customs. I. Title.
    GV863.N72D46 2013
    796.35709747—dc23
                                                                        2012034516

Printed in the United States of America on acid-free paper that meets the American National Standards Institute Z39-48 Standard.

Potomac Books
22841 Quicksilver Drive
Dulles, Virginia 20166

First Edition

10 9 8 7 6 5 4 3 2 1

To my father, who lived in Brooklyn
when the Sunday observance laws were in full force,
and to my brother,
who learned to love baseball

Contents

Acknowledgments

Every book is to some degree a collective effort, requiring the thoughts and help of many people. No less important is the kind support and interest expressed by sundry people who have encouraged me greatly over the years while I have been working on this project. I would like to give thanks to the staff at the National Baseball Hall of Fame and Museum's A. Bartlett Giamatti Research Center for their help—especially Freddie Berowski and Tim Wiles, who supplied me with much useful resource material and ideas. Special recognition goes to Gabriel Schechter, who read through my manuscript with a fine-tooth comb and whose comments and corrections contributed greatly to its quality. My thanks go also to Scott Fiesthumel, who supplied me with material on Utica baseball; Lisa Neilson for some documents on Hudson Valley baseball; Katherine Chansky, librarian/archivist at the Schenectady County Historical Society for information on Schenectady baseball; and to Tony Kissel for his beneficial suggestions. Thanks to my friend Dr. William J. Armstrong, who kindly read through the manuscript and proffered his opinions. Help with photographs and illustrations was rendered by Cecilia Tan, editor at the Society for American Baseball Research; Boris Hristov Michev, maps and geospatial information librarian at Cornell University's Olin Library; Donna Eschenbrenner, archivist at the History

Center in Tompkins County; Pat Kelly, photo archivist at the Hall of Fame Library; and Sarah Kozma, archivist at the Onondaga Historical Association. My deep appreciation goes to Elizabeth Demers, senior editor, and the staff at Potomac Books, for making this book possible. Lastly, thanks to my wife, Jane, for her past, present, and future love and support.

Introduction

Living as we do in a secular and commercial society, the old blue laws that once conditioned behavior on Sundays would appear to be as quaint as the proverbial dodo bird. But to those of us who have lived far into our mature years, the twilight of Sunday restrictions are within memory. Largely forgotten is the reality experienced by my father and those of his generation of a time when Sunday laws, if not absolute in their enforcement, defined the mode of life on the first day of each week.

It is easy to overstate the importance of one's topic. Sunday observance never had the transformative power of other contemporary moral and social movements such as temperance, woman's suffrage, and urban reform. Nevertheless, it had tremendous symbolic importance, which gave the Sabbath significance far beyond its social impact. Baseball, as the national pastime, stood near the pinnacle of this controversy, and to some extent the fight over Sunday baseball reflected the tensions within society and gave them expression.

Sunday baseball was woven into the fabric of social life in New York State over the last quarter of the nineteenth century and the first two decades of the twentieth century. While other studies touching on Sunday restrictions have focused on major league baseball, the approach of this book is to explore the many levels of the sport within a particular state. Whichever way one cares to view the origins of modern baseball, whether the invalidated Doubleday myth or as fact, it all began in the Empire State; hence, technically, baseball is the New York game. Also, as the most populous and influential state at the time, with a more diverse mix of people than the rest of the nation, New York stands as a representative composite of the nation.

Second, concentration on a particular state provides a more distinctive and precise contrast of urban and rural values, mentalities, social connections, and the patterns of life that framed the Sunday baseball debate. A hundred years ago America was a society dominated by regional concerns, intimate networks, and the predominance of local government. Sunday baseball was defined by state laws and politics, local ordinances, and traditional customs. Life was parochial for the vast majority of those living in New York and elsewhere, so to get an accurate historical picture one needs to take a more grassroots approach.

Finally, no one social and moral phenomena, such as the battle over Sunday observance, can be understood without its relation to other such movements (e.g., temperance, the crusades against gambling, boxing, and other such activities). The debate over Sunday observance laws covered not only baseball but these other sports and recreational pursuits. By the same token Sunday drinking, theatrical productions (and later motion-picture shows), as well as a plethora of commercial activities, were affected by such restrictions. In an increasingly complex society where the demand for more leisure time cut across all classes, rigid Sunday restrictions would eventually prove untenable. Sunday baseball was thus a thread woven into the complex web of the state's moral and social order.

Deep cleavages in New York society prolonged the battle over Sunday baseball. Class, racial, religious, and ethnic divisions conditioned the mindsets of people who formed the generations of the late nineteenth and early twentieth centuries. Class snobbery was rampant. Middle-class industrialists, merchants, bankers, affluent farmers, professionals, and others looked with distain and suspicion upon the lower orders whose numbers, thanks to immigration, were growing exponentially. Nativist rural Protestants saw the city as a multicultural cesspool, causing a threat to law and order, and spawning a host of legal and moral reform initiatives. Urbanites viewed country folk as ignorant and backward and, borrowing a phrase from Karl Marx, were dismissive of "the idiocy of rural life." African Americans in New York during this period of heightened segregation were largely invisible and always susceptible to overt forms of violence, discrimination, and abuse.

Shifts in demography underscored an unprecedented array of social changes. Between 1790 and 1830 the state's population increased at a faster rate than the entire nation, but somewhat less so between 1830 and 1890. The population of New York again mushroomed from 5,082,871 in 1880 to 10,385,227 in 1920. After a dip in the 1890s, immigration soared to unprecedented levels during the first two decades of the twentieth century. Between 1900 and 1917, over 17 million immigrants entered the United States, mostly through the port of New York, with a single-year total exceeding one million in 1905. Only World War I and immigration law reform, culminating in the Quota Act of 1924, stemmed the tide. Not surprisingly, the New York City area accounted for much of the state's population. Between 1880 and 1920 the percentage of population in the city, compared to the rest of the state, rose from 23.7 to 54.1 percent.[1]

Natural increases accounted somewhat for a share of this growth given that the age structure of the population was relatively young. The biggest impetus, however, came from an unprecedented wave of incoming aliens—mostly from Central and Eastern Europe, who passed through Ellis Island in tsunami proportions. Many, if not most, of these newcomers remained in the metropolis but a significant number fanned across the state, attracted to jobs in mills, fields, and smaller commercial enterprises. Erie County, inclusive of Buffalo, the state's second-largest metropolitan region, received over 100,000 foreign-born residents each decade between 1890 and 1940. Rochester and Monroe County claimed between 51,000 and 72,000 immigrants over the same period, while other mill towns and cities attracted a more modest number.

By contrast, nineteen of New York's sixty-two counties actually saw its population decrease between 1875 and 1915. Furthermore, counties such as Chenango, Lewis, Madison, and Tioga saw the numbers of aliens decline over this same period. According to the 1900 census, Schuyler County alone lost nine hundred residents over a ten-year period, leaving behind many vacant farms. Unable to attract tenants due to a lack of employment options, immigrants had a relatively small impact in rural areas, and the many small cities, towns, and villages across the state remained overwhelmingly Protestant and native-born in contrast to the sizeable Catholic and Jewish demographic compositions of the larger cities, particularly New York.[2]

Local newspapers were contemptuous of foreigners, and accounts of alien residents depicted with ethnic and racial stereotypes abounded. Violence and depredations attributed to Italian "Black Hand" societies only reinforced these images. A report by Baron Edmondo Mayor des Planches, the Italian ambassador to the United States, sought to refute the widely held notion of Italian immigrants depicted in the press as stupid, violent, and capable only of the most menial jobs. Drawing upon sociological research, he suggested that Italian immigrants were industrious, willing, frugal, well behaved, and progressive. At the same time, the ambassador characterized the immigrant as simple and natural. Second-generation Italians, he claimed, quickly adopted American ways. President Theodore Roosevelt believed that the country's size and stable institutions could accommodate the great mass of foreigners but that laws should be passed and character assessments made so as to allow only the "better sort" of immigrant.[3]

In the metropolis, however, immigration was the catalyst that fueled an acceleration of manufacturing, which established New York as the financial and industrial hub of the nation. The city was home to the great financial and industrial barons of the age such as J. P. Morgan, W. K. Vanderbilt, August Belmont, John Jacob Astor, and others who, by hook or by crook, amassed huge fortunes that they invested in railroads and a host of other heavy industries. Bankers and wealthy capitalists engineered mergers that produced leviathan trusts and monopolies, placing the vagaries of state and national economies in the hands of the few. As an engine of commerce, the metropolis generated a free-market culture that spawned myriad individual entrepreneurs, sweatshops, business ventures, gamblers and shysters, and petty and not-so-petty criminals, all driven to get ahead by the competitive ethos of predatory capitalism. Commercial values favored a lifestyle of incessant activity, whether at work or play, thus increasingly marginalizing the quiet and more contemplative aspects of daily life.

Outside New York City and the larger urban centers the state was a different world. Depopulated rural villages and landscapes stood in contrast to the teeming multitudes of the metropolis. The idyllic image of virtuous rural life in reality consisted of long hours of grueling work, too little leisure time, and a narrowness of intellectual pursuits leading to psychological lethargy and the instinct for exclusion. Rural life centered on local churches that provided spiritual comfort and a venue for social engagement. The traditional folkways of those living on farms or in villages structured the rhythms of life week by week, month by month, and year by year. Hard manual work was the norm Mondays through Saturdays, punctuated by seasonal picnics and fairs, patriotic and religious holidays, meetings of fraternal orders, tent meetings and traveling entertainers, social clubs, and general neighborliness.

Sunday was largely sacrosanct. Growing up in the 1890s near Ithaca, Mrs. Elsie Williams Robinson recalled that Sunday was different from every other day of the week. They went to church and then to Sunday school. Sunday afternoons were long, as the children could neither go outdoors to play nor enjoy card games indoors. They could play the piano and sing hymns and perhaps have a game of dominoes or checkers, but for the most part all activity came to a standstill.[4]

In a society divided along class, ethnic, racial, and geographic lines, the maintenance of moral and legal authority was of utmost concern. "Close to the center of each theory of social change," writes Robert Wiebe, "lay the problem of society's cohesion." Inherent in this statement is the question, what was the glue that held populations together? Clearly, structured societies are characterized by reinforcing layers of authority. Customs and folkways establish a rhythm of life that provides one level of cohesion. Institutions such as family, church, and school are another such level. Finally, the formal apparatus of law, police, and the courts are the coercive level of control.[5]

It stands to reason that in the rural and less populated regions of the state, traditional folkways and personal relationships ensured some degree of control backed, of course, by the full weight of the law. In the largely impersonal metropolis, and a few other places where widely accepted conventional norms and values were less binding, formalized types of control were more pervasive and necessary. In either case the tension between law and order and massive deviance and disorder was a delicate balance. During times of rapid changes, such as the period under consideration, even the slightest challenge to this balance conjured up strong fears and resistance. This was one reason why the Sunday baseball question loomed so large.

The center ring in the battle over Sunday baseball in New York was in Brooklyn. The borough was one of the fastest-growing regions in the country during the late nineteenth and early twentieth centuries. Unlike Manhattan, Brooklyn was a city of homes and communities where baseball could rely on an overspill population moving into previously open spaces. It was an area where impersonality outside of intimate social networks was the norm. As a region containing a mixture of classes, a strong denominational presence of many faiths and churches, a blend of nativist and immigrant peoples, and a home to professional, semi-pro, and amateur baseball, Brooklyn was a composite of the diverse and conflicting tensions and interests that characterized New York as a whole.

The place of Sunday baseball within the shifting tides of moral and social order is the central theme of this book. Since Sabbath observance preceded the formation of the republic, it posited a moral structure based on custom. The prevailing idea of order in Puritan Massachusetts, writes David Hackett Fischer, was a condition of putting everything in its proper place so as to achieve organic unity. Putting things in their proper place meant there was a time for work and a time for play, a time for activity and a time for rest, a time for commerce and enterprise, and a time to perform one's spiritual and religious duties. Upholders of Sabbath observance rode the wave of a traditional moral order based on folkways, narrow interpretations of religious doctrine, and the savvy use of political power to hold the line on Sunday baseball, despite shifting demographics and changes in public opinion.[6]

The need to establish a balance between community control by adherence to traditional norms and reform predicated on personal liberty dominated the period when the Sunday baseball issue reached its height in New York. This was especially the case with respect to the working classes, who were perceived by the more conservative elements of the middle class (particularly the nativist Protestant faction) as requiring constant government, which the blue laws to some degree afforded. Whether one was a Sabbatarian or a proponent of a more liberalized or continental Sunday, the problem of securing order within a free society remained the same. Although extreme language was often used in debating the question of Sunday baseball, the courts and to a lesser extent legislative bodies worked to find a balance compatible to opposing moral ideals and social sensibilities.

Moral conflicts in American society can largely be seen in terms of shifting mentalities, usually reflected in public opinion, from which laws are made. Changes in laws and policies involve modification of previously held ideals. One such instance was temperance and the crusade against saloons that evolved in tandem with the Sunday observance question and in many ways overlapped it.

The temperance movement, supported by a coalition of women's groups, rural churches, and a host of religious-related organizations such as the Women's Christian Temperance Union and the Anti-Saloon League, saw alcohol as the source of many, if not most, social problems. Grassroots organization, political pressure, and a little manipulation led to the passage of the Eighteenth Amendment in 1919 and the Volstead Act. The consequences of banning the sale and trafficking of alcoholic beverages aroused widespread opposition among all classes, which caused a shift in public attitudes. The Twenty-First Amendment, repealing prohibition, took the federal government out of the enforcement business and returned it to the states. Many states soon required bars and taverns to operate within restricted hours, to close on Sundays (or at least part of the day), and to prohibit the sale of liquor to or in the presence of minors.

In many ways Sunday observance was the reverse of the temperance question. Up into the early years of the twentieth century it was widely accepted that playing baseball and other sports on Sunday constituted a violation of divine and civil law. Within a few decades, however, open violation of the legal Sunday prohibitions provided evidence that a growing number of New Yorkers were indifferent at best to restrictions imposed on the first day of the week. In time, indifference translated into serious questioning about the viability of the penal laws related to the Sabbath. The result was a protracted battle in which the more traditional forces held sway until the period of the First World War. When liberalization of the Sunday law with respect to baseball finally came about, it did not tread too harshly on the toes of those folks who believed the Sabbath to be a sacred day. The war of words, the legal battles, and the various legislative initiatives led to efforts to find some point of reasonable compromise.

1

The Battle Lines: Blue Laws, Religion, and the Evolution of Baseball

When the Puritans arrived on the shores of North America in the early seventeenth century, they brought with them a vision of a moral community based on a social order that was normative, homogeneous, hierarchical, and local. Moral communities, so conceived, were derivatives of the twin concepts of order and liberty. It was generally accepted that liberty, or individual freedom, meaning freedom from restraint, could only occur in an environment where order was perpetuated by hierarchies of enforced discipline. To the Puritans, order was a self-reinforcing concept that preserved the stability. The image of a society predicated on moral communities had a persistent lifespan and endured well into the twentieth century.

The Puritans were Calvinists, a theology rooted in independent churches that stood as pillars of moral authority. The Puritans looked to Christian scripture as the basis for their new society. Even a casual reader of the Bible would have been aware of the many pronouncements upholding Sabbath observance. As the fourth of the Ten Commandments, the sanctity of the Sabbath was not only a directive from God but was, according to the Puritans, an imperative for a civil society. Among the hundred-plus references to the Sabbath in the Old Testament, most of them in the Pentateuch, which are the first five books of the Old Testament dealing with Jewish law, one could turn for instance to Exodus 35:27 and be told, "Work is to be done for six days but the seventh is to be a holy day for you, a day of complete rest consecrated to Yahweh," the Hebrew word for God in the Bible. The question is, of course, what constitutes work? This was a matter that not only troubled Old Testament scholars but Sunday observance advocates as well, since nowhere in the Pentateuch is work actually defined. Puritan folkways interpreted cessation from work as not engaging in ordinary weekday activities, although later generations would develop their own interpretation.

Moreover, since not one of the commandments carried any more weight than any other, keeping the Sabbath could be seen to be as important in God's eye as the strictures against murder, adultery, bearing false witness, worshiping other gods, and so forth.

Puritan moral communities saw all of their daily activities in light of religious obligations. Hard work and obedience to authority were concerted virtues that assumed the status of moral imperatives. There is some debate with regard to how the Puritans viewed leisure. The image of the Puritans as dour, humorless killjoys has largely been debunked, which is not to say that they were amenable to the various forms of recreation at their disposal. Sanctioned games and sports played during the week may have been looked upon with suspicion and contempt, but they would not have resulted in a prosecution unless a disturbance was created, usually from too much rowdiness or noise. Such activities on the Sabbath, however, were a completely different story. Essentially, ball sports were tolerated during the week but never on Sundays. Blood sports and all forms of gambling were always strictly forbidden.[1]

The Blue Laws

Central to Puritan theology was the idea of a covenant that established a binding relationship between God and his people. Not long after the first settlers put their feet on American soil, the civil authorities imposed strict codes of conduct regarding Sunday observance. The term "blue laws" seems to have come into use among liberal thinkers in England sometime during the seventeenth century as a reference to strict moralists of every persuasion, most particularly the Presbyterians. The first codified blue laws in the American colonies originated in Connecticut in 1656. This law forbade all ordinary labor on the Sabbath, or any work that may have been lawful on other days. The Massachusetts laws of 1672 charged the tithingmen to apprehend and arrest Sabbath breakers, tipplers, and keepers of licensed houses. After the region of New York was liberated from the Dutch, the Duke of York's Law of 1664 made it a violation to affront or disturb any congregation on the first day of the week. In 1695, the colonial General Assembly of New York passed an Act against Profanation of the Lord's Day, which forbade Sunday fishing, sporting, or playing games of any kind. These statutes were later incorporated into the state constitution in 1777 and became part of New York's penal code.[2]

What emerged in 1778 was the Act for Suppressing Immorality, which became the first state statute in New York dealing with Sabbath observance. This piece of legislation was essentially a restatement of the 1695 act. Prohibitions against Sunday sports were, directly or indirectly, scattered throughout the penal code. The principal clause was section 2145, pertaining to sports on Sunday, stating that "all shooting, hunting, playing, horseracing, gaming or other public sports, exercises or shows upon the first day of the week, and all noise unreasonably disturbing the peace of the day are prohibited."[3]

This restraint was reinforced by section 263 of the penal code, limiting all manner of servile labor on Sunday excepting works of necessity and charity. Section 265, which pertained specifically to public sports, was essentially a restatement of section 2145. Prohibitions against commercial activity on Sunday were contained in sections 266 and 267 of the penal code. Willful disruption, interruption, or disquietude of any assemblage of people met for religious worship constituted a violation under section 274 of the law, whereas section 275 specifically defined these infractions. All Sabbath day offences were misdemeanors subject to punishments laid out in section 269 of the statutes. With only minor changes, these provisions remained in effect until 1919.[4]

New York City, because of its size and stature, became the focus of laws of special application relating to Sunday observance. An 1860 law forbade various kinds of exhibitions on Sunday under the threat of heavy fines. Moreover, an 1872 law eliminated processions on the Sabbath, except for funerals and religious services. Theatrical and operatic shows in the city on

Sunday were forbidden by a special act passed in 1882. In each case the penalties for violating the law were more stringent than those previously prescribed under the penal code.[5]

Although the legal restrictions on Sunday activities contained particular admonitions, there was still ample scope for interpretation. Did the prohibition on all public sports include a group of boys having an innocent game of catch in the park, as opposed to more organized games? Were games and recreational sports played at a distance from residential areas permissible? What actually was meant by "unreasonable noise and disturbing the peace of the day"? How far could a baseball team go in soliciting financial support for Sunday games without falling afoul of the law? As we shall see, these were questions that would entertain the courts with respect to Sunday baseball in New York for years.

A careful reading of the statutes also indicates a clear distinction between public and private activities. Thus a baseball game, or any other form of recreation, on private grounds would appear to be legal under the statutes, whereas similar activities on a municipal lot would be in violation of the law. However, any such game, private or public, would seem to contravene certain sections of the penal code if it disturbed the repose of the community or the sensibilities of any one individual.

Further, there is little mention in the literature pertaining to the obvious question of constitutionality. Does the state have the right to restrict all public activities on Sunday that have no religious connection? An answer to this question was given by Judge Walter Cain Ong, who handed down a ruling from the bench in Cleveland in 1897. He held that the Sunday baseball law in that state was unconstitutional because it was impossible to prohibit citizens from doing anything on the first day of the week that was not unlawful to do other days of the week simply because that day happened to be a Sunday. Since Sabbath laws and ordinances varied from state to state and even from locality to locality, constitutional issues were subject to a more limited interpretation. Sunday observance questions were largely seen by contemporaries in light of their impact in upholding morality and social order. Little mention was made of the rights of the individual to do what he or she pleased on the Sabbath.[6]

While most states (with the exception of those in the far west) had laws prohibiting Sunday activities, there was great variation as to specifics and levels of enforcement. Illinois law forbade any disturbance of the peace on Sunday, but did not specify any restrictions on sports played that day. On the other hand, Kansas outlawed all games and public sports on Sundays. So did Minnesota, until the law was amended in 1905 to allow sports if engaged in an orderly manner. The Missouri statutes prohibited the sale of liquor on the Sabbath but were mute on the question of Sunday sports. Ohio law prohibited persons over the age of fourteen from engaging in sporting activities on the first day of the week, yet was vague enough to enable localities to pass ordinances allowing or inhibiting games as they saw fit. Public sports were specifically disallowed in South Carolina, but not in Tennessee. If a ballpark in Texas opened on a Sunday, it could be classified as a place of public amusement, making the owner liable for a fine.[7]

In the Northeast the Puritan interpretation of the Sabbath dominated, whereas in other parts of the country local norms tolerated orderly forms of recreation and amusement within a framework of regulations. This more flexible interpretation of the law, known as the continental Sunday, was imported by immigrants, largely from Germany, during the nineteenth century. Such variations were widely seen by nativist groups as a threat to American democratic institutions. Certainly the issue aroused strong passions. When the state government of New York introduced a police force into New York City in 1857, rumors that beer would no longer be sold on Sundays led to rioting. For their part, Germans became an important voting bloc within the Democratic Party, which was more favorably disposed to relaxing Sunday restrictions. In time, the continental Sunday would gradually supersede more rigid social conventions; however, legally, the Puritan Sabbath remained in place in New York and its neighboring states for a much longer period. As was so often the case in the United States with respect to moral issues, pluralism eventually trumped universal absolutes.[8]

Religion and Sunday Observance

The first European immigrants to New York were the Dutch, who initially settled in Manhattan and the surrounding area, then later extended their claim and influence up the Hudson River valley. The Dutch were also Calvinists but had a more relaxed view of the Sabbath than that of the Puritans. They were not opposed to legal restrictions but displayed a more casual attitude toward enforcing Sunday laws.

Even before the period of English rule, the religious picture in New York had grown more diverse. In the metropolis the Reformed church held a dominant but not exclusive position. After the British conquest of New Amsterdam, English Anglican churches began to appear. The colony quickly established a policy of toleration toward other Protestant churches, including Congregationalists, Baptists, and Quakers. Immigration from Northern Ireland and Germany brought Presbyterians and Lutherans respectively, which further added to the religious mix.

After the Revolution, central New York was surveyed and divided into lots known as the Military Tract, with land taken from the native inhabitants and given to soldiers, based on rank, in lieu of payment for their services in the war. Sales of land led to greater subdivisions, and soon farms and small settlements dotted the landscape of the various townships, which then coalesced into counties. Migration from New England was also a major factor in the population growth of upstate communities in the region controlled by the Holland Land Company, which was the largest private land developer in the state. The New Englanders brought with them their Puritan religious values and work ethic, and they prospered.

Concern over maintaining a strict adherence to the Sabbath dated back to the early years of the republic. Descriptions of family life on the Lord's Day, which appeared in journals, almanacs, and newspapers, served to reinforce moral Sabbath admonitions and traditional hierarchies. "What can be a more beautiful and interesting sight," so stated one mawkish account, "than to see the principal of a family, surrounded by his children, and all his household formed, from the humble domestick to the valued friend or relative, seated on a Sabbath evening with the book of holy law before him, reading and expounding to them its contents; deterring them from evil by its awful threatening, encouraging to virtue and piety by its delightful promises."[9]

Since the penal laws prohibited nearly every kind of nonreligious activity on Sunday, their violation was inevitable and a constant source of consternation. Religious and civic groups in states like New York, where the Puritan influence was more pronounced, petitioned Congress, on constitutional grounds, to prohibit transportation and the delivery of mail on the Sabbath. The Synod of Philadelphia's Presbyterian Church explicitly condemned "all excursions, whether by walking or riding, for pleasure or amusement, or worldly business: all dining parties given to others, or partaken of an invitation received from them; all visiting or receiving of visits, beyond what is manifestly demanded by hospitality or Christian charity. . . " Other prohibitions were directed at household occupations, discussions of politics, or worldly concerns "calculated to detach the mind from serious thought or to break in on devout feeling."[10]

The *Tioga Eagle* lamented that canals and railroads had opened the gates to travel from remote and peaceful towns and villages to great cities, which was a source of serious Sabbath desecration, "and excitement for the collection of rabble 'who fear not God nor regard man.'" Violations of the Sabbath were also blamed for the dangers of social mixing whereby young men "in the dew of their youth" came to "associate with the inebriate and drink from the cup of sin." The theme of Sabbath desecration as a first step in the descent from virtue and prosperity to ruin was a pervasive and popular statement. At the same time, the proper observance of the Puritan Sunday was seen as the antidote to crime, the violations of property rights, and the enhancement of individual liberty. Well into the nineteenth century the proper adherence to the Sabbath was widely accepted, within the religious spirit of the age, as a bulwark against "moral anarchy."[11]

The sanctity of the Sabbath became a cornerstone of the Protestant evangelicalism that swept across New York during the nineteenth century. Dating back to the hellfire and brimstone sermons of Jonathan Edwards in New England in the first half of the eighteenth century, periodic outbreaks of religious enthusiasm were a defining characteristic of American life. The evangelical revivals of the early Republican era were significant in shaping the religious character of New York. Evangelicals, including Methodists, Baptists, and to a lesser extent, Presbyterians, united Christians who believed in the authority of the Bible, rather than of Rome. Many of these Protestant denominations saw rapid increases in their membership, and the number of churches expanded, especially in rural areas. By the mid-nineteenth century, Methodists across the state had more than twelve hundred churches, the Baptists had nearly eight hundred churches, and the Presbyterians could claim roughly seven hundred churches.

The growth of religious communities, and religious enthusiasm, was offset by the emergence of secular trends. As early as the eighteenth century, jeremiads echoed from the pulpits of the more established congregations about the loss of piety and a disregard for religious fervor. Many of the newer immigrants lacked the spiritual intensity of their Puritan forebearers and opted for a more rational and less literal form of religion. The spread of deism and freemasonry among the colonial elites also contributed to a more relaxed religious atmosphere.

This is not to discount the importance of religious enthusiasm. Puritan-based fundamentalism has risen to prominence and declined in seasonal regularity throughout the course of American history. Such a pattern characterized the George Whitefield revivals of 1739–1742, known as the "Great Awakening," and later in the 1820s and '30s it coalesced into a broad evangelical movement dedicated to eliminating sin and bringing about moral reform.

While evangelical preachers created a groundswell of converts, religious enthusiasm often divided churches between thoughtful communicants who favored a religion based on the word of God and those whose faith was predicated on feeling. Fissures within congregations, fueled by revivals, have been a latent or manifest hallmark within American Protestant religious life for much of its history.

Evangelical forms of religion caught on quickly among the business classes in the emerging industrial towns of New York. Industrialists and many members of the middle class were attracted by the values of sobriety, hard work, and social discipline inherent in the evangelical message. Central and western New York, home to a number of new religious movements, underwent a series of revivals from the 1820s through the Civil War era. Evangelist Charles Finney's travels and tent meetings through the upstate region created a community of militant followers, which affected the religious and social climate for decades to come. His efforts, highlighted by an important revival from 1830 to 1831, sparked an upsurge of religious enthusiasm in Rochester and Utica that had far-reaching consequences.[12]

Concerned businessmen in Rochester turned to the Sabbatarians in an attempt to gain lost authority over workers and to stem the tide of social disorder. Rochester may have looked like a country town in the 1820s, but underneath it was a manufacturing center with the sort of class conflicts that characterized the age. Efforts to control the working masses and the flow of transients through Rochester moved in the direction of limiting the drink trade and tightening restrictions on Sunday activities.[13]

The opening of the Erie Canal in 1825 increased the flow of freight and passenger traffic through the city during the week, including Sundays. Appeals to the state legislature to shut down the locks on the Sabbath fell on deaf ears. Thwarted in the legislature, Rochester's ministers put pressure on the owners of steamboats, canal boats, livery stables, and other transportation businesses by boycotting those firms that contributed to Sunday travel. Led by local Presbyterian minister Josiah Bissell, and with the support of wealthy businessmen, they organized a Sabbath-keeping stage and boat line, known as the Pioneer Line. Opposition by business interests to the ban on Sunday travel and mail deliveries initiated futile efforts to secure post-office contracts for the Pioneer alone. Bissell and others, in concert with the renowned Lyman Beecher of Massachusetts, then formed the General Union for Promoting the Observance of the Christian Sabbath, a national organization devoted to preserving sanctity of the first day of the week principally by lobbying Congress to stop Sunday mail deliveries. The crusade against the mails ultimately failed but, as seen by the conflicts over the propriety of Sunday travel on the waterways, the rolling stone of Sabbath observance was gathering no moss.[14]

Sabbath defenders and nativist groups joined forces to oppose traditional social gatherings by Catholic Irish and German immigrants in public parks on Sundays. Such actions had the double effect of marginalizing groups that did not fit into Protestant middle-class society as well as preserving the integrity of the Lord's Day. Between 1850 and 1880 there was widespread consternation over the running of trains on Sunday to recreational venues and camp meetings at places like Chautauqua in western New

York. The battle over Sunday rail service was significant, not only because camps and recreational centers depended upon railroad traffic for their survival, but because it pitted religious congregations, such as the Methodists, against railroad executives and local business interests.[15]

From mid-nineteenth century the hostile encounters over Sunday closing focused primarily on the drink trade. A number of upstate cities opposed Sunday sales of alcohol. Readers of the Syracuse newspapers were entertained by frequent accounts of efforts by the police to curtail the sale of alcohol on Sunday. The "friends of temperance," meaning the local evangelicals, were in the thick of the fray and, in the words of one article, "the temperance cause in Syracuse has instituted rigorous measures to prevent this wholesale violation of the law. . . " Pious evangelical churchgoers thought that Sabbath breaking tended to deteriorate a sense of moral obligation and open the floodgates of iniquity. Therefore, so the theory went, the state had the right and the duty to forbid it.[16]

The perceived moral danger brought about by rising rates of alcoholism led to the formation of the Women's Christian Temperance Union (WCTU) in 1874. At the local level, the WCTU played a dominant role in mobilizing support for temperance and other moral issues, including Sabbath desecration. The tentacles of the WCTU reached into virtually every city, town, village, and hamlet in rural New York and proved to be a reliable base from which the defenders of Sunday laws and the proponents of temperance restrictions could draw support. Members of the WCTU were not averse to giving local authorities a nudge on the moral questions that concerned them. For instance, when Mayor Frederick E. Bates of Ithaca was perceived to be lax in his enforcement of state and county laws and local ordinances in relation to Sunday closing, the WCTU did not hesitate to remind him of his duty.[17]

Of all the Christian-based youth organizations that lent their voices to the cause of religious and moral instruction, the most predominant was the Young Men's Christian Association. Originating in England in 1841, the YMCA soon became a significant urban institution in the United States. It was a place for supervised residential accommodations and recreational activities within a Christian context. The YMCA attracted youths from the lower middle class or skilled working class, but rarely factory workers or common laborers. Those who joined were almost exclusively native-born Protestants. The evangelical clergy, many of whom were revivalists and Sunday school pioneers, backed the YMCA and other such organizations. Using their connections, they exercised a certain amount of influence over YMCA operations and promoted the cause of Sunday restrictions as a way of preventing large congregations of youths from falling into the dangers of idleness.[18]

During the late nineteenth century and beyond, Protestant churches and congregations lived in separate moral geographical universes, both figuratively and physically, from their Catholic brethren. The growth of industry in New York, coupled with increased immigration, particularly among the Irish and Germans, many of whom were Roman Catholics, led to further class and ethnic tensions and opposing attitudes regarding the Sabbath. The position of the Catholic Church with respect to Sunday activities was less severe than its Protestant brethren. James Cardinal Gibbons, archbishop of Baltimore, was an enthusiastic supporter of baseball, which he referred to as a clean and innocent sport. Since he believed that the American public demanded recreation, he "heartedly approved of baseball as a popular pastime." Demurring slightly, the cardinal thought there needed to be a balance with respect to Sunday baseball between rigid Sabbatarianism and lax indulgence.[19]

The Right Reverend John J. Keane, addressing a crowd in Buffalo in 1895, was equally cautious in stating that while he opposed the continental Sunday the church did not object to "popular enjoyments consistent with the pleasure of the day," provided Catholics did not frequent places where liquor was sold. He cited as his authority the official position of the Church set forth in 1884 at the Third Plenary Council of the Church bishops.[20]

Conservative trends in American Protestantism reached a climactic point in the years between 1880 and 1885. Aside from the crusades against alcoholism and vice, the Puritan Sabbath was probably the most distinctive symbol of evangelical civilization in the English-speaking world at this time and remained a major reform issue where religious and social interests coincided. From the perspective of orthodox Protestant Christianity, Sabbath concerns were not issues of a particular class but were in the interests of everyone, including the working classes, who had a right to a day's rest. In spite of looming clouds to the contrary, evangelicals held to the Sabbath as one of the chief cornerstones of the Church and of Christian civilization.[21]

By the 1890s Protestant religious orthodoxy had become noticeably weakened by the emergence of new social issues and the rising tide of immigration. Country and village churches, which had been numerous earlier in the century, began to suffer from depopulation. Since the rural churches were the foundation of the Protestant establishment, this was a serious matter. Urban churches often dealt with the changing times by deemphasizing the message of personal salvation and stressing matters more pertinent to the concerns of urban dwellers.

At the same time, the conservative approach to Christianity was challenged by the spread of a liberal theology, which would be a significant if not a dominant feature of Protestant Christianity during the early decades of the twentieth century. Many urban churches were awakening to broader social and moral issues brought on by ills such as homelessness, poverty, prostitution, and child abuse. In fairness, many evangelicals and Sabbatarians had a genuine concern for the plight of the poor and downtrodden, but their perspective was more paternalistic, whereas their liberal counterparts framed the question of poverty and vice in terms of social action. Christians were also divided over intellectual challenges to the accepted view of creationism counterpoised by Charles Darwin's theory of evolution.[22]

The focus on a social gospel had the effect of easing some of the tight restrictions and legal sanctions so favored by the orthodox clergy. Some liberal ministers, for instance, supported opening saloons on Sunday since the present law was impossible to enforce and its disregard begot disrespect for the law, which was seen as unhealthy for public morals. Toward the end of the century an idea emerged that social problems were not so much the fault of immoral people as immoral institutions. The focus then shifted away from the drunkard and the fallen woman to the saloon and the brothel. The owners of theaters, fledgling movie houses, and ballparks, along with the proprietors and operators of professional baseball teams, who were targets of attack with respect to Sunday violations, were also denounced as promoting immorality.[23]

Sabbath issues thus brought to the forefront the various cleavages and fault lines that existed within churches, organizations, and social classes. By the late nineteenth century, the Puritan disdain and suspicion of spare time had imperceptibly given way to an appreciation of sports and recreational pursuits. Such pastimes were exemplified by the vast number of Sunday excursions, games and recreational sports, and parks that were filled to capacity on the Sabbath.

This raised questions as to the circumstances by which such activities should be tolerated. Individualized pursuits such as cycling, golf, and tennis, which appealed more to the middle class, came into vogue as the result of a culture of leisure and fitness that spread among the respectable classes. As baseball became more organized and gained popular support among the masses, social tensions over what would or would not be permissible on Sunday increased. As one historian noted, "a commercial culture in the early 1890s began to make itself increasingly felt on Sunday," which reflected developments in baseball within a society that was becoming increasingly complex.[24]

Baseball: The New York Game

In his groundbreaking book *Baseball Before We Knew It*, David Block cites numerous literary references to early forms of baseball such as cat ball, trap ball, stool ball, and the various types of town ball that evolved over the centuries. In compiling evidence from sundry sources, Block suggests that bat and ball games were more pervasive and more ancient than previously thought. In time two sorts of town ball emerged: the Massachusetts game and the New York game, the latter of which proved more successful. The term "baseball" became a cover for any of a number of such games, often with their own unique rules.

Informal types of baseball were played around the state. In 1825, New York journalist and politician Thurlow Weed observed that in the industrious town of Rochester a baseball club numbering fifty members, featuring a wide range of ages, met every afternoon during the ball-playing season. They played on a ball ground covering eight to ten acres. By 1845 baseball games had become so popular in Syracuse that city officials banned the sport from Clinton Square and Hanover Square because of the congestion.

The formation of modern baseball has been attributed to Alexander J. Cartwright, and his Knickerbocker Base Ball Club, however the origins of the game are far more complicated. In his book *Baseball in the Garden of Eden*, John Thorn argues that as early as 1831 there were more than a few teams playing town ball, which had a number of the characteristics of baseball. Moreover, several men with forgotten names such as William Rufus Wheaton, Daniel Lucius, "Doc" Adams, and William H. Tucker have some claim to being called the originators of baseball. The legendary first match game, based on Knickerbocker rules, which took place at Hoboken on June 19, 1846, between the New York Ball Club and the Knickerbocker, is of greater mythological than historical importance. Cartwright soon went west and eventually ended up in Hawaii. The notion that he taught Native Americans the game on his journey appears to be another myth. Whatever the origins of baseball, the game quickly took off. The vitality of baseball in the New York City region was illustrated by constant experimentation and changes in rules that occurred during the Civil War years. During the war, soldiers on both sides of the conflict played various shades of baseball and were encouraged to do so by their officers so as to relieve boredom and take their minds off impending dangers. Not unmindful of the tremendous sacrifices by Union soldiers, ball-playing fraternities helped to raise funds for the wounded and their families. Over the next fifteen years more than sixty baseball clubs sprang up in the New York City area. As with the members of the Knickerbocker club, the men who played baseball considered themselves to be part of an exclusive fraternity, and teams resembled social clubs where ball playing was just one of a number of activities.[25]

The gentlemanly spirit of mid-century baseball was often seen in the detached or dismissive attitudes that players felt toward the sport. Quoting Henry Chadwick, an early baseball pioneer, Warren Goldstein writes that baseball during the late 1850s and early 1860s was defended as "healthful recreation" and "invigorating exercise and manly pastime." Such attitudes were reflected in a game between the Lightfoot Baseball Club of Oxford in Chenango County and a Harpersville team, which led to a 37–37 draw. Rather than play extra innings, the visiting team made their excuses that continuing the game would prevent them from getting home at a decent hour and so departed. For early practitioners, the outcome of the game was secondary to an opportunity to demonstrate manly skill, enjoy the fresh air, and associate with worthy opponents.[26]

Town teams playing standardized baseball, or an approximation of it, were prevalent on the eve of the Civil War, by which time the Knickerbockers' style of play had begun to move out of the metropolitan area and across the state. In upstate cities, teams sprang up in various neighborhoods and among diverse social groups. Baseball in Rochester during these early years was hampered by the lack of appropriate fields, so players, much to the annoyance of many townsmen, would transform public squares and quiet neighborhoods into ball diamonds. Initially ministers questioned the morality of such forms of recreation, especially on the Sabbath, but the sport soon gained wide acceptance. Some have suggested that by 1858 there may have been several hundred teams in the Rochester area, although this figure, as well as even more extravagant estimates put forward in the local press, is highly suspect. Nevertheless, games appeared to be popular. Reports of thousands who turned up to watch the Rochester club play its first intercity match with a Buffalo team are evidence of the game's sudden popularity.[27]

With the close of the Civil War, baseball mushroomed until it could be found in every little town and hamlet. Baseball soon appeared in Newburgh and small Hudson Valley communities such as Goshen. After it was introduced into Kingston, organized baseball generated a hotbed of interest in Ulster County and, according to one local historian, no other county of its size in the state took to the game so fervently. Ulster County was the locale of seven leagues and a number of purely hometown teams ranging from amateur to semi-pro. The most predominant was the Hudson River League, formed in 1885–1886.[28]

Enthusiasm for baseball was further aroused when one of the crack New York City teams, the Brooklyn Excelsiors, organized a ten-day road trip to upstate cities in 1860, including games against inferior clubs in Albany, Troy, Buffalo, Rochester, and Newburgh. In western New York the Niagaras of Buffalo played clubs from Lockport and Auburn. By the mid-1870s towns like Monticello, Port Jervis, Binghamton, Owego, Norwich, and Oneonta fielded teams.[29]

There were also teams of young women who solicited games from both men's and women's teams. Male promoters in the 1860s organized women's baseball teams as a novelty entertainment. In 1867 an all–black women's baseball club, known as the Dolly Vardens, provided theatrical enjoyment by playing the game wearing what was described as red calico dresses. The first white women's professional teams to gain widespread attention were the Blonds and the Brunettes, consisting exclusively of ladies with those hair shades. One patronizing account advertised an exhibition of baseball and other sports "participated in by twenty handsome young ladies to the accompaniment of a brass band in uniform." Around the turn of the century, a team known as The Bloomer Girls reportedly went on barnstorming tours through central New York playing clubs in the larger towns. There were a number of teams of that name, such as the Boston Bloomer Girls, the Texas Bloomer Girls, and the Chicago Bloomer Girls, that traveled the country. It is unclear whether those teams comprised men as well as women, but press reports indicated they played excellent baseball. Nevertheless, fan reaction was often mixed. In a game played at Louisville, Kentucky, spectators hooted down a touring team of female ballplayers and threw stones at them as they were leaving the ballpark. Needless to say, they were happy to leave town and head for their next match in Cincinnati. Upperclass women's colleges like Vassar, Smith, and Barnard fielded baseball teams before exaggerated sentiments of femininity and female frailty closed down many ladies sports.[30]

Reports claimed that this capital sport was all the rage in cities throughout central and western New York. From the late 1860s there were numerous accounts of baseball games played in Ithaca. At Utica and Oswego even the newspaper-carrier boys engaged in matches. The printers took up the game and rival offices organized teams to play one another. The lawyers of Oswego challenged the doctors, and in Rochester even the shoeblacks were looking to arrange a match. The Ilion Clippers, a team from a town east of Utica, formed in 1869, and played against a number of major league teams that barnstormed through the region. The Clippers gave way to the Independents in 1898 and then to a number of amateur and professional teams. Teams of

African American players thrived in the 1860s; however, the New York State Baseball Association, consisting of teams of white players, plunged into the stream of segregation swelling up during this time. At their 1870 meeting, the National Association of Base Ball Players modified the rules for the admission of new clubs so as to bar teams that included "gentlemen of color."[31]

From New York the growth of what had become known as "the national pastime" followed settlers westward across the country, leading to concerns that some sort of oversight should be required. The game's first governing body, the National Association of Base Ball Players, was formed in 1858. By 1866 the National Association had grown to include 202 clubs from seventeen different states, including Washington, D.C. Meanwhile, the forces of change were moving swiftly and would soon override the ability of the association to control the course of baseball.[32]

Challenges to baseball's amateur status were soon forthcoming. The initial step toward professionalism commenced with gate-money, or "passing-the-hat," among patrons with the receipts shared by players and team officials. It was then only a short step to charging admission. On July 20, 1858, a contest between the New York and Brooklyn Clubs at a race course in Queens resulted for the first time in a fee of fifty cents charged to patrons. A further stride toward professionalizing the game came through the introduction of a free-agent market. Clubs sought to strengthen their teams by acquiring players from other organizations. The top three players on the Excelsiors, for instance, joined the rival Atlantics in 1862. One of these players was Jim Creighton, a multiskilled ballplayer who also distinguished himself at cricket. After jumping to the Atlantics, Creighton's career was cut short after his own mighty swing of the bat caused an internal rupture and hemorrhaging, leading to his untimely death shortly thereafter. Soon New York players were in demand by clubs in other parts of the country.[33]

While technically non-amateur teams were not allowed in the association, the press began referring to association clubs as "professionals." The National Association overlooked the pervasive practice of charging money for games, since many clubs engaged in unofficial gate-money practices. They made some effort to bar professional players from participating in matches and in 1866 threatened the expulsion of any club that paid its players, as well as any rival club that played against them. This threat, however, proved to be hollow. Essentially, the National Association's attempt to preserve amateur baseball was "a voice crying in the wilderness." By 1868 it was clear that the National Association had insufficient power and, judging from the many internal conflicts, a lack of authority to act as the governing body for baseball.[34]

The emergence of commercialized baseball begs the question of what constitutes professionalism. Many so-called amateur clubs were forced to raise money to meet expenses, and no doubt a number of teams charged admission to games. As competition between leagues and clubs became more formalized, the next logical step was to use some of the receipts to pay players, particularly the better players, and to entice players from other teams through the promise of monetary rewards. Complaints appeared in the press as to the prevalence of "gate money teams" whose members claimed to be amateurs while practically transforming themselves into professionals. The line between amateur and professional, while obvious at first glance, was anything but, which would prove challenging especially with regard to Sunday baseball.[35]

Nevertheless, the pace of professional baseball advanced quickly from the late 1860s. In 1869 the New York Mutuals became the first baseball team to pay its players, closely followed by the Cincinnati Red Stockings. The Red Stockings went on to be undefeated in 1869 led by one of the outstanding figures of the game, a former cricket player named Harry Wright. The success of the Red Stockings proved that the public would happily pay to watch top-flight players in action, which only professional baseball could provide. After a few glorious years at the top of the baseball world, the Cincinnati club declined and folded. Wright was invited to put together a team in Boston and immediately stocked the club with the best players he could find. Among those players was Albert Goodwill Spalding, who came from a prosperous Illinois farm family. As a teenager, he displayed a remarkable ability to play baseball and was soon a star pitcher on the local Rockford team from 1868 to 1870. Spalding acquired a national reputation as a ballplayer and was enticed by Wright to sign a contract with Boston for $1,500 a year. Spalding would later become baseball's foremost promoter and would make a fortune as a manufacturer of baseball equipment.

On March 17, 1871, the National Association of Professional Base Ball Players was formed in New York, including teams from the New York City area such as the New York Mutuals (1871–1875), the Brooklyn Atlantics (1872–1875), and the Brooklyn Eckfords (1872), along with the upstate Troy Haymakers (1871–1872). The National Association of Professional Players remained in the hands of the players who often made decisions based on what was good for themselves and their respective teams, not the league. Serious problems soon arose. The Association was saddled with an abundance of clubs and heavy expenses causing a considerable turnover. Good ballplayers do not necessarily make capable businessmen, and since professional play required a more sophisticated level of organization, the National Association of Professional Players was doomed. By the 1870s, however, the trend toward professional baseball was irreversible.

The fortunes of the Syracuse Stars chronicled the transition from a strictly amateur game to professional baseball. Syracuse's first entry into organized baseball began with the formation of the Syracuse Baseball Club in the winter of 1857–1858. In the late 1850s the Syracuse team challenged clubs in Utica, Cazenovia, Oswego, and Union Springs. With the outbreak of the Civil War, baseball in Syracuse paused for four years. The sport returned to the city in 1865 with the emergence of the Central City Ball Club, which toured the region playing local teams and was something of a powerhouse in upstate New York.

Several local men, including John J. Dunn, Edward Thurston, and Charles Holden, joined forces in 1866 to form the Syracuse Stars, which featured the top ballplayers in the area. Within a decade they were a first-rate amateur team and became attractive to ballplayers in other organizations. The economic potential of the Stars brought together a number of local businessmen who put up the money that enabled the club to join the professional ranks. During the 1876 season the Stars compiled a record of forty-six wins and thirteen losses, including victories over the St. Louis Browns and the Chicago White Stockings, both of which were in the newly formed National League.

Success gave the Stars national attention. Joining the International League in 1878, the team captured first place with a record of sixty-five wins, thirty-three losses, and four draws. Welcomed into the National League in 1879, the Syracuse club finished its only major league season with a dismal record of twenty-two victories, forty-eight defeats, and a single draw. Professional baseball disappeared from Syracuse until 1885, when the Stars returned to the International League. Like so many teams of the period, the Stars jumped from league to league hoping to stay afloat financially in a highly competitive market. During one of the country's cyclical economic depressions in 1892, the Syracuse Stars were forced to abort their season when the franchise moved to Utica in July.[36]

Like a phoenix, the Stars re-emerged from the ashes in 1894 under new ownership. They continued playing, this time in the Eastern League, where they performed with reasonable success. Switching to the New York State League in 1902, the Stars established an uncharacteristic degree of continuity, although financially they were always touch and go. The Stars filed for bankruptcy in 1914, and for a brief time the team was under the control of their bank's attorneys. The club rebounded by winning the New York State League in 1916. After that league folded in 1917, the city adopted the defunct Jersey City franchise and resurrected the club as the new Syracuse Stars, returning to the reconstituted International League in 1918. Pulling themselves together again, the Stars regrouped under new ownership and in 1920 appeared as a reincarnation of the Newark franchise. The Stars' light finally burned out during the 1928–1929 season, aptly just prior to the stock market crash and the start of the Great Depression.[37]

As a footnote to the Stars' see-saw history, the club was remembered for fielding the last black professional ballplayer prior to the self-enforced apartheid that lasted until Jackie Robinson broke the color barrier anew in 1947. Moses Fleetwood Walker, like most educated African Americans during segregation, lived in the twilight zone of two worlds. A student at Oberlin College, and later briefly a legal student at the University of Michigan, Walker entered professional baseball in 1883 as a catcher for the Toledo ball club. One of a handful of black players in professional baseball, Walker suffered a multitude of physical and emotional indignities from white opponents and teammates alike. In the mid-1880s there were about twenty black professional ballplayers, but by the time Walker arrived in Syracuse in 1888 he was virtually the last. The unwillingness of white teams to play against a club with a black player and the unwritten agreement among club owners that athletes of color were no longer wanted ended the century's brief chapter of integrated baseball.

Apart from Syracuse's professional team the city also had a number of amateur clubs and leagues. The Syracuse Base Ball Club sponsored a host of matches in the late 1850s between married and single men. The city's mechanics played teams centered around various trades and neighborhoods, and the ministers demonstrated their physical, if not spiritual, superiority over the lawyers in several games in which they won. Teams in the city were also organized geographically on the basis of wards. Games of "old fashioned" baseball, probably meaning town ball, were also played into the 1860s.[38]

Later in the century Syracusans were treated to good amateur baseball played by teams known as the Clippers, the Shamrocks, the Foresters, the Jacksons, the Mikados, the Maroons, the Eagles, the Pastimes, the Ironsides, and the St. Cecilias. Several of these clubs were rooted in Syracuse's immigrant neighborhoods. The Irish on the west side, for instance, supported the Shamrocks whereas the Germans on the north side rooted for the Pastimes. East-side fans backed the Ironsides. For a while, indoor baseball played at the armory became a popular diversion for Syracuse fans. In time new teams emerged, such as the Seymours, who were the toast of the amateurs in 1905 while others fell by the wayside. The H. H. Franklin Car Company fielded good teams from 1906 to 1910 and drew upon much prized local talent.[39]

The Syracuse experience exemplified how fragile baseball teams and leagues were in the late nineteenth and early twentieth centuries. Teams often relied upon the goodwill of their prosperous citizens as well as receipts from the gate. The prospects for creating a professional team in Ithaca in 1906 got a boost when a group of local businessmen stepped forward to promote the enterprise. Speaking with hyperbole, the president of the newly formed Ithaca team set forth a plan that would allow the club to achieve financial support through subscriptions. At the end of the season the money raised would reimburse the subscribers. Estimates that $400 a month would be needed to clear expenses reinforced a promise that if there was a shortfall the club would disband.[40]

In the short term the news was good. The Ithaca ball club completed the season, winning twenty of twenty-nine games. Although receipts were slightly below the level the promoters had hoped for, they were satisfied with the team's performance and were optimistic about their future. Rumors began to emerge about the formation of a stock company to finance the Ithaca club for the next season. The *Ithaca Weekly Journal* reported that the wish of many in the community was to have a team in the Empire State League.[41]

The New York State League franchise in nearby Cortland was not so fortunate. The team, known as the Wagonmakers, had joined the league in 1897, but its financial survival was always a struggle. In spite of doubts that Cortland would have sufficient cash to field a team in 1901, club officials put on a positive face and set about fund-raising. A baseball fair held in February was a huge success, netting $1,160, but left the club still $1,500 short of the capital needed to meet expenses to start the season. The sale of stock made up the difference. The directors of the club then set about hiring a manager and recruiting players, some of whom had previous league experience.[42]

The season commenced with enthusiasm and promise. The club, however, never seemed to rise above the level of mediocrity. By the end of the first week in June, there were signs of bickering among the players, costly defeats, and disgruntled fans who felt that their support had been betrayed. In mid-June Cortland took a nosedive and dropped several positions in the standings. The *Cortland Standard* reminded the players that the team was in business at the expense of the people of Cortland, "who have a right to expect anything but the utterly indifferent playing that was indulged in by them. . . " Rumors began to circulate that the team would soon have new players and a new manager, but nothing materialized. Within a couple of days league president John H. Farrell abruptly announced that the team was being transferred to Waverly. The local press eulogized them and with the postponement of the Schenectady match: "The last professional game to be played in this city has been witnessed."[43]

The financial collapse of the Cortland franchise had a ripple effect that affected league schedules. When considering the transfer of teams to other cities, club owners sought out venues where Sunday games would enhance revenue streams. Cities such as Schenectady, Utica, Binghamton, and Troy were considered relatively safe bets due to the low level of ministerial opposition but Cortland was not on the list, which may have helped hasten its departure. Soon after the team left for Waverly there was a disquieting report that the New York State League might be broken apart by the question of Sunday baseball. This did not happen, but such a scare, coupled with ongoing financial issues, clearly exposed the fragility of the league.[44]

Prior to the turn of the century, many sizeable cities in New York fielded minor league franchises. The Auburn Maroons were active in the New York State League from 1888 to 1889 and 1897 to 1898. The Binghamton Bingoes were in the same circuit in 1885 and later became the Crickets in the International League from 1886 to 1887, moving to the Central League in 1888. Binghamton baseball adopted the Bingoes name once more as an Eastern League team from 1892 to 1894. Binghamton clubs then alternated between being called the Crickets and Bingoes in the New York State League from 1895 to 1900. The Bisons were a continuous presence in Buffalo from 1878, jumping from league to league. Elmira was represented by minor league baseball in 1885, 1888, 1891, 1892, 1895, and 1900. Rochester entered professional baseball as the now-familiar Red Wings, later adopting a host of curious names such as the Jingoes and the Hop Bitters.

Meanwhile, professional baseball at the top continued to expand. Major league baseball achieved some stability when the National League was formed in 1876. The league included three upstate franchises, the Buffalo Bisons (1879–1885), the Syracuse Stars (1879), and the Troy Trojans (1879–1882). A team called the New York Gothams joined the league in 1883 and became the Giants in 1885. From the league's inception there were disputes between member clubs over admission charges, which the league had set at fifty cents. Buffalo delayed joining the league over this issue, while Syracuse balked repeatedly at the standard charge before agreeing to increase its admission to the required level. Initially the league banned Sunday baseball, which was in keeping with the moral sentiments of the period and was deemed necessary in order to win support among the respectable classes. Such a policy would later be put to a test by competition from less scrupulous rival leagues.[45]

The National League clubs, in assessing the 1878 season, issued a report saying that efforts to present a distinctly national game in the best possible manner and under the most stringent regulations had been met. They thought that baseball was appreciated and approved by lovers of this "pure and manly sport" and that the moral tone of the game had been elevated. The experience of the league clubs in 1878, however, showed that the business depression that gripped the country had affected receipts to such an extent that such losses might impact salaries for the coming year.[46]

At a meeting of the National League held in Buffalo the following year, the owners were again satisfied with the performance on the field, and the enthusiasm of the general public. Some concern was expressed in the pages of the *New York Clipper* over "evil influences" that surrounded such contests, particularly gambling, and what was referred to as control by unprincipled managers. The rules adopted by the National Association, according to the *Clipper*, had the effect of elevating the moral tone of the game and educating players to recognize the truth of the old adage "honesty is the best policy." Financially, the 1879 season was better than 1878, but the expenses of many clubs exceeded their receipts due entirely to salaries. To remedy this so-called evil, clubs decided on the use of mandatory uniform player contracts that restricted the money paid to players until it was earned. In other words, no advances would be given. Picking up on their "honesty is the best policy" pledge, National League owners sought to wrest control of the game from the influence of gambling rings, claiming that "honest play is the life of professionalism and honesty in professional play can never exist in the same atmosphere that gives life to 'pool rings.'"[47]

The league meeting in Buffalo was further significant in that the owners introduced a reserve clause that would become one of the hallmarks of professional baseball. The idea, originally formulated in 1879, was to hold salaries down by reserving the five best players on each club, thus guaranteeing them a job but making them ineligible to sign contracts with other teams. By the mid-1880s the policy was expanded by club owners to include all players. Since all contracts were uniform, except for salary designations, the reserve clause would apply to every club. Players could be retained by a team even though they had not been paid a salary or were unable to play.

Such was the case of Charles Foley, who missed the entire 1883 season and received no pay during his illness. Nevertheless, the Buffalo team, which held his contract, refused to sign him or release him from the reserved list. Opposition to the reserve clause was muted in the face of its gradual adoption by professional teams. As with so many changes, its effectiveness was the product of gradual implementation.[48]

In keeping with the high moral tone the National League had set for itself, the owners, in addition to banning Sunday baseball, prohibited beer sales at ballparks. Moreover, they did not shy away from enforcing these restrictions. The League subsequently expelled the Cincinnati ball club in 1882 for playing baseball on the Sabbath. Questions related to Sunday matches came up at a meeting of the National League in Chicago in 1886. Several managers favored a plan put forth by Harry Wright to permit clubs who wanted to play on Sunday to do so. This proposal spoke to the reality of varying state laws and local ordinances that allowed or prohibited some or all recreational activities on the Sabbath. It was not until six years later (1892) that the National League, after some controversy, finally sanctioned games on Sunday.[49]

A quick return from this change in policy was the increased revenues afforded by playing games on the first day of the week. This was especially true in some of the western cities, such as St. Louis, where the laws against Sunday baseball were lax and the influence of evangelicals and church groups was scattered or lacking. Sunday games failed to lure clubs in the northeast, including those in Boston, Brooklyn, Cleveland, New York, Philadelphia, Pittsburgh, and Washington, that were in the league during the 1890s. Players who had troubled consciences for violating the Sabbath were allowed to take the day off.

The National League's change of heart was due unquestionably to the emergence of a rival league that did not hold to the National League's "high standards." The American Association, formed in 1882, structured its constitution after the National League's but allowed for some degree of revenue sharing. It parted company from the Nationals in that the new league allowed Sunday baseball, charged a cheaper admission fee of twenty-five cents, and sold liquor at ballpark grounds. The latter point was not surprising considering that large amounts of brewery money had been invested in the league. At the same time, on pain of expulsion, clubs were forbidden to allow betting on their grounds, and the league came down hard on teams that sanctioned "dishonest play" or permitted drunkenness. Like so many other professional baseball associations, the "Beer and Whiskey League" was gone after 1891.[50]

One of two other brief challenges to the National League came from the Union Association formed in 1884. While that league included clubs from Baltimore, Boston, Chicago, Cincinnati, Philadelphia, St. Louis, Washington, and Altoona, Pennsylvania, it surprisingly fielded no teams from the Empire State. The Union Association signed players who were under contract with other major league clubs, which unsurprisingly became the object of much litigation. The association lasted only a year. Franchise shifts, bankruptcies, and the threat of blacklisting by National League owners caused some players to change their minds about jumping to the Union Association.

The other challenge came in response to the parsimonious policies of the owners, when in 1890 the players banded together to form their own league, which included three teams from upstate New York. The plan of the so-called Players' League called for pooling gate receipts from which operating expenses and players' salaries would be paid. Share and share-alike socialism has rarely profited within the bounds of American capitalism, and the Players League was no exception. Like the Union Association, it disbanded after one season.[51]

With the turn of the century, the creation of a permanent rival league to the Nationals under the leadership of Byron Bancroft "Ban" Johnson, helped to solidify organized baseball. Conflict between the American and National Leagues was averted through the creation of a National Agreement for the Government of Professional Baseball Clubs in 1903. The National Agree - ment gave equal recognition to both leagues and established a three-man commission to oversee compliance with the articles and provisions contained therein. The National Commission continued as the governing body of professional baseball until 1920.

From 1903 to 1957, with the brief exception of the years 1915–1916 when the Federal League was in business, New York was home to three major league teams, all in the metropolitan area. Plagued with constant financial troubles and insecure franchises, New York's minor leagues and franchises had a more difficult time. Even so, the chaos of the late nineteenth century, when the game was establishing its identity, clarifying its rules, and creating a fan base, was passing into a new era of greater stability. At the same time, there were a number of unresolved questions pertaining to both organized and amateur baseball, such as the imposition of Sunday observance laws in New York.

Yearning for a Simpler Age

As amateur and professional baseball evolved over the latter half of the nineteenth century, religious proponents and opponents of Sunday restrictions were not idle bystanders. A broad coalition of New York reformers, including labor leaders, progressives, settlement house workers, and social gospelers, supported amateur Sunday baseball. Some clergymen wanted to make the church more relevant to the needs of urbanites and felt that those who supported Sabbath restrictions were driving working men away from the church. Whether the urban working classes cared that much for the religion of the churches was beside the point. More relevant was the reaction of clergymen to changes in the nature of the game itself.[52]

It is on this point that public views on the impact of amateur and professional baseball collided, and upon which the orthodox Protestant clergy had more than a little to say. Sermons delivered from the pulpits of evangelical churches came down heavily against baseball as a business. One such sermon preached by a Syracuse Methodist minister took the form of a tirade in which he equated the devil with professional sport. Not only should a Christian citizen take an uncompromising position on these matters, he asserted, but he should avoid the seductive temptations that came in the wake of professional baseball. Underscoring his text was a kind of domino theory, positing that if Sunday baseball were accepted it would open the door for picture shows and other activities on the Sabbath, which would lead the unsuspecting Christian into grave sin.[53]

A debate over whether the Cleveland National League team should be allowed to play baseball in the city on Sunday touched off a firestorm of protests among the Ohio clergy, similar to those from ministers in New York, which resulted in sermons denouncing baseball. One such minister, the Reverend D. G. Newton, moaned that "baseball, like everything in this country, was a profession, a profession that had prostituted innocent games and pastimes and forced decent and hard working men to abstain from harmless and commendable amusements." Working himself to a fever pitch, the Reverend Newton compared the followers of professional baseball to "worthless vagabonds" and the "bloodsuckers of society," the enemies of thrift, honesty, and industry. Returning to his initial theme, he noted that "no language is too strong in commending baseball in its original simplicity and primitive innocence." Using a variety of mixed metaphors, he characterized amateur baseball as a legitimate child and professional baseball as a pool of unhealthy germs that threatened to kill off that which was good and pure.[54]

While the *Sporting News*, ever the champions of baseball interests, jumped in to defend professional ballplayers and owners against such "monstrous charges," the morality of baseball was not the real issue. Such rich allusions, as noted above, reveal much about the attitudes of many clerics in the 1890s toward a society that was changing in ways they could not understand or appreciate. To them, baseball was the symbol of a bygone era when life was simple and decent, the sanctity of the Sabbath was respected, and everyone knew their place. Such a view of the immaculate conception of baseball, suggested by this idyllic image, would later be reinforced by the Cooperstown myth in which a Civil War hero (Abner Doubleday) laid out a purely American game in one of New York's most pleasant environs. The culture of baseball is one of nostalgia, and together with the holiness of the Puritan Sabbath, this yearning for a better time in a better place among better people spoke to the hearts and minds of many rural native Protestants during this period of great transition.

2

The Emergence of the Sunday Baseball Issue in the Nineteenth Century

Reminiscing while crossing the East River on the Brooklyn Ferry in 1856, Walt Whitman contrasted the ample hills of Brooklyn with the bustling crowds on Manhattan Island. This image was deceptive. From the 1840s to the twentieth century, Brooklyn became one of the fastest growing urban centers in the nation as immigrants swarmed in, initially populating the riverfront from Greenpoint to Red Hook, then moving south. By 1860 Brooklyn was the third-largest city in the United States. Thirty years later, it could boast a population of well over half a million, which would nearly double by the turn of the century. The completion of the Brooklyn Bridge in 1883 facilitated access to Manhattan and expanded cross-river traffic and commercial growth.

At the same time, Brooklyn had its own distinctive pattern of development. Known as "the city of churches," this expanding urban region took on the appearance and ambience of a cluster of residential neighborhoods as one town after another was incorporated. Both urban and rural, the densely packed west side of the city stood in contrast with the sparsely populated eastern regions. In some ways Brooklyn took on the character of Manhattan. Brownsville, home to a large immigrant Jewish population, resembled the Lower East Side, the upscale Park Slope neighborhood mirrored the Upper

West Side, whereas Bedford-Stuyvesant replicated Jacob Riis's portrayal of the city's slums. However, even after Brooklyn was incorporated into Greater New York in 1898, it retained a distinctive identity and a strong sense of independence.

Baseball was central to this unique identity. The evolution of baseball in the nineteenth century was connected to the growth of Brooklyn as a city. For a population that worked indoors, baseball offered working-class residents a few hours of outdoor pleasure. Unlike Manhattan, with the exception of Central Park, where streets and small lots provided the only fields, Brooklyn was blessed with many parks bordered by wide open spaces. Ballparks were matters of real estate, and together with trolley lines and connecting streets they formed part of the borough's infrastructure.[1]

Sunday Baseball in Brooklyn

From the start, complaints and arrests for playing baseball on the Sabbath in Brooklyn, and throughout the metropolitan area, focused on men and boys playing pick-up games in city streets and public parks. As early as 1855, newspapers complained of boys from the metropolis playing ball on the outskirts of urban areas in New Jersey. The police in Hoboken experienced similar problems from young men who crossed the river to play Sunday ball in the Elysian Fields, where allegedly the first baseball game was played. On one such occasion the Hoboken police nabbed twenty lads and young men who wound up in the police court. Having been given a warning about more severe penalties in the future, those boys who could afford the one-dollar fine quickly paid up while the rest spent the night in the lockup. It would not be surprising to learn that the same youths returned to the playing fields soon thereafter—such was the lure of the game.[2]

By the 1870s, reports that the police were arresting boys for playing baseball in crowded areas started in earnest. Kings County added 329,393 new residents between the years 1875 and 1890, forcing baseball-loving youths to play in regions where they were more likely to cause a disturbance. Efforts by the borough police chief to enforce the city ordnance against ball playing on public thoroughfares prompted some officers to crack down on youths playing baseball in vacant lots. More particularly, arrests were instigated by complaints that ball playing along busy city streets and residential areas disturbed worship services at local churches and interrupted the repose of the day. It is not known how many incidents were handled informally by citizens shooing away groups of would-be Sunday ballplayers, accompanied no doubt by stern admonitions. Nevertheless, the many reports of youths congregating in populous neighborhoods on the Sabbath suggest that these matters were a common occurrence.[3]

Policies aimed at minimizing such disquieting activities prompted a certain amount of overzealousness, no doubt in reaction to public pressure. Conversely, there was a push against heavy-handed policing. For the most part, the approach taken by constables toward ball playing tended to follow a pragmatic line. Not for the last time did the Brooklyn police chief take a qualified approach by asserting that no policeman had the right to interfere with boys playing baseball in open spaces unless they were guilty of disorderly conduct, willful trespassing, or participating in games on Sunday. Given the additional burdens placed on the police by an expanding population, such a policy was not only reasonable but necessary.[4]

Reports suggest that disorderly behavior seems to have been the most persistent excuse for arrests from the 1850s to the 1870s, although playing ball on Sundays figured prominently as well. The suspicion of strangers passing through the neighborhoods of Brooklyn was often sufficient to invoke a response by the authorities. In the spring of 1876 pressure was put on the Brooklyn police to arrest anyone playing baseball on Sunday, with special attention to those who resembled "idlers." Of particular concern were youths who had wandered into Brooklyn from New York and Hoboken, creating a disruption during the course of a game. The determining factor appears to have been the dictum pertaining to causing a disturbance, as the police were on record for allowing games that had unobtrusive consequences.

Official responses to Sunday ball playing were not only generated by public complaints but by changes in the law. A revision of the penal code in 1882 was interpreted by the police throughout the New York area as a green light to clamp down on all Sunday activities except for works of necessity and charity. For a brief time police efforts at curtailing Sunday pastimes resulted in a reduction of Sabbath violations, leading some observers to question whether the New York police seemed more interested in prosecuting boys playing the national game on Sundays than in arresting young men paying for drinks in a bar on that day. Given that bars and saloons were cash cows for the political machines in Brooklyn and New York, the regulation of Sunday drinking was spotty at best.[5]

As with numerous other attempts to enforce the penal laws, vigilance soon gave way to laxity. Inconsistent enforcement of the statutes in the outer boroughs and metropolitan areas of New York was simulated elsewhere. Professional teams from St. Louis and Hartford, for instance, were able to take time off from their league schedule to play Sunday matches with amateur clubs in the safe havens of Elizabeth and Orange, New Jersey. The persistence of ball games on the Sabbath, which was a source of constant annoyance to churchgoers and persons wishing for a day of peace and quiet, aroused only mild sympathy from the political bosses on either side of the Hudson and East Rivers.[6]

Stymied in their attempts to stage ad hoc Sunday games in parks and open lots within Brooklyn's most populous neighborhood districts, baseball teams sought to establish a more permanent address. As early as 1858 Brooklyn teams played at the Fashion Race Course in the Flushing region of Queens County. The field was an enclosed park, the first such venue used for baseball, although it had been designed for other purposes. Brooklyn's first official ballpark was the Union Grounds in Williamsburg, which had originally been a skating rink but was modified for baseball in 1862. It became home to the Atlantics, the Eckfords, and the Mutuals, who enjoyed rent-free accommodations during the mid-1870s in exchange for a share of the profits that went into the pocket of William Cammeyer, who owned the grounds. Although the field was located within a residential area, the wooden fence surrounding the park offered a semblance of exclusivity.[7]

So successful was this arrangement that the owner of the Capitoline Park, located south of Williamsburg in Bedford Stuyvesant, converted his skating rink into a baseball field with a seating capacity for about five thousand. Thus a pattern arose. The benefit to the owners was that they could make money on their real estate year-round with skating in the winter, baseball in the summer, and perhaps racing in between.[8]

Complaints by some members of the public about the noise occasioned by a spirited game of baseball were one of the drawbacks to contests within residential neighborhoods. Such disturbances sometimes led to unwelcome attention by the police, followed by a disruption of the games and even arrests. This state of affairs eventually encouraged baseball clubs and leagues to migrate to the eastern and less-populated part of Brooklyn in search of a safe haven where the reach and interest of officialdom were less intrusive. Just over the border in Queens County, Ridgewood Park was situated in what was then rural Long Island, five miles beyond the convenience of urban amenities.

In the 1880s more professional and semi-professional leagues and teams began to appear, adding further complications for those charged with upholding Sunday restrictions. Ridgewood Park became a magnet for weekend holiday-makers who made the trek to the northeast regions, bringing with them their love of baseball. Sensing that Sunday matches would have a better chance of success farther away from home, the professional Brooklyn Grays (later the Bridegrooms) of the American Association played fourteen games at Ridgewood in 1886, interspersed with Sunday matches at Washington Park, their permanent home in the Red Hook section of Brooklyn. This was a shrewd decision as Sunday games at Ridgewood Park were popular, averaging about four thousand fans for each contest.[9]

Even though Sunday games were illegal, the enforcement of the law remained inconsistent. Fans attending the Sabbath-day match between the Athletic baseball team of Long Island City and the Nameless Club of Brooklyn, won by the Athletics 13–10, were in no way inconvenienced. Since no one seems to have been bothered by the game, no complaints were made to the police, who were not inclined to initiate arrests on their own. A Sunday contest between the Grays and Baltimore at Ridgewood Park was remarkable for its loud fireworks but did not occasion any interest by law enforcement.[10]

This is not to say that such games on Sundays went unnoticed. Since the beginning of the season there had been interventions by the police in Sunday matches at Ridgewood Park. The first intrusion occurred in a game played by the Grays on April 25, 1886. Later in the season on a September Sunday afternoon, the police raided all the ballparks in the vicinity and notified the

owners that no games would be allowed on that day, much to the consternation of the shocked proprietors. Ignoring this warning, a scheduled game
between Brooklyn and the Athletics went ahead. The police dutifully arrived
at Ridgewood Park during the sixth inning and shut the game down while
the disappointed spectators looked on.[11]

Police crackdowns on Sunday games that took place on the fringes of
Brooklyn did not occur out of the blue. Pressure from groups opposed to
Sunday recreation existed all over the city by the 1880s. On April 10, 1887,
the Law and Order Society of Newtown informed the sheriff on Saturday
night that if baseball playing was allowed on Sunday a committee would go
before the grand jury and have him indicted for dereliction of duty. The sheriff ordered the police chief to prevent a game at Atlantic Park between the
Cuban Giants and the Newark ball club. The spectators who had paid good
money to attend the game were not amused to see a phalanx of police enter
the field, and a few fans pelted them with stones as they retreated from the
park. At the same time, to make sure the laws were respected, police commissioner Henry Johnson made a turn around the ballparks of Long Island
City and let it be known he was keeping a close watch on all outdoor activities. Meanwhile, the mayor of Long Island City issued a statement that he
was in favor of allowing baseball on Sundays, but he, fortunately, did not
have the Law and Order Society breathing down his neck.[12]

Amateur clubs, in contrast to those teams that charged admission, took a
more casual attitude toward Sunday baseball. Games on the first day of the
week were openly reported in the press, and the names of players were listed.
The Vernon Athletic Club in 1896 noted that Saturday and Sunday dates for
August and September were available and hoped to hear from teams within
two hundred miles of Brooklyn, for whom they would pay travel expenses. The
Sidney baseball club, champions of the Brooklyn Amateur Association, was
busy during the same year, playing weekend games in Brooklyn and towns
around Long Island. The Orient Athletic Club, after changing its name to the
Bedford Baseball Club, announced that the team would play on Saturdays,
Sundays, and holidays at the newly renovated Washington Park, with clubs
offering suitable inducements. In the meantime, they were looking to find a
second and third baseman and two outfielders to round out their squad.[13]

By the 1890s, recreational associations of all sorts had sprung up around Brooklyn. While the Varuna Boat Club was primarily concerned with sailing, they did field a baseball team that played on Sundays. When the Bay Ridge Athletic Club held its fifth annual outing over the last weekend of July 1899, a Sunday baseball game was among a variety of activities that included track and field events and a bicycle race. African American clubs had their own athletic organizations, such as the Fruition Cake-Walk Society, that cultivated outdoor sports. Baseball was near the top of the list but even middle-class pastimes, such as lawn tennis and croquet, were played. So prevalent and open was Sunday baseball by the last decade of the century that amateur athletes would have considered themselves exceedingly unlucky to have ended up in court for violating the Sabbath day sanctions of the blue laws.[14]

The desire to escape the hustle and bustle of city life led those who could afford it to look further afield. Resorts, hotels, and inns located in the scenic Catskill Mountains and as far away as the Adirondacks offered the vacationer and weekend traveler a variety of amusements and sporting opportunities. Fishing, hunting, boating, bathing, cycling, and games such as golf, tennis, croquet, and bowling were available, as was baseball. Since these activities took place in relatively secluded areas on private grounds, little heed was paid to blue law restrictions.

Sunday school and church-sponsored outings were also frequent occurrences during the summer months. One such excursion involved a steamboat trip up the Hudson River for a picnic where a number of activities, including baseball, would occur under the watchful eye of the superintendent of Sunday Schools, Mr. A. W. Webster, and another minister. It is presumed that these events took place during the week, or on a Saturday, so as not to despoil the Sabbath. However, Sunday baseball was sometimes condoned if it was slotted into church group activities. Catholic youth groups, which had fewer scruples about the sanctity of the Sabbath, formed Diocesan leagues for the express purpose of playing Sunday baseball.[15]

Brooklyn in the late nineteenth century had become a magnet for pleasure seekers from all over the metropolis. "The public parks and parkways of Brooklyn," one newspaper boasted, "are perhaps more largely devoted to amateur sports than any other borough in New York, or any other city in the world." And there was no pleasure spot more magnetic than Coney Island. By the 1880s Coney Island became the main attraction within the city of Brooklyn. Aside from its obvious seaside advantages, "the Island" offered vaudeville shows, dance halls, hotels, and long boardwalks, occupied by the cacophony of street vendors, where visitors could enjoy the salubrious benefits of ocean air. Coney Island and Far Rockaway also attracted sportsmen of all sorts. The Coney Island Jockey Club pulled in the racing crowd from far and wide, and the west end of the island gained a certain notoriety from the gamblers and hangers-on who flocked there.[16]

Baseball was a part of this picture. Brooklyn Grays president Charlie Byrne planned games at the new ballpark situated between the iron piers behind the South Beach hotel. The masses of people that gathered on Sundays posed a problem for the police, who were under pressure to maintain order and uphold, to some extent, the sections of the penal code related to Sabbath-day fun. Increased police involvement led to the arrest of six players on the Brooklyn Club for playing a May 3, 1885, game on the grounds of the Sea Beach Railroad Company. Byrne made an appeal arguing that the game was played away from churches, dwellings, and schools, and did not interfere with the religious services or the repose of the neighborhood. Moreover, the game had the consent of the Sea Beach Company. This argument was convincing enough for the appeal to be granted. Subsequent police vigilance meant that Coney Island enjoyed a number of quiet Sundays after the May 3, 1885, incident.[17]

The blue laws were also enforced at nearby Rockaway Beach. Among the amusements was a curious form of baseball that consisted of patrons throwing baseballs at wooden figures. Sometimes the sport was changed so that, barbarously, a live Negro was positioned as the target with only his head exposed through the canvas. Concern that the beach was being invaded by "objectionable characters," the Seaside Businessmen's Association put pressure on local authorities to have amusements closed down on Sunday. Blame was directed at the sheriff, Capt. George DeMott, who was accused of not doing his job. A report circulated by a New York newspaper, based on circumstantial evidence, noted that DeMott had taken a bribe of $50 from gaming and concessions interests. The sheriff blamed the seaside business-men, whom he believed had paid for the story in order to get rid of him. Under pressure, Captain DeMott soon saw the writing on the wall and was quick to capitulate. "I intend to give this Law and Order Society all the law enforcement they or anyone else can desire," he said. "No beer or liquor will be sold on Sunday, no games or sports of any kind will be open, and the only thing people can do is bathe and eat their meals."[18]

One Christian Sabbatarian did an accounting of the various Sunday games played around the country. He observed that the schedule of the National League comprised 792 games, of which thirty-six were arranged on Sunday in states where such games were against the law. Looking at the full scope of organized baseball, he calculated that there were 128 Sunday games in all the professional leagues played around the country. The worst aspect of this violation of the law, he thought, was the demoralizing influence Sunday baseball had on the young. "Why should we enforce our laws against other places of amusement . . . and not against the league players?" the writer astutely asked. "Here is work for Sabbath committees in at least twenty states in the Union and probably in all."[19]

Throughout the 1880s and 1890s a number of organizations devoted to preserving the integrity of the Sabbath, along the lines of the Law and Order Society, came into prominence. The Lord's Day Alliance, founded in 1888 as the American Sabbath Union, had as its agenda to maintain and cultivate the first day of the week as a time for rest, worship, Christian education, and spiritual renewal. That same year the Society for a Better Observance of the Sabbath was founded in the village of Jamaica, east of the borough, to uphold traditional Sunday norms and values. The leader of the group, the Reverend William James of the Woodhaven Congregational Church in Queens, observed that the movement set itself against all violations of the Sabbath, noting particularly the prohibition against Sunday sales of liquor in saloons.[20]

Like the WCTU and other moral reform organizations, such Sabbath protection groups were locally based, having some influence in nearly every Protestant church, in every town, and in every local community around the state. Ministerial associations brought together concerned clergy from denominations within a given region, and served as watchdog committees on the lookout for violations of the Sabbath laws. Sunday schools not only imparted to youth edifying bible stories but also preached against the dangers of drink, the evils of the flesh, and, directly or indirectly, the error of Sunday sports. Crusaders like ex–baseball player Billy Sunday toured the country, haranguing and simultaneously delighting audiences with lectures on the dangers of alcohol and other sins. Mass meetings, sermons from the pulpit, and even Christian ladies' tea parties were also occasions for speaking out against Sabbath desecrations.

Blue law advocates mobilized community opposition in 1889 to stop noisy ball games in Brooklyn and to secure indictments against the managers, players, and proprietors of ballparks alike. The persistence of amateur, semi-pro, and professional teams playing Sunday games brought the Sunday Observance Association into action. Sabbath protection groups noted that Sunday ball games at Ridgewood Park occurred in open defiance of the law. It was widely believed that the Christian Sabbath must be maintained, or Christianity itself would be imperiled. The Sunday Observance Association addressed letters to Sheriff Matthew J. Goldner of Queens County accusing him of knowingly allowing Sunday ball and the opening of saloons. Behind the letters were veiled threats of legal action if the sheriff did not comply.[21]

The Sabbath Observance Association's overall plan was to arouse public opinion by communicating to all churches the need to prevent Sunday baseball. On at least one occasion the Law and Order League of Queens joined forces with the New York Sabbath Committee in the neighborhood of Ridgewood Park to prevent the riot and revelry that was reportedly taking place. Convinced that public sentiment in Brooklyn and the vicinity was behind them, these organizations put pressure on local officials to halt baseball on the Sabbath. Sunday protection groups, however, were often confronted with overlapping political jurisdictions, as in the case of Ridgewood Park on the border of Queens County, making it difficult to pin down the proper authorities to make arrests.[22]

The Women's Sabbath Alliance, organized in 1857 to combat the increasing amount of Sabbath desecration, was another supporter of Sunday legislation. Apparently, the primary function of this alliance was to encourage parents to teach children to observe the Sabbath. The role of women in defending the integrity of the Puritan Sunday cannot be overestimated, and the efforts in this direction by women's organizations were neither passive nor inconspicuous. Among the alliance's various missions was an unlikely crusade against Sunday golf. As a sport of the middle classes, golf was a more obvious and pressing concern for respectable Sabbatarian ladies than were Sunday baseball games. Like the more male-dominated Sabbath organizations, women's groups sought to organize branches and engage in overt activities in places where Sunday recreations were of a concern.[23]

Proactive efforts by Sabbatarian organizations were galvanized by a measure of public opinion that conveyed the feelings of ordinary citizens through letters to the local press. One such letter writer was puzzled as to why policemen were not dressed as private spectators in the stands so as to give Sabbath breakers no warning and thus arrest and convict "these lawless and God defying persons." The correspondent also complained of flagrant assaults on the peace and quiet of well-behaved citizens (meaning white, middle-class property owners) caused by ball playing and other games.[24]

Another letter, penned in 1888 and signed by "A lover of the National Game," objected to Sunday ball at Ridgewood Park. The letter's author pinpointed an important distinction that was beginning to form in the minds of Sunday baseball opponents between professional and recreational baseball. He noted that baseball contests on Sunday, especially by "big salaried players, are a perennial nuisance not tolerated in other parts of the state." Like many other citizens of Brooklyn, the author distinguished between the bother caused by boys playing ball in the street and that of professional and semi-professional teams. Ball-playing youths were merely pests, he thought, whereas organized baseball called for strong law-and-order measures to which the public would give their blessing.[25]

The rapid growth of population in the Brooklyn (encompassed within Kings County), which more than doubled in size between 1875 and 1900, aroused fear among the propertied middle and upper classes of being swamped by hordes of newcomers. Sunday street ballplayers increasingly became less of a concern, as were the amateur teams that drew smaller crowds, unless they proved to be rowdy. Popular clubs, attracting thousands of supporters on a Sunday, and amusement parks for the masses (Coney Island and Ridgewood Park) were another matter. In an age that was fixated on moral and social order, the Sunday blue laws were a convenient tool for keeping "the great unwashed" at bay and alleviating the threat of riot and mayhem.

The persistent activity of Sabbath observance groups in combating Sunday baseball in Brooklyn was reinforced by various sermons emanating from pulpits around the borough. Reflecting a changing climate of moral uncertainty, one clergyman remarked, "I am persuaded that nothing now concerns human society more than the question of Sunday observance." Until recently, he thought, religious or social conventions determined what actions were permissible on Sundays. "Now the code is so confused," he lamented, "that one's conscience does not know what to do."[26]

Between the years 1868 and 1888, while several hundred thousand immigrants poured into the metropolis, Protestant churches in working-class neighborhoods disappeared, reinforcing the impression that these religious organizations largely entertained the middle class. As one minister put it, "to the mass of workingmen Sunday . . . is a day for labor meetings, for excursions, for saloons, beer-gardens, baseball games and carousals," instead of a time for church. While for many churchmen Sunday observance remained an article of religious doctrine, the lay supporters of Sunday laws saw more perceptively that it was an issue of class and moral decline.[27]

The Reverend Dr. Leander Trowbridge Chamberlain, a Presbyterian minister in Brooklyn, spoke for many in lamenting that the experience of the past few years had demonstrated how the old law, which enforced an observance of Sunday, was becoming less rigid. Casting a glance at his less orthodox colleagues and the liberal clerics opposed to the blue laws, he noted that the people who should advance the cause of good were permitting nonobservance to increase. This sentiment was carried forward by the Reverend Dr. William H. Ford, who from a Brooklyn pulpit decried the fact that "the fear of improper observance of the Sabbath is founded upon the increasing cry for recreation, which is but an apology for desecration." On this point, he surmised, the church must stand firm since a lukewarm attitude could only lead to the encouragement of evil.[28]

Another clergyman, the Reverend Jesse W. Brooks of the East New York Reformed Church predicted that in a few years the American Sunday would become a battleground between the powers of God and mammon, and there was no mystery as to the composition of either side. The Reverend Charles Buck, a Methodist minister, thought that the desire for gain and pleasure came from the foreigner "who had no more right to force on 'true Americans' their Sabbath activities any more than their language or marriage laws." Suspicion of alien influences would be a constant theme for the next quarter century and beyond, as white middle-class Protestants wrestled with an inner misgiving that they were losing ground to those elements who, according to the Anglo-Saxon pecking order, were far lower on the food chain.[29]

A constant theme running through the various Sabbath-day sermons was the church at war against the forces of secularism. Baseball, although casually alluded to, was not necessarily the central point of concern but was part of a more global problem. The perceived desecration of the Lord's Day naturally involved sports but also the casual enforcement of laws against the sale of liquor and other items, the flagrant running of theaters and shows, and at a later date movies, which carried the added burden of being morally objectionable.

As usual, the *Sporting News* in 1891 overstated its case when it gleefully declared that Sunday was getting to be a great day for sports in America and that the Puritan Sabbath was becoming a tradition of the past. "We simply recognize the growth of liberal thought on religion," it was observed. "Such liberality is pronounced unchristian by our zealous divines." A *New York Times* editorial more aptly described community attitudes toward Sunday observance by stating that "Sabbath breaking is no longer regarded as sacrilegious in this country is yet disreputable" in those communities which are not too large to have any effectual neighborhood opinion. The editorial concluded that public sentiment was in favor of the Sunday laws but "the Puritan element should not push its observance too strongly since their position owes much more to sentiment than to argument."[30]

Whether anyone was convinced or took to heart the pronouncements of the Brooklyn clergy, whose sermons were often printed in the press, their arguments were primarily a front for the status quo. In the last analysis, the clergy and their supporters had only to point to the appropriate sections of the penal code to state their case, a subject on which all who held to the notion of a Puritan Sabbath were well versed. Efforts to uphold the law were further bolstered by the formation of the New York Civic League, which claimed to be a nonpartisan organization intent on lobbying for moral reform and the preservation of Sunday observance laws in Albany. In fact, it was anything but nonpartisan, and throughout the period when the battle over Sunday baseball was raging various church advocacy groups and pro-Sabbath elements within the Republican Party courted favor with the League for their own advantage.[31]

Constant vigilance of Sabbath observance codes by blue law protection societies could not prevent Sunday games, as more and more teams, professional and amateur, chose to evade the law and suffer the consequences, if any. Police attentiveness had the effect of limiting the number of professional games played on Long Island during the early 1890s. At the same time, law enforcement turned a blind eye to amateur games sponsored by the Brooklyn Amateur Association at Bay Ridge and other spots around the borough. Semi-pro games on Sunday at Ridgewood Park and elsewhere were increasingly advertised and played openly, drawing together some of the best clubs in New York. Even so, amateurs and semi-pro players were still liable for arrest when the police were otherwise not occupied.[32]

Such inconsistencies in law enforcement were a source of confusion for the public as well as for the police. The problem was complicated by the fact that the fortunes of Sunday baseball were sometimes linked to those of prizefighting. Professional baseball, as we shall see, became increasingly associated with all kinds of roughhouse and disreputable behavior, which put it into the same category as boxing, a pervasive and popular entertainment of the working classes. For those citizens accustomed to a moral climate that defined social behavior in terms of absolute right and wrong, exceptions to the illegality of Sunday baseball and prizefights were bewildering and distressing—all the more so since both sports had acquired a reputation for attracting gamblers and other perceived seedy characters.

The issue was partly resolved when Justice William Jay Gaynor of the New York State Supreme Court ordered the mayor of Brooklyn to issue special licenses so that ball games and fights could be carried out at limited times in restricted places. At the same time, Gaynor hoped to put the matter to rest since he was tired of complaints from the boys and young men who were constantly being picked up on Sundays for playing baseball. Gaynor responded by ordering Police Commissioner Leonard Welles yet again not to interfere with boys playing baseball in isolated areas. Welles was glad not to strain police resources by chasing down "hard working boys" from enjoying some innocent fun. With the amalgamation of Brooklyn into Greater New York in 1898, the *Sporting News* predicted that Sunday baseball would be available to the Brooklyn club somewhere in the metropolitan area. However, considering that a good segment of public opinion remained hostile to any deviation from the letter of the law, such a prognostication remained premature.[33]

The Darker Side of Baseball

It was on moral grounds that the opponents of Sunday baseball felt most at home. No other issue divided the classes more than the question of drink. While the respectable middle classes (especially the rural Protestant church-going middle class) were traveling the dry road of temperance, many urbanites, immigrants, and working-class folk were drowning in a sea of alcohol. New York City, the most populous metropolitan region in the country, also ranked first in the number of bars, saloons, and taverns. As late as 1914, over thirteen thousand drinking establishments were scattered around the city, and in some districts there was a saloon for every six inhabitants.[34]

During the late nineteenth and early twentieth centuries alcohol flowed through baseball, both on and off the field. Club owners often conducted their business in bars, making the tavern their home away from home. Nearly every team in Harry Wright's National Association of Professional Baseball Players found their games marred by "drunkenness and riot," as the result of the sale of liquor at games. It was unusual for teams not to have at least one player who was an alcoholic. Regardless of fines, the threat of suspension, or blacklisting, the problem continued. Players sometimes hid whiskey bottles in a corner of the dugout or in the outfield so as to take sips during the game. Pete Browning, who played centerfield for Louisville of the American Association in the 1880s, was usually drunk on and off the field, and although he had a career batting average of .341, he claimed that he couldn't hit the ball until he hit the bottle. In some cases liquor was passed from the stands on to the field. With lots of time on their hands, the bar or tavern became the off-field resort for many players. Given the pervasiveness of alcoholic consumption, and the culture of drinking that permeated urban society, teams often had little choice but to tolerate its drunkards and hope their antics would not embarrass the club or compromise the game. While clubs frequently criticized their players for drunkenness, they did little or nothing to confront the problem.[35]

Alcoholism often contributed to ruined careers and ruined lives, a prime example being Hall of Fame pitcher Grover Cleveland Alexander. Another victim was Bugs Raymond, who pitched for the New York Giants in the year they won ninety-nine games and finished in first place. In a game against Pittsburgh near the end of the season, Raymond was called in from the bullpen to pitch to Pirates' star shortstop Honus Wagner. With two outs and two runners on base, Bugs's first pitch hit the grandstand, bringing in a run. Wagner hit the next ball back to the pitcher. Rather than make an easy toss to first base for the third out, Raymond tried to get the runner coming in from third base and threw the ball over the catcher's head, allowing another run to score. Manager John McGraw then pulled his inebriated pitcher from the game. Raymond walked directly out of the park and across the street to a gin mill, where he traded the game ball for three shots of whiskey. Bugs never played again for the Giants and he was last seen, in uniform, plying his trade in a Sunday game with a New York sandlot team.[36]

The most enduring and insidious affliction to befall professional baseball, and to some degree amateur ball, was its long-standing association with gambling. Reports of gambling emerged as early as the 1860s, and the problem never went away. "One of the greatest drawbacks to the progress of healthy sports and pastimes and their popularity with the best classes of society," noted the *New York Clipper*, was the tendency of the professional class of the sporting fraternity "to enter into fraudulent collusion with knaves to wager bets." Gambling was the benchmark that divided respectable society from the sporting and uncouth crowd, and for those among the "better classes" gambling was the brush that smeared professional baseball.[37]

Gambling was situational and rampant at many ballparks, hotel lobbies, betting shops, restaurant bars, and other places where the sporting crowd tended to congregate. What amounted to a version of insider trading during the 1879 season was carried out by two telegraph operators in Syracuse. Using their position, they took advantage of advanced information about the outcome of games and so issued a false report for the purpose of buying pools (pools being the amount staked by a combination of bettors). The scheme backfired when Western Union got wind of the scam and proceeded to discharge and blacklist the operators, who pocketed only the measly sum of $32 for their efforts. So pervasive was gambling on sports over the latter decades of the nineteenth century that organizations such as the Society for the Prevention of Crime took upon themselves the task of reporting on the activities of gamblers and passing along useful information to the police.[38]

Gambling money was sometimes used to acquire ball clubs. On January 25, 1885, Dave Dishler, a colorful local character, purchased the Utica team in the New York State League. To raise the $5,000 necessary to buy the club and to secure operating expenses, Dishler, head of the city's Democratic Party, joined forces with Thomas Wheeler, the local Republican boss, to operate one of Utica's two gambling dens. The profits from this operation were enormous. This political tag team proved beneficial at election time since whoever won would serve the interests of the Dishler-Wheeler gang. So egregious was this partnership that a reform group of businessmen and politicians formed a party to combat Utica's "back room politics." As an owner, Dishler was popular with his players—no doubt because he paid them well.[39]

In spite of stepped-up law enforcement, gambling on baseball games continued unabated. After refusing to play the 1904 World Series against Boston, manager John McGraw of the Giants participated in post-season play the following year against the Philadelphia Athletics. McGraw was lambasted by the American League president for refusing to let his team play the previous year and for overall boorish and bad behavior. The Giants manager got his own back by beating the Athletics in five games, and by winning the bets he placed on the outcome.[40]

Betting on matches was occasionally singled out for close attention by the police, but for the gamblers themselves this was merely an annoyance.

The police were further hampered because the law did not cover individuals who made personal bets. In any event, gambling at the ball park was easily concealed from the few police detectives assigned to keep an eye on the betting crowd.[41]

Game fixing had a close association with gambling. The first reported case of a game that was thrown occurred in a match played on September 28, 1865, in Hoboken, New Jersey, between two New York teams. Players on the New York Mutuals were said to have received $100 to lose a game to their archrival, the Brooklyn Eckfords. Two months later, club officials charged William Wansley as the person who organized the fix and handled the negotiations. Wansley was later expelled from the team. Although the frequency of throwing games cannot be determined precisely, it was well-known that professional players on some teams, especially the Mutuals, which was controlled by the infamously corrupt William Magear "Boss" Tweed, leader of New York's Tammany Hall political machine, were more than willing to take money from gamblers in exchange for sloppy play on the field.[42]

In spite of the National League's moral posturing in the 1880s, the vigilance against gambling and its consequent evils appeared to collapse into humbug in the 1890s when owners, players, and managers made little effort to mask their gambling activities. Monte Ward of the New York Giants, for instance, was supposedly said to have won twenty shares of stock from a club director in 1892 as a result of betting on where the team would place in the standings that year.[43]

Not surprisingly, those clerics most dismayed by the desecration of the Sabbath were equally disturbed by the gambling that took place at many ballparks. The close association between betting and sport reinforced the perception that baseball was corrupt. During the high point of the summer in 1901, the Greenpoint Ministers Conference in Brooklyn circulated a petition protesting against nuisances in that region, including gambling. While baseball wasn't considered the worst, the crowds of men and boys who gathered near the games on a Sunday and indulged in gambling were more problematic. This was in spite of the fact the police had tried unsuccessfully to put a stop to these illegal activities. With the start of a new baseball season, the gamblers returned to Greenpoint and carried on business as usual.[44]

Concern about gambling at ballparks was briefly overshadowed by the burning issue of racetrack gambling. The penal code was full of provisions against gambling. With the passage of the Ives Law in 1887, betting at race courses was permitted with some restrictions. The matter became a hot topic in 1908 when several bills were presented to the legislature, with the backing of Gov. Charles Evans Hughes, to outlaw it. The defenders of moral rectitude were nearly unanimous in support of the antigambling bills, but the sporting interests had a powerful lobby and won over a number of men who could usually be counted on to support the agenda of the churches. Sen. Owen Cassidy of Schuyler County, who stood against earlier bills, quickly changed his position and voted to abolish racetrack betting in response to an overwhelming response from constituents in his district. Less fortunate was Sen. B. M. Wilcox of Auburn, a twenty-year trustee of the First Methodist Episcopal Church in that city who, after casting his ballot against the antigambling bills, lost his position on the board when his friends determined that his vote made him an undesirable church officer.[45]

Baseball also had to contend with violence. Mistreatment of the arbiters of the game by partisan fans was particularly noteworthy. The abuse of umpires was as old as organized baseball itself. Umpire baiting during the 1879 season was almost as disgraceful as in the previous season, cried the *New York Clipper*. It was bad enough that umpires were verbally harangued by the "betting crowd" and physically attacked by players, but they also had to endure humiliation from the press over alleged bad decisions. The abuse of umpires occurred at all levels of organized baseball. An assault on an umpire by a Poughkeepsie player in the Hudson Valley League, which appeared at a later date in the *Sporting News*, would have only raised a few eyebrows since the practice was so common.[46]

Even in the rough and tumble world of late-nineteenth- and early-twentieth-century New York baseball, there were limits. During the ninth inning of a game between the Metropolitans and the Alleghenies at the Polo Grounds, the general round of focused abuse led one fan to go so far as to suggest that the umpire was being paid off to make improper calls. The game was immediately stopped and the fan was arrested. Physical violence was one thing, but demeaning the integrity of a man in authority was, according to the moral climate of the age, unconscionable.[47]

A week later the same newspaper noted that at no other time had it been so dangerous to be an umpire at a baseball match. The umpire's bodily safety was threatened by extreme partisanship, and it appeared that no legislation on the part of professional baseball could protect an umpire from such abuses. The irony was all the more galling because it was generally agreed in baseball circles that "good umpiring is essential to the life of baseball."[48]

For those concerned with what was perceived to be the overall erosion of authority in society, umpire abuse was a reinforcing symbol. The context for such abuse was a climate of rowdiness marred by violence and dirty tactics among players, fights among fans, and even fisticuffs between fans and players. The ganging up of both fans and players on umpires was yet further proof to the respectable classes in urban and rural regions alike that professional baseball was a sport of ruffians and drew to itself obnoxious and dangerous elements. To punctuate the point, reports of fights and brawls that occurred at picnic parks and ballparks every Sunday in Queens frequently appeared in the press around the turn of the century.[49]

In light of ongoing misbehavior, by 1900 interest in the national pastime continued to divide social classes, which had ramifications for Sunday baseball. The local press reported a riot that took place on a Sunday game at Star Park in Syracuse during the 1902 season as "an incident shameful to the city and injurious of its good name." While many people in Syracuse maintained a conscientious scruple against public sports on Sunday, the press reported that there was tacit acceptance of such games provided there was no disturbance. Public confidence had become so shaken that the future of Sunday ball in the city was in doubt.[50]

Violence on the field was no less pervasive than it was in the stands or in train cars. Fights among professional players, often leading to injuries, were so widespread that they barely merited mention in the press. One such brawl on July 15, 1906, between players on the Pittsburgh Pirates and the New York Giants, was so egregious that it managed to get some coverage. The fight, witnessed by Pittsburgh mayor Charles F. Kirschler, resulted in the arrest of Giants pitcher Joe "Iron Man" McGinnity, who unmercifully pummeled his opponent and left him bleeding on the ground with a black eye. The Pittsburgh mayor ordered McGinnity's arrest. The pitcher was taken from the field amid cries and catcalls from the fans. The Pittsburgh crowd, still in an uproar, kept up a running fire of abuse for the rest of the game. The affair did not faze the "Iron Man," who proved to be as effective a pitcher as he was a fighter and went on to win twenty-seven games that year for the second-place Giants.[51]

Hooliganism by fans also affected innocent bystanders. The cause of Sunday baseball could hardly have benefited from the actions of a crowd of hoodlums who attacked passengers on a train from Long Island heading to a Sunday ball game in New York. A similar fate befell beleaguered passengers on a New York Central train from the metropolis to Albany, who were terrorized by drunken New York Giants players. The team members took possession of a train car, causing a small riot that was further aggravated when outfielder Mike Donlin ("Turkey Mike") drew a pistol and pointed it at the conductor. Donlin was among three players arrested, but the man Damon Runyan later called "the most picturesque, colorful ballplayer I ever saw," was able to reap the rewards of celebrity when a local politician paid his $1,000 bail bond.[52]

League officials were not unaware of the climate of violence that marked baseball. Byron Bancroft Johnson, the driving force behind the creation of the American League and the dominant figure on professional baseball's governing committee, the National Commission, was forced to take steps to address the problem. Initially, he sought a self-correcting approach by admonishing American League umpires to adhere to the rules regarding rowdy behavior on the ball field. Later, after an incident in which Detroit outfielder Ty Cobb threw his bat into the stands after striking out, Johnson was forced to take a tougher stand by threatening to suspend unruly managers and players and further promising dire measures unless players curbed their tempers.[53]

How effective efforts were to restrict gambling and baseball violence remains an open question. Ironically, Arnold Rothstein (the alleged instigator of the Black Sox scandal in 1919) described in the press as a sportsman, made the extraordinary claim in 1917 that there was little high-stakes betting in professional baseball on a daily basis, and that huge bets on the outcome of a game were few and far between. Whether Rothstein was being disingenuous or just cagey, nobody knows. What is known is that periodic crusades against the long and ignoble tradition of gambling at baseball games continued until the 1920s, when Commissioner Kenesaw Mountain Landis, and belatedly club officials, sounded a call to order for players and gamblers alike. Still the problem continued, since there were far more people willing to place bets in every big league city than could be countered by the resources available to curtail the problem.[54]

By the second decade of the century, professional baseball remained a rough game full of provocation and fisticuffs. As one cleric noted, "baseball cannot be played by temperate men." Nevertheless, it could be said with some degree of accuracy that by the eve of the First World War, the trend in professional sports toward greater commercialism was offset by the more extreme incidences of rowdy and violent behavior that had previously marred the game. Still, it was not until two game-fixing scandals came to light during the winter of 1926–1927 that regulations were tightened and baseball turned a corner.[55]

Sunday Baseball Upstate

Opposition to Sunday baseball in cities and communities upstate mirrored that experienced in Brooklyn. One fundamental difference was that in Brooklyn, and in the rest of New York City, both organized and informal Sunday baseball games suffered from the sporadic attentions of law enforcement, while the Sabbatarians upstate directed their full attention to the professional game. Essentially, the issue of baseball on the first day of the week in places like Buffalo, Syracuse, and Rochester did not rise to importance until the end of the nineteenth century. When it did, the ramifications affected not only the players, managers, and fans in those particular cities but the status of organized minor league baseball throughout the state.

In 1888, President E. Strachen Cox of the International League prevented several member clubs from scheduling Sabbath games and thus set back professional Sunday baseball in a number of upstate cities. This was in spite of the fact that the Syracuse Stars and the Rochester Baseball Club (called then the Jingoes) had signed contracts with several other teams to play Sunday ball, so as to enhance their revenues. Sunday baseball and economics were closely tied together. Club financial accounts were thrown into disarray by a lack of clarity about when and if Sunday games would be played. Problems arose since many games were already scheduled.[56]

Often team owners had to wait on the political process before determining the schedule, as was the case in the Eastern League and the New York State League, whose fixtures in 1899 were contingent upon a bill to legalize Sunday baseball in New York. The bill was quickly put to rest. As it turned out, no team in either league scheduled games on Sunday, although four International League cities—Syracuse, Rochester, Toronto, and Montreal—entertained professional baseball matches on that day.[57]

Sunday baseball in Syracuse was not without its headaches. As the 1897 season approached, Stars owner George N. Kuntzsch was in a quandary as to where his team could perform without arousing opposition from local residents who were overtly in favor of Sunday observance. Hostility to Sunday sports forced him to abandon plans to hold games in the western suburb of Solvay. Turning his attention to amateur grounds, Kuntzsch was faced with the prospect of having to lay out considerable funds to make these parks suitable for professional Sunday ball, such as enclosing spaces so he could charge admission. He also encountered opposition from those who were not anxious to have their parks turned over to professional baseball and were content with hosting amateur games. The suggestion was made that if the Stars wanted to play on Sunday, they might have to find a venue in another town.[58]

The potential crowds for Sunday baseball reflected the growth of urban population centers in cities like Syracuse, which absorbed immigrants from overseas and migrants from rural areas. Thanks to its geographical location in the center of the state, Syracuse developed as a noteworthy industrial city after the creation of the Erie and Owasco Canal systems in the 1820s and later became a major railroad thoroughfare. Settled by Protestants who migrated from New England and eastern New York, Syracuse's population grew dramatically with the influx of large numbers of German and Irish immigrants in the 1840s, who by the 1860s comprised the largest foreign-born groups in the city. Attracted by the lure of railroad and construction jobs, people from southern and eastern Europe were later drawn to Syracuse, where they found employment as laborers in mills making china, caskets, agricultural machinery, and steel.

Despite the diversity of Syracuse's population, the largely Protestant middle class dominated its political and cultural life and played a pivotal role on Sabbath issues. Strong opinions on the subject from different quarters bubbled to the surface. When the Syracuse *Evening Herald* solicited from newspapermen in the region their views on whether the State Fair should remain open on Sundays, they were besieged with letters expressing sentiments on both sides. While the responses were favorable, they did not reflect the silent majority of public opinion that was far less supportive of popular Sunday activities.

Those behind the retention of the Sunday blue laws had the energetic backing of several ministerial groups. The ministers in the many Syracuse pulpits directed their guns against Sunday baseball using a battery of well-trod arguments. A group of ministers called a meeting at the YMCA hall in May 1897 to voice their objections. They expressed fear that Sunday ball would be used as a wedge to promote and legitimize other Sabbath activities. In opposition to the contention that baseball on the first day of the week would give the laboring classes a wholesome outlet, one of the ministers argued that the Sunday laws were designed to protect the working man from toil and unnecessary activity. "Workingmen ought to be the first to uphold the moral and civil law enacted first of all for their own good. . . . To sit three hours in the sun is not the sort of rest men need on Sunday."[59]

The Barber's Fraternal Union was less than appreciative of what the ministers were doing "for their own good." They were also quick to respond to the insinuation that their successful fight for a rest day on Sunday was in any way connected with the baseball issue. While thanking the various churches for their support in the battle to obtain a day of rest, the spokesman for the barbers stood firm against the magnates compelling players, "to work in hopeless slavery while they ought to be free." The position of the union should be "to assist them to regain their liberty." As for Sabbath-day baseball in general, the barbers emphatically believed that they had a perfect right to enter into or witness a game on Sunday if they so choose. What is interesting about this letter is that the barbers took the unusual step of showing solidarity with professional ballplayers, not as performers or athletes, but as skilled labor entitled to the respect and dignity deserving of all other working men.[60]

This was certainly not the sentiment of the ministers, whose support for workers' rights did not go much beyond vague platitudes of fair treatment and advocacy for Sunday rest. Hostility to the influx of foreigners, who were seen as undermining both personal liberty and the integrity of the Sabbath, was relatively common. The Reverend Wilbur F. Crafts, PhD, a supposed well-known lecturer on "reform," gave a talk to the Syracuse chapter of the YMCA, which turned out to be little more than a study in ethnic stratification. Society, he surmised, descended in hierarchical fashion from the exalted Anglo-Saxon, who was a lover of personal freedom and an advocate of the Puritan Sabbath, to the army of ignorant aliens with their notion of a continental Sunday, which would result in a slave society devoid of fundamental liberties. Most of the foreign hordes to which Dr. Crafts referred comprised a significant portion of the working class of Syracuse, revealing a hypocritical disdain for those very people in whose best interests many of the clergy theoretically claimed to be acting.[61]

Faced with opposition from the defenders of the Sabbath, the promoters of Sunday baseball were not sitting on the sidelines. In May 1897 they gathered a petition of some eight to ten thousand names, which they presented to Mayor James K. McGuire, asking for support in allowing baseball games on Sunday for the benefit of working men. At the same time, the petitioners wondered if the ministers could secure as many names from their party of followers.

The mayor proved wholly sympathetic in believing that baseball played on Sunday was neither illegal nor improper, provided that public order was maintained. He did not think that the majority of liberal-minded Christians would object to enjoyment gained by a Sunday afternoon of baseball, especially since the city did not offer any other place for amusement and recreation on that day. Ignoring the gambling and outbursts of violence that were associated with the game, he also thought that Sunday baseball was a sufficient deterrent to vice.

To back up his case, the mayor offered some statistics that showed that the city's 115 churches had a seating capacity of 60,000, yet the average Sunday church attendance was only 30,000 communicants. Since very few of that number were poor or laboring people, it followed that the masses of working men had little interest in attending church services, which they considered the exclusive clubs of the well-to-do. As a Christian, Mayor McGuire said he would hypothetically ask the ministers that if one had a city in which there are forty thousand working people, what harm would it be to allow ten thousand of them to attend a Sunday ball game?

The upholders of the Sabbath laws were less interested in answering such questions than in engaging in the practical details of how to prevent Sunday games from occurring, especially those of the Stars, the city's professional team. Throughout the early weeks of May 1897 the ministers busied themselves looking for opponents of Sunday baseball who would be willing to sign a petition, stating that such events would be of injury to property and a disturbance of the peace. They also pressured their attorneys to force injunctions to stop games which were not altogether successful, since those few cases that came before the courts were dismissed for want of evidence. In the meantime the ministers looked to public forums to advance their cause.[62]

At a mass meeting held at the Alhambra Hotel in Syracuse on May 31, the Sunday baseball question drew a large audience of businesspeople and professionals, including a sizeable delegation of clergymen. Dr. James R. Day, who chaired the proceedings, noted that local politicians would be mistaken if they believed the public was indifferent to the Sunday observance issue. He further stated that the toilers of the city "would decide with their feet" whether there would or would not be Sunday baseball in Syracuse. At the end of the day, he predicted that ball games on the first day of the week would win out, backed by many loyal supporters.

Numerous other speakers took the opposing view that the majority of people in Syracuse did not want Sundays to be desecrated by ball playing. Arguments ranged from the notion that Sunday was a sacred day and should be observed as such, to legal defenses that baseball on Sundays was in clear violation of the various sections of the penal code. A German clergyman, speaking on behalf of the German citizens of Syracuse erroneously declared that, contrary to accepted public opinion that his fellow countrymen favored Sunday ball, the German community of the city would fight to the end for the enforcement of the Sabbath laws. One proposal called for the creation of a municipal playground that would be open six days of the week for public relaxation and for baseball between the hours of 2 and 4 p.m. on Sunday afternoons.

In the end there was little doubt that the cards were stacked against the proponents of Sunday ball. The meeting wound up with the passing of a resolution to adopt a committee of twelve clergymen and twelve laymen, appointed by the Ministerial Association, to take every step to enforce article 265 of the penal code. By taking a firmer stand on Sunday sports, the Sabbatarians sought to ratchet up the pressure on law enforcement and political officials alike.[63]

A day prior to the Syracuse gathering, amid circulating petitions both favoring and opposing Sunday baseball, a mass meeting was held in nearby Auburn under the auspices of the local Ministerial Association to protest the desecration of the Sabbath with the intent of encouraging legislative action. Most of the attendees were opposed to the violation of the Sunday laws. The gist of their arguments was that the custom of strict observance was a commandment from God, and it was thus the most vital question that the American people should consider. One minister spoke in favor of "all healthy sports" and thought that time should be made available to give working men a chance to attend games during the week should they wish to do so. Commercial interests were also opposed to Sunday baseball. Such were the proprietors of Owasco Lake resorts who believed that games would cut into their business and would create noise and congestion.

Spokesmen for the various labor unions, including cigar makers, barbers, shoemakers, stonecutters, machinists, and brewers, among others, presented the other side of the case. They accused the Ministerial Association of creating antagonism among the working classes through their condescension and the masking of their intensions under the guise of moral reform. Many churchgoers, they pointed out, spent Sunday freely playing lawn tennis or croquet, and driving around the country while at the same time loftily condemning baseball as a desecration. The day was sufficiently long, so the spokesmen for the workers thought, to accommodate both church attendance and afternoon sports.[64]

Feelings in Auburn on this question ran high during the spring and summer of 1897 and reached the tipping point when unknown persons entered and desecrated a church at Sand Beach on the shores of Owasco Lake. The pastor of the church had been active in the local Law and Order Society's fight to do away with Sunday baseball, and the police looking for a cause made the obvious correlation. A reward of $25 was offered for information leading to the arrest and conviction of the guilty parties, but there is no evidence that the perpetrators were ever caught.[65]

The situation in Utica was far less climactic. Returning to the New York State League in 1898, the "Pentups" benefited financially from large crowds whose attendance at fewer than ten Sunday games equaled that of their other forty-five home matches. Envious of Utica's success, the nearby Rome club joined the league the following year, but in June several Rome players were arrested for playing on Sunday, which mobilized evangelical groups in Utica to push for similar action. In both cases the jury handed down not-guilty verdicts, which cleared the way for Sunday baseball to continue. Utica carried on its winning and profitable ways in spite of occasional Sabbatarian interference.[66]

Sabbatarian influence had been clearly present in Utica years earlier. In 1891 the debate over Sabbath-day baseball came to light in a game with many clergy in attendance, which became the focus of an elaborately documented case. During the trial that followed the arrest of a dozen ballplayers for playing baseball on Sunday, Chief of Police Charles M. Dagwell testified that he had attended Riverside Park the previous Sunday with other officers, having been apprised of the planned game. He saw a gathering of men in uniform preparing to play baseball in front of a crowd of about three hundred people. After the men had taken their positions, the park's owner ordered an announcement to be read to the effect that "this is not going to be a match game but an exhibition of three innings to show the science and skill of baseball." Police chief Dagwell then intervened, saying that if the event continued, the players would be arrested. After three balls passed over the plate, he stopped the game and dutifully took a number of the participants into custody. The police chief reported that no admission had been charged and the crowd departed quietly.

When the case came to court, lawyers on both sides presented lengthy arguments. The counsel for the defense challenged the prosecution to show how the defendants had violated the law in letter or in spirit. "The object of the law," he said, "must not be lost sight of." The notion of rest, referring to section 265 of the penal code, meant proper relaxation and recreation. "The grounds," he went on, "were private and the announcement made before the game clearly stated that this was to be an exhibition of skill not covered by the law." In conclusion, he argued that the players were not guilty of any offense either by accident or design.

The counsel for the city's corporation, Mr. Josiah Perry, summed up for the people by appealing to the jury's common sense. Calling the defense arguments preposterous, he laid down the facts by noting that prior notice was given of the event, which in itself was a violation of the law. "A reasonable observance of the Sabbath is necessary," he said, "because experience shows the decadence of all nature is the result when the Sabbath is neglected." He further commented "that there has got to be a line drawn somewhere, or the Sabbath goes." Looking ahead to future debates, he observed, "and if it goes there will be ball playing, circuses, races, and everything else, including all manner of commercial activity." The question, he thought, "is whether the law of the state is to be obeyed, and if the integrity of the day is to be preserved."

In the end, Perry's eloquence landed on deaf ears. The corporation counselor later stated that he was sure of the verdict after the jury was impaneled. Those claiming a prejudice against playing ball on Sundays, he thought, excused themselves from the case, whereas those who had an opinion the opposite way remained silent, and thus the jury was packed. In a criminal case, he went on to say, the jury may render a verdict that is contrary to law. "What occurred last Sunday was just as much an exhibition as if Barnum's circus had exhibited."[67]

In the aftermath of this remarkable case there was much analysis of the events. The consensus of opinion was that the verdict could not be well received by thinking people. By analogy, a crowd may gather at a racecourse to observe horses running around the track only to be told that it was not a horse race but a demonstration of a jockey's skill and a horse's endurance in running. Indeed, any number of things could be done, under this interpretation of the statutes, which hitherto could be regarded, even by the most liberal people, as Sabbath breaking and unlawful. The prevailing sentiment was that if the verdict was sound in sense and law then the Sunday statute would be of little account.[68]

Such cases of baseball's version of "the emperor's new clothes," though rare, were not unheard of. Some years later Charles Sellers, manager of the Logansport team in the Northern Indiana League, was arrested on a complaint by the Reverend E. C. Richardson for hosting a game against Huntington near his church on Sunday in contravention of Indiana law. Three witnesses called to testify said that the exhibition was so bad that it could not be considered baseball. The judge agreed and the case was dismissed.[69]

The comparatively lax approach that prevailed in Utica was less so in other upstate industrial cities. Throughout the 1890s Sunday baseball supporters in Rochester experienced problems similar to those in Syracuse. On June 9, 1890, a day after the Rochester Hop Bitters of the American Association hosted the National League Philadelphia club in a Sunday game, an Irondequoit farmer named Frank Towle swore out an affidavit claiming that players on each team had violated the Sunday baseball law. Subsequently, a number of players were arrested, taken to jail, and eventually released; this, however, did not put the matter to rest.[70]

An aroused Towle, along with like-minded residents, then formed the Law and Order League of Irondequoit. Shortly thereafter, following a Sunday game played surreptitiously between Rochester and the Brooklyn Gladiators of the American Association at the Windsor Beach Park in the town of Irondequoit, the players on both clubs, upon hearing that the Law and Order League had sworn out a warrant for their arrest, beat a hasty retreat from town one step ahead of the police. The players arrived in Elmira early the following morning, but within an hour or two a Rochester constable and the attorneys for the league had caught up with them, and warrants were served on both teams. Upon returning home, Herbert Agate, one of the attorneys for the Law and Order League, told reporters they were determined to stop play at Windsor Beach and if the Rochester club played there again that further arrests would be made. "We have nothing against baseball," said Agate, "but we don't propose to have it played on Sunday in our town if we can stop it, and we think that we can."[71]

The Hop Bitters picked up the gauntlet when later in the season Rochester scheduled a Sunday game against Columbus at Windsor Beach Park. The match predictably was interrupted when members of the Law and Order League ran onto the field. Fearing a riot, the Rochester manager cut a deal with the intruders. If they let the teams complete the game, the offending manager and players would agree to appear in municipal court the next day. Clearly the writing was on the wall. A few weeks later, after the New York State Supreme Court refused to throw out the indictment against the players, the team owners thought it prudent not to schedule any more Sunday games and thus suffer the loss of revenue.[72]

Between the end of 1892 and the start of the 1895 season, Rochester was without baseball. During the summer of 1895 the city got back a team in the Eastern League, nicknamed the Browns. A sense that things were not going well in Rochester came to light before the start of the 1897 season as team officials waited to see if bills introduced by legislators would change the legal status of Sabbath-day games. New York City Republican Jerry Sullivan, a former umpire who had campaigned for his seat by advocating Sunday baseball, introduced the first of a series of bills into the legislature. His bill, which would permit games on the first day of the week, was unsurprisingly roundly defeated. Soon after, several other bills sought relief from the blue laws. The one given the best chance to pass would have circumvented the relevant statutes by imposing a small fine on baseball promoters. Predictably, the legislature refused to seriously consider any of the reform proposals.[73]

The failure of Sunday reform legislation cast a dark shadow over Rochester's season. The sense of gloom was further exacerbated by a grand jury decision in a Sunday desecration case reinforcing the general consensus that playing baseball on the Sabbath was against the law. Not excited about having to pay a fifty-dollar fine for each violation, coupled with the anti-baseball atmosphere in Rochester generated by the Law and Order

League of Irondequoit, the three saloon keepers who owned the club decided they had had enough and sold the team, most likely to men who thrived on challenges, who then moved the club to Montreal.[74]

Hopes were raised when it was reported in December that another baseball bill would be introduced at the next session of the legislature by assemblyman-elect Jacob Haight of Monroe County. The *Sporting News* optimistically and naively predicted that the measure would sail through both houses based solely on the recent elections that had apparently brought a number of Sunday baseball advocates into office. It did not. Notwithstanding, the so-called "bible of baseball" grossly underestimated the opposition, dismissing them as "a few narrow-minded cranks," oblivious to the strength of religious groups opposed to Sunday baseball and the sympathies of the large number of communicants they represented. The good news for Rochester fans was that the team, now under new management, would make sure the city had baseball for the following season.[75]

As the century drew to a close, the *Syracuse Post Standard* predicted there would be a strenuous effort in favor of legalizing Sunday baseball in New York State. Agents of the various lobbies, pro and con, would actively petition members of the legislature. Glancing at the local scene, the paper painted a picture of resistance to change, if not downright opposition to legalizing Sunday baseball. It noted that there were many people in Syracuse who believed as a matter of business that Sunday ball gave injury to those in the city. Were it legalized, the novelty would soon wear off and there would be a visible reaction against it. There were many people who were far from being prudes, so the article continued, who found Sunday ball at Star Park, with all its boisterous features, jarring to their sensibilities. While good crowds might turn out on Sundays, it was thought that many would otherwise withdraw their patronage from the game, causing weekday attendance to fall. Sunday baseball may have its advantages from a box office standpoint, but it also had its downside. There were hundreds of men who would shun the game if played on Sunday. The practical question was whether Sunday attendance offset the general loss of credibility to the game as a whole? [76]

Exorcising the demon of Sunday baseball during the late nineteenth century seemed a clear and absolute necessity to many people. One Presbyterian clergyman in Olean took the church's General Assembly to task for its compromising position on Sunday activities. Noting that many proponents of the blue laws were "the men who give the denomination substantial support," he affirmed that the church must stand firm against any deviation from the Sabbath laws. Another Presbyterian minister pointed to the open stores and saloons in his town on Sunday, and the foreign element "who try to break up our Sunday laws." "The grandest thing that as a nation we had to show these foreign friends," he said, "was our American traditions." Foremost among these traditions was the preservation of the Sabbath. If the nation stood at a moral crossroads, if America did not draw the line at Sunday baseball, the country's future would slide downhill, as did Rome and other hedonistic societies. More than a few clergymen believed that, according to God's word, a man who broke the Sabbath was a ruin to society and that no nation which did not respect the Lord's Day could prosper. Such was the weight of opinion as the people of New York prepared to face a new century.[77]

3

The Sunday Question:
Commercialized Baseball, Evasions,
and the Courts, 1900–1909

A decision by the U.S. Supreme Court in 1922 concerning a claim for compensation by the Baltimore club of the defunct Federal League against Major League Baseball was baseball's most important case during the twentieth century. The argument of the Federal League Baltimore Club (Balt-Feds) was that organized baseball was controlling a relatively limited supply of talented players, thus establishing a monopoly in defiance of the antitrust laws. By the turn of the century America was dominated by large trusts that controlled entire industries. While baseball was not in the same league as John D. Rockefeller's Standard Oil Company of Ohio, it entertained many of the restrictive practices of trusts. Since a number of major and minor league teams played each other in different states, it was reasonable to conclude that they were subject to rulings by the Interstate Commerce Commission. It would seem therefore that the Balt-Feds had a clear-cut case of antitrust violation.

However, the Supreme Court saw things differently. Justice Oliver Wendell Holmes presided over the unanimous decision in rejecting the plaintiff's case. While admitting that baseball was a business, the court took a very narrow interpretation of interstate commerce. Since baseball was not food or some other tangible product, it was put into the category of exhibitions for profit. Personal effort, not related to production, could not be construed as commerce. Not being subject to interstate commerce prohibitions nullified further consideration by the court for baseball being a trust.[1]

Amateurs, Professionals, and the Baseball Trust

The justices on the Supreme Court were swayed not only by legal arguments but by sentiment. Numerous articles appearing in magazines and in the press around the turn of the century had characterized baseball as a wholesome outdoor exercise, emblematic of manly virtue. Albert Spalding, perhaps baseball's strongest promoter at the time, went to great pains to show that baseball was a reflection of American character. In his book *Baseball: America's National Game* (1911), he recounted the history of the national pastime as a truly American phenomenon which, in the tradition of American heroism, had overcome adversity to become the great game of the people. As a self-proclaimed embodiment of these attributes, Spalding was a key figure in persuading the National League to prohibit games on the Sabbath. Later, he was willing to forego his principles when the opportunity to make a profit by playing on Sunday arose.[2]

Nevertheless, Spalding's version of baseball mirrored the prevailing sense of national history as one of progress and expansion, guided by a wise administration with a sense of destiny. Imbued with the close association between "America's game" and American nationalism, the justices could not bring themselves to think of baseball as something similar to a shoe factory or any other such industry subject to the antitrust laws, thereby perpetuating an anomaly in legal thinking that has endured until the present day.

The ministerial opponents of Sunday baseball in New York, however, knew better. A reading of God's word with respect to the fourth commandment, "For six days you shall labor, but on the seventh day you shall rest . . . ," (Ex. 34:21) easily interpreted labor as activity for which one earned a livelihood, or engaged paid employment, by the "sweat of one's brow." While pressure to limit all Sunday sports continued, the guns of New York's clerical conservatives were aimed directly at commercialized baseball. Curiously, the growth of the professional game stimulated, rather than stunted, amateur ball and there was no reason to doubt that baseball "is played more than ever on the simple village greens." While many of the respectable church-going classes frowned on vulgar commercialized sports, the professional game by the turn of the century had taken a strong hold on the working classes as never before, much to the annoyance of their so-called betters.[3]

While any form of Sunday activity might arouse the ire of the strict upholders of the Puritan Sabbath, clerical opposition had gradually weakened toward less invasive amateur sports including rowing, cycling, tennis, golf, as well as collegiate and recreational baseball in most parts of the state. The distinction over who was an amateur or a professional mattered not only to those who supported the traditional Sabbath but to colleges and other organizations where the two overlapped. One issue that divided amateurs and professionals involved an interpretation of the rules. When the American League decided to alter the rules in 1901, marking a significant change to the game in an effort to speed up play, a number of colleges—led by Cornell University—pushed to continue playing by the earlier rubrics. Their obvious argument was that since college men were not connected to either major league, or to professional sports in general, they could adopt whatever rules their institutions so chose.[4]

From the 1870s when a number of New York colleges organized baseball teams, the rules regarding who could play and under what circumstances were very loose. Member clubs in the League of Upstate Teams hired non-school and even professional players to perform for them. In the spring of 1883 all league clubs, except Cornell University, which was guilty of other infractions, hired professionals. There was also an easy relationship between college and professional teams who often played against one another.[5]

By the early twentieth century the cozy intercourse enjoyed by amateur and professional teams had largely dissipated, making the growing cleavage between the two an irreconcilable gap. Some colleges and schools took an elitist attitude in promoting the purity of amateur athletics. President Charles William Eliot of Harvard University articulated the view of many of his peers that sports should be regarded as nothing more than play and should be indulged in only to strengthen the body so as to invigorate the mind. The Public Schools Athletic League (PSAL), formed in 1904, emphasized the unique status of amateur sports. The PSAL staged seven hundred district competitions over the course of a single year, involving 100,000 competitive members in New York. Whereas the PSAL, so it was said, "is considered mainly in its athletic aspect, it will be regarded as a potent moral force."[6]

In 1906 the Intercollegiate Athletic Association was formed (forerunner to the National Collegiate Athletic Association, NCAA), at the insistence of President Theodore Roosevelt in response to the serious injuries and deaths occurring in college football. The organization quickly set about solidifying rules for amateur athletics. The integrity of one's amateur status was a constant concern, and on at least one occasion the NCAA warned colleges and universities against allowing students to play baseball for money. Some athletes, Eddie Collins for example, used phony names to hide their identity as pros and so maintain their status as an amateur. The legendary athlete Jim Thorpe was stripped of his Olympic medals after it was reported that he played in a semi-pro baseball game. In the racially charged atmosphere of the times Thorpe, being Native American, was held to a different standard than his white counterparts. Thorpe went on to have a career in professional sports, specifically baseball and football, and is remembered as one of the country's foremost all-around athletes.[7]

One of the intersecting points between amateur and professional sports was summer baseball. By the end of the decade more college ballplayers were joining professional and semi-pro teams during the summer. The problems of enforcing an athlete's amateur status, and the recognition that summer ball allowed college players to earn needed money for the school year, garnered some public sympathy. However, a number of persons both inside and outside academia were disturbed by this trend. Professor Judson P. Welsh of Penn State University warned, "To allow baseball men when professionals to compete on college teams would simply introduce anarchy into our intercollegiate sports." By anarchy he meant that permitting college men to play professional baseball in the summer would serve as a Trojan horse for compromising the amateur status of other sports.[8]

Many people were concerned not only with the amateur status of baseball but other sports as well. Remarks made by Chicago mayor Carter H. Harrison that baseball, horse racing, and boxing, in particular, were becoming big money spectacles caused indignation among many sportsmen. Mayor Harrison believed that such pastimes invariably degenerated into fraud and dishonesty, attracting gamblers and bookmakers. Admittedly, however, he had not attended a professional game in fifteen years. In essence the debate was one of contrasting perspectives. To baseball club owners, who freely admitted that they were running a business and were anything but subtle in their pursuit of profits, fans were viewed as customers, players became labor, sport became entertainment, and club owners became management. As the cultural historian Johan Huizinga put it, "we do not play for wages, we work for them." Baseball as a game played by amateurs, on the other hand, was often represented as an amusement, a sport, or a diversion from the routine of life's occupations. For the proponents of amateurism, the focus was on the activity of playing regardless of whether any spectators were present.[9]

Baseball was also caught up in the wake of shifting attitudes toward trusts and the centralizing tendencies of big business. The professional game had grown up with industrial capitalism, and while it was comparatively a small enterprise, organized baseball harbored the same tendencies to monopoly and predatory exploitation as did coal, steel, or other large industries. By the turn of the century the excesses of free market capitalism were coming under scrutiny. The concentration of capital in the hands of a small band of pluto-crats, the extravagance of the few contrasted with the degradation of the many, as well as brazen corruption and unscrupulous business practices had mobilized a disgusted public in support of reform, including reform-minded politicians. Muckraking journalists and those calling for a more competitive market sought to bring to light the greed and corruption of trusts and large conglomerates.

Generally speaking, the history of professional baseball from the 1870s provided a clear record of concerted efforts by the major league team owners to drive out competition, whether it came from the American Association, the Union Association, the Players' League, or later the Federal League. As a consequence, American and National League teams were able to hog all the best players and function as a monopoly, which was what the Balt-Feds Supreme Court case was all about.

At the height of the war between the National League and the upstart American League, Albert Spalding had been behind an idea to turn profes-sional baseball into a trust. John T. Brush, owner of the Cincinnati ball club and an ally of New York Giants owner Andrew Freedman, claimed to have amassed documents showing that Spalding approved a plan for settling the battle between the two leagues, which called for a board of control that would govern the baseball situation in the country, and take power out of the hands of individual club owners. Spalding allegedly had said that such a plan would require a strong man to lead it, presumably himself. Spalding's model for the baseball trust, so Brush asserted, was the Bicycle Trust. Such a trust involved management by a small board of control that would issue licenses to teams and leagues, allowing them to function. Unconvinced by Spalding's analogy, Brush pointed out to him that the bicycle industry was different from the baseball business since manufacturing industries can make choices whether to expand, contract, or relocate plants, whereas baseball was denied the same options.[10]

Spalding strongly denied Brush's assertion that he ever concocted a baseball trust scheme or was eager to see it successful. Turning the table on his accusers, he said, "I positively refuse to have the parentage of this Freedman-Brush busted trust scheme sworn on me." Spalding went on to say that a baseball trust was not discussed at any league meeting. He further denied statements that he was trying to force a trust on the owners. Instead, he sought to formulate a code of rules for baseball similar to what the Jockey Club had done for horse racing. Such a code, he claimed, had raised the sport from bad repute to a position of respectability.[11]

Taking a page from Spalding's book, Freedman, an astute and ruthless businessman and by all accounts an unlikeable person with close ties to Tammany Hall, joined in the controversy. He proposed in December 1901 that the National League create a trust that could move franchises at will and peddle players, like pawns on a chess board, so as to maximize profits. Given that many team owners possessed shares in other clubs this idea was not far-fetched. The so-called Brush plan, proposed by Freedman, would create a cartel by which the Trust would be divided into preferred and common stock, which would provide a dividend of 7 percent that would go to the National League as a body. Profits from the common stock would be divided among the clubs as follows: The Giants would control one-third of the share, with 12 percent each going to club owners closely allied to Freedman and Brush and the remainder divided among the four other National League owners. No wonder Spalding vigorously opposed such a self-serving and lopsided scheme, even though he was spinning his own wheels. At the same time, Spalding attempted to line up support to become president of the National League even though he could interest only half the owners. While ignoring the other magnates, Spalding's coterie of backers dutifully elected him. Prior to the vote, Spalding promised that as president he would immediately remove Freedman from baseball. Freedman took the matter to the state Supreme Court to void the election, and on this occasion he had the last laugh.[12]

Despite evidence of numerous shady practices, Freedman sought to put to rest the rumor that he was looking to join the American and National Leagues into a single combination or, contradicting earlier statements, seeking to form a baseball trust, or any other kind of athletic trust. "I have had some experience in trusts, Freedman observed, "and I know that sport cannot stand modern so-called trust business. When you come to sport it is sentiment for baseball, not business. I want to eradicate baseball from a commercial standpoint and get it down to sentiment." An analysis of Freedman's business interests suggests that he was being more than a little disingenuous. In September 1902 he sold the controlling share of the Giants to Brush. According to one newspaper source, during the eight years that Freedman had been in the National League he had done more to denigrate baseball than any other man.[13]

While sentiment thinly glossed over the commercial realities of professional baseball, the contrasting perceptions of seeing the sport as a game or a business kept bubbling to the surface. According to one article, the matter revolved around status. The baseball magnates knew they were running a business, but in public they pretended it was a game. While the fans believed baseball was a game, they were a vital component of the commercial side of the enterprise. The article went on to compare professional baseball with the operations of an amusement park: "It makes no difference whether it is as vast a public place and enterprise of amusement as the New York Hippodrome, or whether it is only a penny slot machine, or automatic piano. Amusement and sport for the public they may be, but they are all alike operated from a business point of view." In conclusion, the article stated, "does anyone think that owners have invested hundreds of thousands of dollars for the fun of the thing?"[14]

The "trust issue" came to a head in March 1912 when U.S. Rep. Thomas Gallagher (D-IL) charged that baseball was a combination in restraint of trade. He introduced a resolution in the House of Representatives calling for the creation of a seven-man committee to engage in a thorough review of baseball operations, specifically the National Commission and the various leagues that operated under the National Agreement of 1903. He was quoted as saying that the baseball trust was "the most audacious and autocratic combination of them all." In the court of public opinion, Congressman Gallagher's frontal attack on "the great national pastime" fell like a lead balloon. Newspaper editorials and letters, some from the owners, presented the business side of the question, arguing that players were free agents and well-paid for their services. Without the reserve clause, the reasoning went, owners could not afford to pay such high salaries. Garry Herrmann, head of baseball's National Commission, compared the work of the Commission to the Supreme Court, with its powers limited to interpreting the rules and settling cases within its jurisdiction. The difference was that the court adjudicated cases in light of the Constitution, whereas baseball's governing body was held to no such standard.[15]

Trust-busting initiatives against professional baseball may have died a quick death, but that did not enhance the reputations of baseball's magnates, who were widely criticized for being cavalier and hostile to external competition. The evil in baseball, according to one source, was the tyranny placed on professional baseball by magnates of the game who impose their power through exploitative contracts. Some years later, newspaper columnist Jim Corbett wrote, "The loud shouting about the commercial aspect of baseball has been the biggest factor in the loss of the game's popularity." Baseball over the past few years," so it was argued, "had done little else but play up the commercial side of its operations, not the sporting end of the game." In effect, commercialism had always been more or less a permanent part of major league affairs.[16]

Defenders of professional baseball argued that the business of baseball fit within the framework of competitive free enterprise and that any man could own a team if he had the capital to do so. Baseball, from a commercial standpoint, was like the steel industry, noted one source; it was either feast or famine. Club owners knew the risks of the game. They may suffer a loss or earn a small profit one year and make a fortune the next year. While it would seem to follow that poor teams would lose customers and be forced out of the league, they would soon be replaced by other healthier and stronger clubs. This Social Darwinist model did not happen at the major league level after 1903, although some clubs were teetering on the brink of bankruptcy. It took another half-century for impoverished and unsettled teams to move to greener pastures. The situation in the minor leagues, where market forces were less impeded, was a different matter. Supporting arguments pointed to the frenzied bidding for top players to illustrate that there was intense competition among professional clubs for valued resources.[17]

While opponents of Sunday baseball were largely indifferent to theoretical interpretations of the antitrust laws and classical economic arguments, they were easily aroused by the practical, moral, and legal considerations of what constituted commercialized sport. Commercialization had soiled the reputation of baseball and convinced those of the more genteel classes that the sport had fallen from respectability and had attracted followers of the worst sort. Ironically, major league attendance grew from 4.7 million fans in 1903 to 7.2 million in 1909, thanks largely to the mass influx of immigrants and the growing popularity of the game among those considered at the time to be the "worst sort" of followers.[18]

Creating a Social Order

Social control was interconnected with the politics of class. Looking downward from the upper echelons of society, the loftier classes saw commercialized baseball in a similar vein to other seemingly unsavory pastimes, particularly prizefighting. Church groups and respectable middle-class folk, who had an aversion to lower-class entertainment, presumably supported an effort to defeat the Horton Boxing Law, which legalized professional boxing in New York. The passage of the Lewis bill in March 1900, largely along party lines with the backing of Republican governor Theodore Roosevelt, overturned the Horton Law and temporarily derailed prizefighting in the state. Conversely, amateur boxing, which flourished in youth clubs and the YMCA, was popular in middle-class circles and was seen as a vehicle for promoting the virtues of competitiveness and manliness.[19]

Despite the insistence of the sporting crowd that professional boxing was neither brutal nor crooked, moral reformers continued their opposition to prizefighting in whatever form. The celebrated fight between Jim Jeffries and Jack Johnson in 1910 was caught on film and distributed to movie theaters in New York and around the country. The showing of this motion picture became, for a short while, the cause célèbre among evangelical groups and organizations like the YMCA, which sought to have the film banned under ordinances prohibiting indecent public displays. Unlike baseball, the supposed vulgarity and brutality of boxing was an issue, but the real subtext was race. To respectable middle- and upper-class citizens, watching a black man beat up a white man on the screen was too much to stomach.

The social views of the more elevated classes, particularly the critics of Sunday baseball, underscored a sensibility that was gradually becoming more problematic. Religious reformers, who tended to see the surrounding environment as a battleground of good and evil forces, thought that the best cure for society's ills was to raise moral standards. Mayor Randolph Horton of Ithaca, in a speech to the ladies of the WCTU, expressed the belief that the best antidote for the drink trade, Sunday desecration, or the ruin of local girls was to create such high public opinion that the fear of disgrace and ostracism would serve as a correcting force for those who had fallen astray.[20]

Forgetting that the lure of sin could be equally attractive, if not more so, such views seemed to be pervasive among those in more rural areas, whose direct contact with the national pastime consisted of local boys playing a spirited game on the village green. True, a number of communities formed Law and Order Societies, and town after town across the state boasted branches of the Anti-Saloon League. Their primary object, however, was to keep an eye on bars and other such places to curtail the pervasiveness of the drunk and disorderly cases that filled the dockets of local courts.[21]

In surveying the local press, there were not many examples of Sunday baseball violations in New York's small cities, towns, and villages. Some such cases, however, were reported. Protestant pastors in Geneva and Cortland put pressure on local authorities to enforce a whole range of Sunday activities in defiance of local ordinances, including baseball games, which lead to some arrests. The clerical crusade in the western New York town of Medina also led to repeated arrests of ballplayers for playing games on the Sabbath. The management of the local baseball club in Little Falls hoped to thwart opposition from the ministers by agreeing to allow sermons and sacred music on the grounds before each game, guaranteeing an attentive and respectful audience. The Church of Baseball may have had many willing communicants, but that is not what the ministers or those in power had in mind.[22]

The Reverend E. W. DeWitt experienced some bother from the deacons of his church, and from certain members of his congregation, over his love of baseball. The previous year, Rev. DeWitt came to the North Main Avenue Baptist Church in Wilkes-Barre, Pennsylvania, from Corning, New York. He proved to be an able and well-liked minister but had such a passion for baseball that he rarely missed a game played by the local Wilkes-Barre Barons. It is unclear whether his attendance at the ballpark included Sunday games, or if the deacons thought that baseball was interfering with his clerical duties, or whether the church officers were opposed to baseball in principle. Whatever the reason, the deacons requested that their minister refrain from indulging his passion. In the aftermath of what might have been an undignified scene, Mr. DeWitt tendered his resignation. The loyal congregation refused to accept it, and thus indirectly showed their support for the national game.[23]

The fondness Cornell University students had for baseball led to the arrest of a number of young men for violating the Sabbath, following a report to the police by a faculty member. The professor in question might have been Bert G. Wilder, a reputed sourpuss, who seven years earlier had written a letter to the university's Board of Trustees complaining of town boys playing baseball every Saturday on campus within earshot of his classroom. In another irate letter he lashed out against the junior prom, which he objected to on moral and hygienic grounds. The professor's high dudgeon, in spite of the prevailing attitude in some quarters that "boys will be boys," was rewarded by a fine of $2 ($50 in current value) that was slapped on the offenders, which may have been a sufficient deterrent. One supposes, however, that Cornell men continued to play Sunday ball, usually beyond the gaze of their priggish elders. Amateur baseball, organized sport or casual games, remained a clean and wholesome recreation for those living in county towns and in the countryside. The professional game, however, like so much of city life, carried the taint of corruption.[24]

The low-grade reputation associated with commercialized sport provided a contextual environment for hardening attitudes toward professional Sunday ball. Wherever he looked in Syracuse, the Reverend Guy B. Galligher, an esteemed local clergyman and a stalwart member of the Anti-Saloon League, saw nothing but wickedness. Sunday baseball, to his way of thinking, was one of many forms of Sabbath desecration, although he recognized that the existence of such a heterogeneous population meant that combating Sunday baseball entailed many difficulties. Even so, Galligher kept himself busy prosecuting cases against professional baseball in Syracuse.[25]

Behind efforts to curtail Sunday baseball and other public amusements was a visceral fear of crowds by those of the respectable classes. Since large gatherings carried with them the potential for disorder and mayhem, the notion of keeping congregations of lower class persons from assembling was seen as a precautionary step toward solving the problem. Since the laboring classes were kept in check through toiling long hours six days a week in factories, shops, and other workplaces, the upper echelons of society hoped to ensure order and stability by restricting games and public spectacles on the seventh day.

The context for opposition to Sunday baseball upstate was the various ways that local communities sought to enforce social control. Having come to the realization that a strict adherence to the Puritan Sunday was fading away, advocates for a tight moral order put constant pressure on local governments to pass ordinances imposing curfews on young people. One town after another across the state in places like Little Valley, Churchville, Wolcott, Caledonia, and Friendship enacted curfew laws that were enforced in varying degrees. All such laws were pretty much the same. The curfew ordinance adopted in Seneca Falls required children under the age of sixteen to be home by nine o'clock in the summer and eight o'clock in the winter unless accompanied by a guardian. Larger upstate cities, Binghamton and Elmira for instance, also toyed with the idea of imposing curfews. Men in the village of Clyde took the extraordinary step of passing an ordinance compelling their wives to be at home by nine o'clock, as the town's womenfolk apparently were so addicted to attending card parties they were neglecting their husbands and families.[26]

Along the same lines, the WCTU conducted a crusade in Geneva against the use of tobacco, especially by boys. That same organization also began a campaign against the crying of newsboys in the streets on Sundays. The temperance element in the town of Fleming launched a series of crusades against resorts on Owasco Lake for selling liquor on Sundays. An anti-vice crusade swept through Bath, resulting in the closing of a disorderly house. Authorities in Ithaca during the spring of 1908 sought to crack down on the Sunday sale of intoxicants by Italian immigrants in the Klondike region south of the city. An Ithaca newspaper editorial urged the removal of able-bodied prisoners, put to work in public areas on Sunday, as a threat to the general health and moral well-being of the community. Other towns enacted ordinances against cigarette smoking, gambling, dance halls, loitering, billiard rooms, and expectoration on public streets. The list goes on.[27]

The pattern that emerges from moral reform efforts in these towns and villages is a network of measures aimed at reinforcing social control and orderly folkways of behavior. Enacting ordinances is one thing, enforcing them is another matter. Hence, efforts to ensure their compliance probably did little to eradicate the nuisances and threats to the peaceful order of local communities. At the same time, these laws created an attitude of tolerance among the general population and helped, in some measure, to undermine respect for the norms and rules they sought to uphold. The same could be said of attempts to enforce the penal laws against Sunday activities. In the years following the turn of the century, the Sunday baseball issue would again reassert itself in the metropolis, particularly in Brooklyn, where it all began.

Efforts to Evade the Sunday Blue Laws

As the newly enlarged metropolis of New York entered the twentieth century, the city was in the midst of one of its reforming moods. Exposure of corruption, particularly among the police, had tainted Tammany politicians, leading to the election of the Fusion candidate Seth Low as mayor in 1901. Two years later the voters were tired of the puritanical Low, who was a strong supporter of Sunday closing laws, and swept the Tammany candidates back into power. Aware of their precarious position, the new leadership sought to alter their image by adopting policies and appointing men to office that would moderate past abuses.

New York City police commissioner William G. McAdoo was hardly the ideal protector of the Sabbath that orthodox Protestant ministers and their congregations would have hoped for. In his memoir, McAdoo wished not to engage in any controversy with his Sabbatarian friends but was reticent to "repress Sunday baseball among the four million more or less hardworking population of Greater New York." For McAdoo Sunday baseball was a fact of the season, "as the bluebird appears in the hedges in the country, the small boy naturally takes to baseball in the streets. . . . "[28]

Like many people in public life, McAdoo came up through the ranks. He was appointed New York police commissioner by mayor-elect George B. McClellan Jr. and took office on January 1, 1904. His ascendancy to this post followed a steady rise through the political system. Born in County Donegal in Ireland during the post-famine period in 1853, McAdoo came to the United States as a boy. As a young man he found work as a journalist on a Jersey City newspaper. Sometime later he entered state politics and soon became a rising star. After holding several state offices in New Jersey, McAdoo became the leader of the Democratic Party in Jersey City. He served four terms in the House of Representatives, after which he was appointed secretary of the navy during Grover Cleveland's second administration. Later, after moving across the Hudson River, McAdoo became involved in New York City politics, and, although not part of the Tammany political machine, he was not a reformer either.

Drawing upon his experience in politics, McAdoo knew he would be confronted with a daunting task in the country's most populous and ethnically diverse city. Within the hierarchy of police responsibilities, overseeing violations of the penal laws with respect to Sunday baseball was not a high priority, yet it did not escape his attention. The ongoing practice of selective policing and the ambiguities surrounding the permissibility of Sunday games in New York brought a whole set of legal challenges and loopholes that encouraged professional league owners to test the waters.

Four months after taking office, Police Commissioner McAdoo was confronted with his first challenge regarding the Sunday baseball law. Strapped financially, the Brooklyn National League team sought to cash in on the rich returns that matches on the Sabbath would bring. The first regular-season Sunday game played in Greater New York was at Washington Park on April 17, 1904, against Boston in front of a crowd of twelve thousand spectators. Fans were admitted to the game after purchasing a scorecard, which led ministerial groups to immediately complain that such a desecration would eventually erode all religious observance of the day. Subsequently, two policemen were ordered to survey the scene at Washington Park. Satisfied that the crowd was peaceful and orderly, without any roughhousing in the stands or on the field, they did not see any reason to intervene.[29]

After pondering the issue, McAdoo decided to allow games to be played in the isolated parts of Brooklyn. On the other hand, he did not permit matches to be conducted by major league clubs at any grounds in Manhattan. The police commissioner had personally visited both Ridgewood Park and Washington Park and found them to be relatively isolated from any residences or places of worship. Considering that no complaints had been filed, he chose to defer to the decision by Justice William J. Gaynor in the case of *Bedell v. DeMott*. That case concerned the legality of allowing games in remote parts of the borough if no objections were made. Justice Gaynor ruled against the Brooklyn sheriff (DeMott), stating that there was a world of difference between a Sunday game taking place in the outer region of Brooklyn as opposed to one played in the thickly populated regions of Manhattan.[30]

Thinking that an important corner had been turned, the *Sporting News* predicted that before long, baseball would be played at both the Polo Grounds and Hilltop Park in the upper part of Manhattan Sometime earlier, the New York Giants had successfully scheduled a Sunday game against a semi-pro team from Murray Hill at Olympic Park in Manhattan (135th Street and Atlantic Avenue). About seven thousand spectators poured onto the ground admission-free, save for the purchase of a scorecard. Scorecards went for twenty-five cents, but, latching on to an economic opportunity, some enterprising spectators bought large numbers of programs and sold hundreds for one dollar each, thus making a huge profit. The game, with modified rules to accommodate the lack of space, went off without interruption. This, however, was an anomaly, since there was no record of further professional games allowed in Manhattan on Sunday for years after.[31]

The driving force behind the push for Sunday baseball in the ensuing decades was Charley Ebbets, owner of the Brooklyn Dodgers. No one did more to try to circumvent the Sunday baseball laws than Ebbets. He was born in New York on October 29, 1859, and was educated in the city's public schools. Ebbets married his first wife in 1877 and fathered three children with her. Divorced in 1921, he remarried a year later.

Ebbets started as a bookkeeper with the Brooklyn organization in 1883 and became a shareholder in 1890. Ned Hanlon, owner and manager of the Baltimore Orioles, was also a stockholder in the Brooklyn club. With the demise of the Orioles Hanlon sought to transfer some of the best players from Baltimore to Brooklyn and then move the team back to Maryland. Ebbets successfully opposed this shift of value. In 1898 he succeeded Charles Byrne as president of the Brooklyn club. Four years later Ebbets purchased the Dodgers (known as the Superbas until 1910) from the other stockholders. The franchise struggled financially for a number of years until the opening of a new stadium in 1913 and the appointment of an able manager brought new capital into the enterprise. Energetic and personable, Ebbets became a leading spokesman among the National League magnates and a strong promoter of baseball interests. During his tenure as club owner, he proved to be one of the great innovators of the game as well as one of its most colorful personalities.

Ebbets may have originated the plan to sell scorecards as a substitute for paid admission to games, and he was eager to keep a good thing going. He devised a scheme to make the scorecards color-coded in relation to the cost of the seating. They were printed and ready the week following the previously mentioned Boston match and for a Sunday game against Philadelphia at Washington Park. The game was seen as another test case for circumventing the law. A crowd of thirteen thousand spectators was apparently unaware that the police had arrived and arrested three unfortunate program sellers under section 267 of the penal code, which prohibited the sale of such things on the Sabbath. The expectations of the crowd were quickly dampened when a number of policemen walked slowly from the grandstand to home plate immediately after the first hitter had gone to bat. Amid shouts and jeers from the fans, several players, including pitcher Ed Poole and catcher and utility infielder Fred Jacklitsch of Brooklyn, along with Philadelphia catcher Frank Roth, were arrested and, together with the program sellers, taken to the local police station. Captain J. P. White, who engineered the arrests, said that he had not received "a single protest against playing Sunday games at Washington Park from any of the residents in the neighborhood or anywhere else." One suspects, however, that members of the Sabbath Observance Association had made their displeasure known to the police commissioner who ordered the arrests.[32]

Optimism that baseball would become a regular Sunday pastime was quickly squelched when Ebbets, on the advice of counsel, announced there would be no more games played at Washington Park until the case pending against the ballplayers and program sellers was adjudicated. Since John F. Clarke, the district attorney for Kings County, reported that the Court of Appeals had decided that Sunday baseball playing was unlawful, the cases against the ballplayers and program sellers looked solid. However, Judge Gaynor, the presiding judge on the Supreme Court, reversed the decision of the magistrate and chastised the police, saying there should be no interference with Sunday games unless a resident in the vicinity complained that the religious repose and public peace was being disturbed.[33]

The mixed messages handed down by the courts as to the legality of Sunday baseball must have been exasperating for the Brooklyn owner. For some time Ebbets had been annoyed at the hypocrisy of allowing amateur and semi-pro games to be played at Ridgewood Park and Coney Island on the Lord's Day while disallowing professional games on Sunday at Washington Park. To illustrate this point, on the same day the police had halted the game against the Phillies at Washington Park, no attempt was made to stop a semi-pro match at Ridgewood Park between the Star Athletic Club of Newark and the Brooklyn Field Club. Although five arrests were made after the fact, those apprehended were quickly released as the magistrate was in a hurry to get back to the ballpark to witness the second game between the local Ridgewood nine and a Stamford Connecticut team. Ebbets therefore devised plans to skirt the law and remain a step ahead of the Sabbath observance crowd, who were a vocal presence in the borough.[34]

And vocal they were. A number of complaints appeared in the local press, such as the one directed to the *New York Times* by "An American Citizen," charging that Sunday ball playing was carried out on private grounds with the consent of the owner, contravening Section 265 of the New York Penal Code. The writer further noted that the police should heed the wishes of the law-abiding element in the community with regard to Section 267 of the penal code, prohibiting the sale of programs in lieu of admission to Sunday games. It was not hard to figure out who was behind the outcries and legal challenges. Protests against Sunday baseball in Brooklyn had been launched by the New York Sabbath Observance Association and the Kings County chapter of the same organization, which sparked the decision to arrest the three players who took part in the April 24 Sunday game against Philadelphia.[35]

Throughout 1905, the police in Brooklyn closed the lid on Sunday baseball. The Superbas considered filing an injunction preventing the police from interfering with Sunday games but nothing came of it. During the 1905 season, Ebbets was also concerned with keeping players from jumping their contracts to play for rival organizations. Given previous decisions, Ebbets was confident that the courts would ultimately uphold his interpretation of the argument. For the time being, however, the police and the courts were not on his side with respect to Sunday baseball.[36]

Sometime later, in the spring of 1906, Ebbets tried another scheme to get around the Sunday law. He ordered that collection boxes be placed outside the gate at Washington Park so that patrons could drop in contributions if they were so inclined. The legality of this scheme centered on the literal meaning of voluntary. If fans were free to choose whether they wished to contribute or not, then in essence the games would be free and not subject to police concern. If on the other hand, the contributions were a prerequisite for entering the ballpark, then the "voluntary" contributions would be equivalent to charging admission. The determination of what voluntary actually meant fell to Arthur J. O'Keefe, the deputy police commissioner, who sent a detachment of officers to the April 15 Sunday game to see if the law was being violated.[37]

According to their findings the police were not satisfied insofar as the commissioner ordered all Sunday games with admission fees and contributions stopped. If the order was defied, he warned, every player on the field would be arrested. Gate receipts for Sunday baseball, however, were not Ebbets's primary objective at this point. Knowing that the Dodgers (as they were now beginning to be called) were playing well in the summer of 1906 and could pull in a crowd of up to thirty thousand on a Sunday, Ebbets was willing, for the moment, to provide free Sunday baseball to prove to the mayor and other officials how strong a hold the game had on the public.

With games against the western clubs in full swing, Ebbets offered Charles W. Murphy, president of the Chicago Club, $500 to have the Cubs play a free game against the Dodgers at Washington Park. Tempting though the offer must have been, Murphy first agreed but later refused, most likely out of fear of legal repercussions, which resulted in the game being called off by the police before it started. The voluntary approach was not taken seriously by the fans as the containers meant for contributions were found to contain litter along with the far-less-than-expected monetary offerings.[38]

Apart from added travel expenses, Sunday baseball in Brooklyn affected more than the potential size of Ebbets's wallet. Weekend games in the northeast were a scheduling nightmare for western clubs in both major leagues whose series against the Dodgers, Giants, and Yankees, not to mention the four other clubs—Boston, Philadelphia, Pittsburgh, and Washington—had to be cut short, compromised, or rerouted because of the Sabbath. Since a number of major league cities in the Midwest tolerated Sunday ball, complex travel plans were employed to take advantage of games on that day. If the Yankees had a game scheduled in Boston on a Saturday, they might be required to take a train overnight to Detroit for a Sunday game, which was allowed. They would then return to Boston, or some other city, for a Monday game.

Similar scheduling problems affected minor league teams to the extent that franchises were sometimes awarded or denied by the league based upon a willingness and ability to entertain baseball on the first day of the week.

In putting together the New York State League schedule, for instance, it was noted that the Sunday baseball question was not only an annoyance but a fear, leading some owners to purchase racetracks that could be used both for racing and for baseball during the summer months. Indecision as to whether Sunday games would be tolerated only added to the confusion.[39]

In the meantime, Ebbets became embroiled in another tussle over territorial rights. A dispute had originally arisen between Brooklyn and the New York Clubs over the right of the former to play Sunday games in Hoboken, New Jersey. Three years later in 1904 the issue flared up again. The question revolved around whether the New York Highlanders (forerunners to the Yankees) would be allowed to play some games at Ridgewood Park, which Ebbets considered to be a violation of his territorial interest. It appears that the Highlanders had earlier misinterpreted the peace agreement between the American and National Leagues in which the question of territorial rights was never discussed. A spokesperson for the Superbas claimed, perhaps with tongue in cheek, that it was out of the question to give any club special privileges to play Sunday games wherever they liked. The matter fell to the National Commission, which ruled that the New York American League Club could play ball at Ridgewood Park when the Brooklyn team was out of town, although the field was within Ebbets's territorial jurisdiction. Ebbets probably gave way on this issue so as to divert further hostility, which might play into the hands of anti–Sunday baseball agitators.[40]

The Gaynor Decision

The evasions, controversies, surreptitious events, and legal challenges surrounding Sunday baseball in Brooklyn inevitably brought the issue to the attention of the New York State Supreme Court, and particularly to the attention of Justice William Jay Gaynor. Born in 1851 in Oriskany, New York, Gaynor was elected to the New York State Supreme Court in 1893 and was appointed to the appellate division in 1905. Like many Democratic politicians, Gaynor was closely allied to Tammany Hall, and with the backing of the political machine, he won election as mayor of New York in 1910. Assuming a more independent stance as mayor, Gaynor soon lost the support of Tammany but was popular enough among other political factions to be considered a strong candidate for governor. While proving a courageous and honest office holder, Gaynor was not a highly effective mayor. His tenure in office was marred by an assassination attempt on August 9, 1910, the residual effects of which perhaps contributed to his death while sailing to Europe on vacation on September 13, 1913.

Nevertheless, Gaynor played an important role on the Sunday baseball question. During his years on the bench, he had been besieged with complaints from young men and boys who had been picked up by the police for playing innocent ball games in the streets and in parks, sparked by complaints from local property owners claiming disruptions to their peace and quiet. A liberal at heart, Gaynor was more than sympathetic to those favoring Sunday baseball, but as a lawyer and judge he knew that the law was the law and some middle ground would have to be found.[41]

By the spring of 1904 the temperature of the Sunday baseball question in New York was on the rise. Ministerial groups saw great peril in the general drift away from Sunday observance and related this trend to a steady rise in crime. At the same time, ministerial groups from a number of New York churches issued a warning to their advocates within the Republican Party that they would not tolerate any relaxation of either Sunday licensing laws or restrictions on other Sunday activities. Up to that point amateur and semi-pro Sunday games for the most part had been played with relative impunity in many regions of Brooklyn. Yet, on Commissioner McAdoo's orders, they had been prohibited in Manhattan, much to the pleasure of some and the annoyance of others, again raising questions of hypocrisy.[42]

Further, the upholders of Sabbath observance could not have been pleased that the U.S. Army was sponsoring a Military Base League with many games, including Sunday matches. An extensive network of military base teams, including a nine-fort association in New York, played baseball every day of the week. Sabbatarians raised their voice in opposition, but military base games continued unabated. Not that there was much they could do about it. As with all matters related to baseball and the law, it was always a question of interpretation. Responding to a complaint against military baseball in Massachusetts, the U.S. District Attorney stepped in to prevent soldiers from playing Sunday games at Fort Banks in Winthrop. He cited Chapter 575 Section 2 of the United States laws, stating that where no punishment for any offense on federal land was provided, the offender was liable to arrest under state law. In spite of the possibilities for litigation, the ministerial opposition was savvy enough to know that some battles they could win and others they could not. Thus Sunday military baseball in New York had its day in the sun.[43]

In May 1904, Judge Gaynor handed down a significant decision with respect to Sabbath day baseball. In essence he opined that "baseball may be played on Sundays without hindrance unless there be a specific complaint showing that the repose and religious liberty of the community are disturbed." In rendering his opinion Gaynor noted that men and women were constantly arrested on charges that the courts repeatedly decided did not constitute a criminal offense and, so he remarked, "it cannot be said too often to those who rule the police that our government, like all free governments, is a government of laws and not of men." The meaning, of course, was that arbitrary arrests would not be tolerated.[44]

Philosophically, Gaynor was correct in stating that playing baseball on Sunday was not a crime, but his decision did not change the provisions of the penal code that held such activities to be a violation of the law. Gaynor reasoned that a blanket acceptance of the literal meaning of the relevant sections of the law was wrong, since playing baseball on Sunday was only a crime when it interrupted the peace and religious liberty of the community. His second point was that a more flexible interpretation of the Sabbath did not affect, and thus interfere with, all religious activities whether they included worship services, Sunday school, or any other gatherings under the loose umbrella of religion. Such a broad definition of religious activities, he reasoned, contravened the intent and purpose of the statutes. Implied in this line of argument was the fact that many secular activities took place on Sunday under the guise of religion. Moreover, he pointed to the need of the large majority of the population to spend time outdoors on Sundays, since their vocations kept them indoors during the week. Implicit in Gaynor's decision was that one's conscience should be one's guide as to what was or was not permissible with respect to Sunday baseball.[45]

Public reaction to this decision was mixed. The response in some quarters was that since Sunday baseball was now legal in the borough by inference it could be extended to other regions of the state, a point on which Gaynor disagreed. When asked whether the Gaynor decision would enable the Giants to play Sunday games at the Polo Grounds, Giants owner John T. Brush tactfully replied that if there was a popular demand for Sunday games, and assurances could be given that no law would be broken, he was happy to give the people what they wanted. Brush thus reinforced the status quo by showing support for the proponents of Sunday baseball, knowing that such would not be the case as long as the legal restrictions were on the books.[46]

Predictably, a number of Brooklyn clergymen were disappointed with the decision and Gaynor's accompanying explanation. Most of the criticism concerned the excessive noise and commotion stemming from baseball on the Sabbath. This of course was a ruse since Sunday games generated little more perturbation than that caused by crowds gathered for other purposes. However, it provided a convenient excuse. If anything, the ministerial opponents of Sunday baseball stiffened their resolve to use their power to pressure the authorities to stop games. Playing upon an ambiguity in the decision, opponents of Sunday sports could broadly define what constituted a violation to the peace and repose of Sunday worshippers. Doubtful that complaints would be investigated, the well-connected ministerial and law-and-order groups were confident that pressure could be exerted on the police to stop games and make arrests, which proved to be the case.[47]

The legal ambiguities in Gaynor's opinion prompted Brooklyn District Attorney John F. Clarke to take the matter to the New York appellate division. Clarke made it clear that he agreed with Gaynor's view of the case but thought that it raised an important question in law that he believed, considering the divided sentiment of the community, should be settled by the Court of Appeals. Clarke might also have added that his hand was forced by a visit from several ministers who asked him to proceed with the case, arguing that playing baseball on Sundays took young men away from places of worship.[48]

Gaynor's decision on Sunday baseball was embellished and extended by other legal opinions. There was widespread agreement among magistrates and justices that noncommercial baseball was not illegal, based upon a reading of the law that allowed for games that were not public sports. "In my thirty years in the criminal law," observed magistrate James G. Tighe in deciding a case involving amateur Sunday games in Brooklyn, "I have found the playing of harmless games on Sunday by boys and young men conducive to good order and repose of the community." Similar words were uttered by Judge Cornelius F. Collins, a loyal Democrat with a pronounced interest in juvenile delinquency issues, before throwing out a case against three men for tossing a ball on Sunday. "To my mind," he noted, "Sunday ball playing is no crime. I would much rather have a son of mine go out and play ball on Sunday than go to a saloon."[49]

An opposing decision was rendered by Justice Nathan Miller of the Supreme Court in a case brought by four private citizens seeking to gain a temporary injunction against the Binghamton Baseball Club of the New York State League, restraining them from playing Sunday games in the nearby village of Lestershire. A motion was made by attorneys for the ball club to set aside the injunction. In rejecting this motion Justice Miller, a Republican, quoted Section 265 of the penal code that explicitly prohibited baseball, as a public sport, among other activities, on the first day of the week.

On the same day that Justice Miller issued his ruling, Justice William S. Andrews ordered the police commissioners to enforce the law preventing the local professional Stars club from playing baseball on Sundays in Syracuse. In giving an opinion, similar to that in the aforementioned case, Justice Andrews also held that playing professional baseball on the Sabbath was subject to Section 265 of the penal code. He further contended that it was the duty of the commissioner of public safety to enforce the law within his jurisdiction and that the court had the power to compel him to do so.[50]

Justice John A. Blanchard of the State Supreme Court held that in the normal course of events, playing baseball on Sunday was not an infraction. In rendering a decision in the case of *Ontario Field Club vs. McAdoo*, the judge stated, "It is not illegal to play baseball on Sundays, but it may become illegal by attending circumstances. It is illegal when carried on as a public sport, as for example, when the public is invited by advertisements in the news media or otherwise and an admission fee is charged or collected." Blanchard's reasoning was tantamount to saying that it is not against the law to be a prostitute, but to do the things one must do to function as a prostitute is illegal.[51]

He would later opine in a case brought by Thomas Gagan, district attorney of Rockland County, that Sunday baseball may be played on a private ground provided no admission was charged. Far from having any hostility toward the sport, Blanchard claimed that "the game of baseball is our national game and there are very few persons in any community who do not take an interest in it, because it is clean, healthful, and interesting." The judge concluded that the present Sunday statute struck a happy medium, which was something the law rarely did.[52]

But did the law achieve a happy medium? What started out as a seemingly liberal interpretation of the penal code, based on the Gaynor decision, by the end of 1904 had become a trump card that could be used by opponents to overturn Sunday games whenever and wherever they so desired. Local courts may have (as they often did) treated nonprofessional Sunday games as a nuisance and preferred to overlook Sabbath-day baseball cases altogether; however, they could not ignore such violations when brought to their attention by powerful and influential groups. Thus the threat of court proceedings and the sporadic use of police power rendered the exercise of the law arbitrary.

There was also a difference in the view taken by local magistrates and judges on the state supreme court with respect to Sunday baseball. City and town magistrates usually took a more lenient position, seeing nothing wrong with ball playing on the Sabbath provided that assurances could be given that the peace of citizens in their various neighborhoods were not disturbed. Justices on the Supreme Court often took a more stringent position, arguing that the letter of the law must be observed with respect to any commercial transaction that may take place in or around a ballpark on Sunday. The problem for law enforcement was to adapt itself to both of these legal interpretations.

These judicial opinions had wide application for other entertainments since the opening of movie theaters on Sunday, for instance, would also be a crime if admission was charged. As the pace of commercial activity and the number of diverting amusements accelerated after the turn of the century, law enforcement and the courts were increasingly confronted with the rising tide of Sunday infractions. By the end of the decade the courts at least had been provided with a framework for adjudicating Sunday baseball cases. Nevertheless, as with all matters relating to sporting activities on the Sabbath, the issue was not clear cut and remained open to much scrutiny.

The weight of these decisions gave justices and magistrates a clear mandate to close down all commercialized baseball on Sunday. However, within the confines of metropolitan New York, the torch carried by the crusade for an open Sunday continued to burn by the close of the decade. After his election as mayor, Gaynor reached an agreement with District Attorney Charles S. Whitman (himself a future governor of the state) about a broad, liberal enforcement of the Sunday laws so as to balance public order and decorum with the personal liberties of the people. As a result, the mayor promised to consult with prosecutors about the proper administration of Sunday observance in the city.[53]

The Liberal Opposition to Sunday Restrictions on Baseball

The liberal and socially progressive forces within Protestant churches, which emerged as a recognizable movement in the 1890s, became a voice on the side favoring Sunday baseball by the end of the first decade of the twentieth century. The term "liberal" should be used advisedly since it was understood at the time, within the connotation of its nineteenth-century meaning, as individual liberty, both politically and economically.

Both sides of the Sunday observance issue talked about personal liberty, but they meant different things by it. The upholders of the Puritan Sabbath thought that liberty could only be experienced within a moral society, thus liberty and morality were virtually one and the same. For the "liberals" who sought to reform the penal code, liberty revolved around the question of choice and the absence of restrictions. While the so-called liberals argued most eloquently that the justification for Sunday baseball was to give the worker an opportunity to see a game that would otherwise be denied him, the real beneficiaries of such a tack were the club magnates whose pecuniary benefits from Sunday games would greatly enhance their cash flow. Hence the liberal position was essentially a free-market argument. The strongest backers of Sabbath-day ball were those interests which sought to profit from a more open Sunday.

In fact, what people during the first ten years of the twentieth century understood as liberal, in contrast to our present-day perspective, was a modified form of conservatism that saw no contradiction between a market-driven secular society and an orderly society. Among liberal ministers, the desire for a more open Sunday naturally fell in line with a greater degree of secularization. In responding to colleagues holding to a strict interpretation of the "holy Sabbath," the Reverend Dr. F. W. Betts in Syracuse noted that Sunday was not and ought not to be a church day. He, along with a growing number of liberal Christians would have seconded the words of Rabbi Charles Fleischer of Boston, who remarked that twentieth-century man abhorred idleness and sought an active life in the expansive arena of the outdoors. "Give men sunshine and open air," Fleischer said, "and the pleasure of throwing aside Colonial narrowness by making antiquated the law against Sunday baseball."[54]

Such talk had a link to the theme of Muscular Christianity, whose seeds had been planted in the 1870s and 1880s. They soon sprouted forth in the sermons and pronouncements of many preachers and churchmen, who called for vigorous exercise and the strengthening of the body along with the elevation of character and the spirit. The hidden agenda behind Muscular Christianity was the need to strengthen native Anglo-Saxon manhood to become more competitive, not only on the athletic field and in business, but also as a bulwark against the weakening of society brought on by effeteness and the descending hordes of immigrants. Muscular Christianity would play an important role in the growth of a militaristic spirit during the next decade.

One of the spinoffs of this virile brand of Christianity was the Commercial Athletic Association, composed of employees working in the wholesale district of New York City. The organization was formed in 1907 to encourage interest and enthusiasm in healthy athletic sports, and to arouse a spirit of friendliness among employees of different houses with a view of developing muscles and minds—outdoors in summer and indoors in winter. While the association promoted all kinds of activities, baseball was a big part of the program.[55]

The shifting winds favoring a more pluralistic approach to Sunday base-ball, brought on by a more robust liberalism, blew in off the pages of vari-ous printed sources. Newspaper editorials pointed to the discrepancies in the penal code making it difficult, if not impossible, for law-abiding citizens to obey the law, and the need to adjust the Sunday laws to the general sen-sibilities of the community. The necessity for wholesome and energetic diversions on a Sunday, which included professional baseball, was also a popular theme, as was the oft-repeated argument that Sunday ball gave fac-tory operatives, who were also rooters, the chance to see a game.[56]

The answer to a question posed by C. F. Mathison of the Personal Liberty League, in a letter to August "Garry" Herrmann of the National Association, as to why Sunday baseball was a good thing, could have been given by the Liberal Sunday League. The Liberal Sunday League, formed as a lobbying organization in response to the persistent pressure from Sunday observance organizations, jumped into the fray with great enthusiasm. In the spring of 1909 it planned a series of mass meetings at Cooper Union, Madison Square Garden, and various public halls around New York with the objective of con-structing legislative and aldermanic bills that would be taken up by the law committees and presented to the various legislative bodies. In support, it proposed to canvass for votes and thus arouse public opinion.[57]

True to their word, the Liberal Sunday League quickly adopted a plat-form and set about pressing for bills in Albany on a whole range of Sunday observance issues, among them baseball. At a meeting of the league's board of governors, they put forward a plan to draft a bill to be presented to the leg-islature making Sunday a legal holiday, as it was in Germany and other European countries, with the intention of giving working men enjoyment on the one day of the week they had to themselves.[58]

Two days later, advocates for more tolerant Sunday laws appeared before the Ways and Means Committee of the New York State Assembly to argue their case. Meanwhile, assemblyman George A. Voss of Brooklyn introduced a bill that would ease restrictions on certain Sunday activities. Though backing for this measure was insufficient to ensure passage, the Liberal Sunday League garnered strong support from other like-minded groups, such as the German-American Alliance.[59]

As a long-time opponent of the Puritan Sabbath and an advocate for more leisure activities on weekends, New York's German community could always be counted on to carry out the fight for a more unrestricted Sunday. Not only was the continental Sunday an integral part of their culture but as the backbone of the state's large beer-producing industry, many Germans were irritated at the persistent efforts by many Protestant churches to further the cause of temperance, as well as Sunday observance. Since beer and baseball had always enjoyed a close, uneasy relationship, the issues of temperance and Sunday baseball were singular matters to New York's German community.

Consequently, German-based groups vigorously pursued the fight against Sunday laws on a number of fronts. On one occasion, Governor Charles Evans Hughes met with representatives of the German-American Federation pressing for a more liberalized Sunday. He no doubt listened politely to their arguments but promised nothing. Politically, Hughes was no fool and, like so many politicians, he knew that real power in the state rested with the myriad of temperance and Sabbath protection groups, who by the end of the first decade of the twentieth century, and with the help of an army of lobbyists, had become a dominant political force in Albany.[60]

4

Local Opposition to Sunday Baseball and the Legislative Initiative, 1910–1916

A l Smith was born on December 30, 1873, in the multicultural Fourth Ward on Manhattan's Lower East Side. As a boy he received a sociological education by observing the patterns of behavior among the many ethnic groups in his neighborhood. Just prior to his twenty-first birthday, Smith entered politics as a foot soldier in the vast army of Tammany Hall, where he rose through the ranks. A decade later, thanks to his Tammany connections, Smith entered the New York State Assembly. Although he had very little formal education, Smith had extraordinary political instincts, was an excellent judge of character, and possessed a sense of direction that enabled him to hold his own in more elite company. When colleagues in the state legislature would boast of their Ivy League pedigrees, Smith would proudly assert that he was an F. F. M. (Fulton Fish Market) man, a metaphor for his schooling on the docks, in the markets, and at various jobs on the sidewalks of New York.

As a strong proponent of industrial regulation, an opponent of temperance (and later prohibition), and an advocate for changes in the penal code respecting the Sabbath, Smith typified the reform spirit that was bubbling to the surface as progressivism hit its stride over the second decade of the century. When the blue laws in New York were finally amended in 1919, fittingly it was Al Smith, now governor of the state, who affixed his signature to the legislation. The road to that end proved contentious, as the forces backing the status quo retreated behind the shield of the penal laws and effectively repulsed the arrows thrust in their direction by reformers. As with all political battles, the Sabbath observance issue revolved around a struggle for power and the use of power by law enforcement, by lobbyists, and by legislators in the halls of Albany. These are themes that dominated the debate over Sunday observance entering into the century's second decade.[1]

Enforcement of the Sunday Observance Laws Upstate

The legal battles and police operations involving Sunday baseball that had earlier so entertained authorities in the metropolis soon fanned out across the state. With some exceptions, the focus was on cities in the New York State League (NYSL) where tenuous financial considerations encouraged clubs to test the waters of Sunday ball, and where ministerial groups were the most active. Between 1911 and 1917, and from 1919 to 1920, no less than twenty-two towns and cities fielded NYSL clubs at one time or another in a six-to-eight team league. Buffalo and Rochester, the two largest upstate cities, were represented in the Eastern League from 1901 to 1911 and in the International League thereafter. Since those leagues did not schedule Sunday games, baseball in those two cities avoided the kind of ministerial interventions or police activity that existed elsewhere. It is unclear whether other professional leagues in the state such as the Empire State League, the Hudson River League, or the New York–Pennsylvania League allowed Sunday games. However, Newburgh, which fielded teams periodically in the Hudson River League, the Atlantic League, and the New York–New Jersey League, was known to be a hot spot of reaction against Sunday law reform. As a rule, minor league ball in upstate New York was allowed, or not allowed, on Sundays depending upon the attentiveness of ministerial associations and law and order groups, the vigilance of local authorities, and the mood of the public.

Elmira

The ambiguities confronting law enforcement officials at the start of the decade first made their appearance in Elmira. Even though Republican governor Charles Evans Hughes was considered a reformer, he tended to side with the traditionalists on matters of moral concern. Knowing that his support came primarily from the upstate rural counties, he was willing to give a ready ear to complaints by ministers whose congregations were firm on Sunday observance. Since the ministers and their representatives had a direct line to the governor, and the governor held authority over county officials, including sheriffs, Hughes could effectively determine Sabbath-day policies at the county level.

Such was the case in Chemung County when the sheriff, T. Stanley Day, was hauled into court to answer charges brought by the Protestant Pastors' Association and the Elmira Civic Federation for refusing to arrest players in a NYSL game between Elmira and Binghamton. Day's counsel told the court that the sheriff was acting on legal advice not to proceed against the players without obtaining a warrant. The opposition pointed out that Sunday baseball was illegal in the state and that the sheriff had no need to obtain a warrant prior to making arrests. Lawyers filed briefs and Governor Hughes informed the parties that he would decide whether to press charges or not. After due deliberation, the substance of Governor Hughes's decision was "Not Guilty—but don't do it again."[2]

Knowing that the governor was keeping an eye on him, the sheriff may have felt his job was in jeopardy if he did not toe the line. A month later, Day stepped in to prevent a Sunday league game between Elmira and Syracuse. As soon as the first ball was thrown, the sheriff intervened and arrested four players, this time without obtaining a warrant. Although a concert of sacred music preceded the game, this olive branch proved to be no deterrent against local groups determined to stamp out Sabbath violations.[3]

At another Sunday game played against Binghamton, two Elmira players, pitcher Louis Polchow and catcher John Clougher, were taken into custody and released on $1,000 bail. This time there was no concert, no admission had been charged, and the game was played on private grounds. The case followed a set pattern. Token arrests for Sunday law violations were an ever-present possibility. They served more as a warning against further actions than as a determined effort to punish the offenders. While there are questions as to how seriously the local court took such matters, the sheriff was not taking any chances. When the case came before the magistrate, the only witness for the prosecution was the reluctant Mr. Day. After five minutes of deliberation, the players were released.[4]

For reasons that are not altogether clear, the Elmira team refused to show up for a Sunday away game on August 14, 1910, against the Wilkes-Barre Barons. This no-show brought the Elmira club into conflict with the board of directors of the NYSL. The indignant home team filed suit with the NYSL board for compensation to recover $300 in lost revenue from their opponents. Elmira then took the unusual step of filing a countersuit for $500, claiming that the league had violated section forty of the NYSL Constitution, disallowing the director of any club (in this case Wilkes-Barre) from having a voice in a case of which they had an interest. In awarding Wilkes-Barre their requested compensation, the directors indicated there was no reason why parks in cities that allowed Sunday ball should stand idle. The irony was all the more glaring since the reason the Elmira franchise had been restored to the NYSL in 1908 was that the city at that time permitted Sunday baseball.[5]

Such inconsistent behavior was the product of selective and inconsistent policing. Knowing that Sunday baseball was widely played all across the state, and that there was an even chance that a team charging admission could get away with a Sabbath-day game unscathed, team owners, aware of the financial rewards of such matches, were thus caught in a bind. As a rule clubs like Elmira followed the maxim "once bitten, twice shy" in deciding whether or not to play on Sundays.

The fear that Sunday baseball in the NYSL would disappear altogether proved to be groundless. The interference that had marred Sabbath-day games in Elmira earlier in the season was absent with the scheduling of three late-season Sunday doubleheaders, involving the Syracuse Stars and Wilkes-Barre, Utica and Scranton, and Elmira against Albany. The Elmira games were performed in Albany under the auspices of the Knickerbocker Athletic Club, which had previously been refused permission to play on Sunday in the capital district. One presumes that the home teams made a good profit, which for some clubs justified the risk.[6]

Syracuse

As we have seen, Syracuse was another place where the Ministerial Association was alive and active. While there is little evidence during the century's second decade that the city's semi-pro teams experienced any ministerial hassles, such was not the case with the Syracuse Stars, whose Sunday matches were always under threat of interruption by the police. Local authorities on their own were reluctant to stop Sunday games, which a succession of police commissioners considered to be harmless amusements that didn't bother anyone. If pressed by the ministers, however, they were willing and able to enforce the law.

During the summer of 1912 there was increased activity by the police in stopping commercialized Sunday baseball in Syracuse. At grounds where admission was charged a summons was routinely given to players, managers, and umpires to appear before the nearest magistrate. While it was thought that the mayor favored Sunday baseball, he was under pressure from various ministerial societies formed for obtaining a stricter observance of the Sabbath, which had for some time been urging him to take action.[7]

As a matter of formality, players and other personnel brought before the court were released by juries whose deliberations before handing out acquittals often took a matter of minutes. "Sunday baseball is doing less to hurt the morals of the community than the mockeries of trials," noted one editorial. It further observed that by eliminating this pretense, Syracuse would get Sunday baseball and the sheriff would have the satisfaction of having done his duty, thus removing a possible excuse for his dismissal from office. The same jurors who would stand firm to convict criminals and those who threatened the community were prepared to do an about-face when deciding on Sunday desecration cases.[8]

A series of baseball-related cases over several months led the *Syracuse Herald* to assert with confidence that jury acquittals were practically assured. One case involved the proprietors of the Syracuse Stars. Another case the previous week caused pitcher Moyde Cunningham and catcher Charles Koopman of the Stars to be placed in the docket following a regularly scheduled game played under the auspices of the Oneck Social Club. A further case involved six Stars players, including the team's leading hitters John Deal and Mike Wotell, who were taken into custody by Sheriff Fred Wyker after a ten-inning victory over the Wilkes-Barre club before thirty-five hundred supporters. The *Herald* article went on to say (overstated as it turned out) that police interference with Sunday games was a thing of the past and that there was an overwhelming desire by the people for Sunday baseball.[9]

Financial troubles motivated Syracuse's only professional team to persevere with Sunday ball, as was the case with many other minor league clubs. Money woes, whether due to mismanagement or low attendance, had plagued the Stars for decades. Taking a page out of Ebbets's playbook, the Stars owners sought ways of skirting the law. A popular tactic was to appease the community's religious sensibilities by offering concerts of sacred music at the ballpark and charging a fee for the entertainment. Afterwards, the fans were allowed to enter the stands for free. The way "sacred" was defined remains a mystery, but clearly the various hymns and solemn selections performed by local musicians would not have been in keeping with the setting for baseball. In at least one instance, the Onondaga County sheriff and his deputies attended one of these performances involving a game against Albany at Star Park without making any arrests. On the other hand, the ever-attentive Syracuse Ministerial Association was not fooled and filed a complaint. They may well have been assisted by the Law and Order League, which sought to mobilize the moral and religious forces in Syracuse "into a body which will assist any man or body of men in the enforcement of the law."[10]

A long-standing disagreement between local ministers—dedicated to upholding the Sunday baseball regulations—and Mayor Louis Will, came to a head when the two parties met in March 1914. The mayor fired the first salvo, charging the ministers with misrepresenting his position on Sunday baseball by making false statements in telegrams to the city's legislative representatives. The ministers fired back claiming that the mayor had said explicitly that Sunday baseball would furnish a positive outlet for the animal spirits of younger people. While they did not wish "to hamper young men in their pleasures and exercises," the ministers clearly reiterated their opposition to professional baseball on Sundays as legitimizing the commercialization of the Sabbath. Mayor Will countered by saying that the public wanted to see the best players perform. A spokesman for the ministers agreed that they could, but not on Sunday. Shortly thereafter the Ministerial Association backed up their words by forcing the suspension of a Sunday exhibition game.[11]

Continuing the feud, the city's chief executive sent a letter to the Onondaga County legislature reiterating his support for Sunday baseball in Syracuse and his perception that the public shared the same feeling. The ministers set up another meeting with the mayor and again took him to task, warning that Sunday baseball had to conform to the law or else. Mayor Will then took his message to the people, calling on baseball advocates to organize and get the law repealed. He noted that in many parts of the state Sunday baseball was regarded as a dead-letter issue and games went on uninterrupted. His efforts failed to give a green light to the Stars, who once again were put in jeopardy through pressure exerted on the police commissioner by the usual suspects.[12]

To galvanize further support for their cause, the Syracuse Ministerial Association organized a Sabbath Observance Day, which was celebrated in various places around the state. Activities consisted of a field day, including lectures on the evils of Sabbath desecration, sanctimonious music, and innocent games, excluding baseball. Realizing that this plan had insufficient backing from all the ministers, the committee opted for a more modest gathering that would feature a talk by a representative of the New York State Sabbath League. The speaker, a German professor, argued for the spread of German culture but was opposed to German militarism. This unusual and somewhat irrelevant argument during the height of World War I received a cool reception from the ministers, the majority of whom were avidly pro-British.[13]

While the opponents of Sunday baseball in Syracuse could still hold sway over much of the churchgoing public, other voices now arose. Among the liberal clergy there was a groundswell of opinion that Sunday was not, and ought not to be, strictly a church day. They saw the Sabbath as a time for appropriate pleasures, entertainment, and recreation, which afforded many options. Far from viewing Sunday professional baseball as a step down the long dark road of commercialism and desecration, the reform-minded ministers talked about community well-being, an afternoon's enjoyment for the working man, and the virtue of sport as an avenue to spiritual, physical, and moral well-being.

Albany

Professional baseball teams in the Capital District faced similar obstructions to Sunday baseball as those experienced in Syracuse and elsewhere.

The primary difficulty was the highly impressionable and literal-minded sheriff of Albany County, Lansing I. Platt, who by 1910 had gained a reputation for arbitrarily permitting or disallowing Sunday baseball games as he saw fit. Platt's ambiguity over Sabbath-day matches, coupled with persistent complaints from Sabbatarian religious groups, meant that owners of the NYSL Albany and Troy clubs in Albany County played Sunday home games in an atmosphere of uncertainty. On two occasions in July 1910, Sheriff Platt cancelled Sunday games, acting on a threat by the New York Civic League. Subsequent events proved that this was the tip of the iceberg.[14]

Without other apparent options, the supporters of Sunday baseball in Albany looked to the governor's office to see if newly elected governor John A. Dix (a Democrat for a change) would be amenable to some modification. The law forbade Sunday games, but enforcing it was another matter. The constant refusal on the part of juries to hand down convictions led a number of people to conclude that repeal or modification of the law was better than its violation. Those advocating blue law reforms, as was noted earlier in Syracuse and in places like Utica, were of the same opinion.[15]

After so many years of Republican domination of both the governor's office and the state legislature, the hopes of many people for a modification of the penal code were pinned on Dix. An upstate Democrat from a wealthy family in Glens Falls, Dix graduated from Cornell University in 1883 and then entered the lumber and paper manufacturing business in the North Country where he made a name for himself as a conservationist. Long active in the Democratic Party, Dix was hand-picked by Tammany boss Charles F. Murphy to run for the state's highest office. As a shrewd politician, Murphy recognized the changing demographics in the state and the need to realign the machine with the cause of reform. Careful not to push progressive change too far, Murphy, a man of cautious instincts, saw Dix as a moderate reformer and an ideal candidate. Throughout his tenure in office (from 1910 to 1912), Dix tried to balance pressure from progressives with the more wary demands of Tammany. Not surprisingly, he found this to be an incompatible marriage and ended up alienating both factions, which was the reason he was a one-term governor. What must have been an inconvenient few years as governor contributed to Dix's natural tendency for tactfulness and a desire to please all parties.

Nowhere was this more apparent than with regard to Sunday baseball. Before taking office governor-elect Dix, responding to a story that he favored games on the Sabbath, denied ever having so expressed himself on the question but said, diplomatically, that he would give consideration to any legislative bill on the subject. When confronted with the same issue a year later, Dix posited the opinion that there was no need for state regulation of baseball. His comments were in response to Assemblyman Cyrus W. Phillips of Rochester, who wanted to put baseball under the control of the State Athletic Commission due to complaints about the improper sale of tickets during the 1911 World Series between the Philadelphia Athletics and the New York Giants, which the Athletics won. The governor, clearly wanting to avoid the issue, said that baseball was such a popular sport that public opinion should regulate it.[16]

With little hope of comfort from the governor's office, supporters of professional baseball in Albany and Troy were thrown back on their own devices. The two clubs, which played their home games at Chadwick Park in Colonie, hit upon a scheme of automatically making patrons members of the Chadwick Athletic Club through a fee equivalent to the cost of a ticket. This would allow them to attend games without additional expense. A letter was sent to Mayor James Briggs McEwan of Albany by the ever-watchful New York Sabbath Committee, demanding an end to this arrangement. In turn, the mayor handed the letter over to Wallace A. Peasley, Sheriff Platt's replacement, for action. Peasley occupied the post of Albany County sheriff from 1913 to 1917.[17]

Peasley responded accordingly. After a conference with the Albany manager, the Albany-Binghamton game scheduled for the following Sunday was cancelled. Fed up with this constant interference, the Albany management took their case to the courts. The matter fell to Supreme Court Justice Aaron V. S. Cochrane, who granted an injunction to the Chadwick Athletic Club restraining Sheriff Peasley from interfering with the upcoming Sunday Albany-Scranton game. Predictably, the New York Sabbath Committee was on top of the matter, and their attorney filed a complaint. The case was deferred so that further arguments on the injunction could be heard.[18]

Two weeks later, Supreme Court Justice Gilbert D. B. Hasbrouck took up the matter again. He heard arguments on both sides as to whether Sunday baseball played under the auspices of a club that charged no admission and limited entry to club members could take place. Given the serious implications of the case and the complexities involved, Justice Hasbrouck, perhaps wisely, reserved judgment on the question by granting a further temporary injunction similar to the one handed down by Justice Cochrane. Sheriff Peasley, by this time, must have been considerably annoyed and frustrated. Exasperated, the sheriff declared that he was ready to enforce the law, but in view of vague and conflicting opinions asked the court to define his duties.[19]

The answer came in the form of another injunction, issued this time by Supreme Court Justice William P. Rudd, restraining Sheriff Peasley from interfering with Sunday games at Chadwick Park pending further appeal. Undeterred, the sheriff sent word to the Troy club that he would prevent the game scheduled for the following Sunday at Green Island in Albany County. What appears to have irked Peasley was that Troy had indulged in an often-repeated maneuver of shifting a Sunday game to another, hopefully safer, location. Although permitting the NYSL match between Albany and Scranton at Chadwick Park, the sheriff, true to his word, stopped the Troy–Wilkes-Barre game on the same grounds and arrested Troy manager James Tamsett, and several of his players. They were arraigned in court and pleaded not guilty. Their next appearance in court ended with a swift acquittal.[20]

Such inconsistent action probably left the Troy club's management scratching their heads as to why the enforcement of the law involving two teams playing games at the same venue should be so different. The degree of difference was a complaint by John M. Hurley, a police detective who purchased a ticket to the Troy game, no doubt reacting to pressure from the ever-watchful defenders of the Sabbath.[21]

Peasley did not amuse the court by ignoring their injunction. Justice Hasbrouck wasted little time in deciding that it was the duty of sheriffs and other law enforcement officers to ascertain whether baseball played in a respectful manner on Sundays would be in violation of the law. If sufficient evidence was found then it was the duty of county and city police to apprehend and punish the violators. If the law was not transgressed and the sheriff made an arrest, Justice Hasbrouck maintained that he did so at his peril. In essence, this was a classic case of passing the buck by making the sheriff of each county and the police of each city responsible for determining whether Sunday baseball violated the law. Thus the Sunday baseball question reverted back to square one, with the added difference that law enforcement was now on the hot seat and could be held accountable for making the wrong choices.[22]

The upholders of Sabbath restrictions in the Capital District were not the only ones galvanized by this issue. In an open letter to George West of the New York Civic League, Samuel A. Spellman of Albany, a proponent of reform, outlined thirteen reasons why Sunday baseball should be legal. His letter was in response to ongoing Civic League complaints that had resulted in the abandonment of Sunday ball, forcing Albany and Troy to play Sabbath games for free. The reasons were:

1. There was no doubt that the majority of people in the state favored league ball on Sunday.
2. People who work six of seven days should not be denied the privilege of attending a game on Sunday afternoon.
3. Attending one of these games is far better than some other diversions not interfered with, such as loitering or hanging about in pool rooms, to any extent.
4. By protesting against Sunday baseball, Protestant clergymen increase the feeling of indifference of other people toward attending religious services.
5. The ballparks in the league are well removed from dwelling houses, which eliminates a cause of objection.
6. A person could not possibly choose a more desirable way of spending a Sunday afternoon than by attending a ball game. The writer noted that the league bans betting, no objectionable language is heard, and games are played in a spirit of good fellowship.
7. Sunday baseball will never drive anyone to hell or turn anyone into an undesirable.

8. People who attend these games are law-abiding persons and have no desire to interfere with the rights of others.
9. The hour at which Sunday games are played does not interfere with church services.
10. If the question was submitted to a vote it would without a doubt receive the support of 50 percent of the voters.
11. Protests by religious groups mean that opposition to Sunday baseball is the cry of the minority.
12. The league depends on returns from Sunday games to cover its large investments.
13. The Civic League and other like groups could best spend their time on matters requiring more urgent attention.

Eleven of the above thirteen points relate to the ability of persons to watch a game with no reference to those who staged the games. These statements implied that the rights of spectators—and consequently those of management—to make a profit off professional baseball, were the driving forces behind blue law reform.

Mr. Spellman concluded with a fourteenth point by referring to the Civic League's "unreasonable and narrow minded ideas as not worthy of endorsement by anyone having at heart the best interest of the ordinary American citizen." These were hardly words to endear one to the opposition, but then again the letter was mostly designed to play to the public gallery than to convince those whose heels were deeply dug into the soil of their cause.[23]

Undeterred by the various legal maneuverings, the Albany club put together a plan to raise a public subscription among businessmen and others so as to collect sufficient funds to cover Sunday games, thus enabling the team to play free on Sundays. Without Sunday baseball, State League clubs would stand to lose thousands of dollars as weekday crowds did not raise enough money to meet payroll demands that averaged about $2,500 a month. This plan was predicated on the assumption that the public in Albany was behind Sunday baseball. Considering the fact that professional baseball in Albany closed down after the 1916 season and did not return for another four years, such optimism may have been unwarranted.[24]

Binghamton

Like many New York towns and cities, Binghamton was a product of the nineteenth-century industrial revolution. While not exactly a company town, the region around Binghamton became a center of shoe manufacturing. What began as a single factory—located two miles west of Binghamton and started by G. Harry Lester in 1888—within several decades had become one of the largest shoe producers in the country, employing several thousand workers by the turn of the century. George F. Johnson, a senior manager at the Lestershire Manufacturing Company, joined forces with Henry B. Endicott to buy into the firm and expand the factory, which in 1902 became known as Endicott, Johnson and Company.

At a time when unregulated capitalism reached its zenith, Johnson sought to create a model of corporate paternalism along the lines of the industrial communities established by George Pullman, Harold McCormick, William Cooper Procter, and other philanthropic factory owners. Johnson was not only a benign employer and a successful businessman; he was also a baseball enthusiast and an advocate of community athletics. He purchased the Binghamton NYSL club in 1912 to go with a new stadium he had built in Lestershire that would eventually bear his name. Johnson was a supporter of Sunday baseball and scheduled games on the Sabbath with the proceeds going to charity, much to the annoyance of local Protestant ministers and their supporters.[25]

Opponents of Sabbath-day baseball were not passive for long. The Anti-Sunday Baseball Citizens Committee sent a warning to the Broome County sheriff that he would be held responsible for suppressing Sunday games at Johnson Field whether admission was charged or not. Attorneys for George Johnson responded by producing a petition said to have been signed by eleven hundred working-class persons, many of them presumably Johnson's employees, favoring games on Sunday.[26]

Unfazed, the attorney for the Anti-Sunday Baseball Committee contacted William Sulzer, who followed Dix as governor. Although a Democrat, Sulzer was known to be sympathetic to those who opposed Sunday baseball. Campaigning in 1910, Sulzer delivered a speech in Batavia in which he lambasted the Republicans as a party that had deviated from the vision of

Abraham Lincoln and was without a conscience. Declaring himself a candidate for governor, Sulzer trotted out his conservative credentials, claiming on one hand to be a loyal advocate of Democratic Party principles, while at the same time criticizing some of its leaders. He characterized himself as someone who could unite and harmonize the dissident factions within the party. Addressing himself to the disinterested voter, Sulzer's conciliatory approach to politics, coupled with his image as someone who could uphold the status quo, no doubt appealed to the bosses at Tammany Hall.[27]

Several years later Sulzer was elected governor, but his tenure as the state's top executive officer soon ended in personal tragedy. Upon his election, Sulzer broke with Tammany and adopted an independent stance. His plan to introduce a primary system and remove Tammany appointees from office cost him considerable support and made him politically vulnerable. The machine-dominated Democratic majority, in turn, prevented Sulzer from making those appointments and refused to confirm his selections. Hints of wrongdoing, no doubt instigated by the Tammany leadership, were brought against the governor for making false statements (perjury), and for the misuse of campaign funds for private use (embezzlement). On August 13, 1913, the assembly voted seventy-nine to forty-five to present to the Senate eight articles of impeachment. The senate clerk, Patrick McCabe, an advocate for Sunday baseball, then served Sulzer with notice of these charges. The governor was tried on September 18 and convicted on three of the eight counts, leading to his removal from office.[28]

Six months before the roof caved in, Sulzer was focused on the Sunday baseball issue. After consulting with the governor, the representatives of the Anti-Sunday Baseball Citizen's Committee received assurances that the appropriate sections of the penal laws would be enforced in Binghamton. Sulzer further added that if local authorities would not uphold the law, he would. The governor, in a letter to Dr. Bernard Clausen, representative of the Binghamton opponents of Sunday baseball, promised to see that the sheriffs around the state did their duty on pain of dismissal. One of the first sheriffs to feel the heat was Arthur M. Seaman, sheriff of Broome County. Seaman had allowed two Sunday games to be played at Johnson Field. Further, he had permitted the advertising of other such matches later in the

season. Seaman's attorney, James K. Nichols, moved to have injunction proceedings against the Binghamton ball club dropped. This engendered a
lengthy local debate as to the proper role of the sheriff with respect to
Sunday games.[29]

Meanwhile, Dr. Clausen was forced to issue a disclaimer that the State
Christian Endeavor Union, of which he was a member, was proposing to
aid Governor Sulzer in his primary battle as a reward for his sympathetic
stand on the baseball question. It is unclear as to the political involvement
of this organization, but the close association between evangelical groups
and politicians who supported the Sunday observance faction in Binghamton
and elsewhere makes Clausen's denial of the Christian Endeavor Union's
active advocacy for Sulzer rather suspect. George Johnson knew the lay of
the land in Broome County as well as anyone, and as a person of prominence and power, he was an equal match for his opponents. On behalf of the
Binghamton club, Johnson voiced his determination to carry on the fight to
every county in the state where Sunday baseball was played.

Amid the threat of lawsuits and countersuits, Sunday baseball continued in Binghamton. A game against Troy played at Johnson Field on June 8
went ahead as scheduled with the proceeds going to the House of the Good
Shepherd, one of George Johnson's charities. Prior to the game both sides
agreed on a binding referendum as to the validity of Sunday ball, to be taken
among the villagers in Lestershire. The result favored Johnson and his supporters. Bitter in defeat, the Binghamton ministers then demanded through
their legislative representatives that Sunday games be suppressed not only
in the town of Lestershire but in other cities around the state. On the strength
of this victory, the supporters of Sunday baseball responded by petitioning
Governor Sulzer to send a special message to the legislature, recommending an amendment to the Sunday law that would allow cities to decide the
question by local option.[30]

The vitriolic passions engendered by the persistence of Sunday games
were grist for the mill in the 1913 fall election battle in Binghamton. Sensing
that the tide of public opinion had shifted over the summer, the Republicans
thought it prudent to back away from the candidacy of the hardliner Mortimer
Edwards, who had declared himself firmly against Sunday baseball, and

choose instead a more moderate candidate: Simon P. Quick, who would later become an advocate for local option bills. The Democrats nominated Arthur Rowland, a Tammany organization man, who had served for two years in the state assembly and had opposed Sulzer. Rowland likewise stood in favor of local option as a means of securing reform, but he never got the opportunity of furthering this cause as he was defeated at the polls in this nominally Republican constituency.[31]

Newburgh

As in Binghamton, the clash between the ministerial supporters of the Sunday laws and their opponents came to a head during the spring and summer of 1913. Upon reviewing the schedule of games played by other teams in the vicinity, the Ministerial Association found that with the exception of Newburgh, other clubs did not play Sunday baseball. Since the Newburgh team played outside the city limits, the Anti-Sunday Baseball Citizens Committee fired off a letter to the sheriff of Orange County asking him to prevent games where a fee was required. The letter referred to the case of the *People v. Demarest* in which Judge John A. Blanchard held that public Sunday baseball was prohibited by statute where an admission is charged. As further evidence, the Ministerial Association cited other court cases to support their position. Self-righteously, the ministers stated that they had been forced to take this action to protect the good name of the city.[32]

Following the usual script, the Newburgh club applied for an injunction restraining the sheriff of Orange County from interfering with Sunday baseball. Upon review, a decision handed down by Supreme Court Justice A. S. Tompkins denied the application of the Newburgh Baseball Club, which was part of the New York and New Jersey League. Counter to some other rulings, the judge reasoned that it was immaterial whether an admission fee was charged or not. Those who believed in Sunday baseball, he opined, must go to the legislature for relief.[33]

The Legislative Battle

By the end of the first decade of the century, the locus of the Sabbath wars had begun to shift from the playing fields and the courts to the state legislature, where bills to legalize Sunday sports were regularly introduced. Indeed, legislative efforts aimed at reform dated back to 1897. During the 1907 session, reformers presented several bills to legalize amateur and semi-professional Sunday baseball. One such bill was introduced by an assemblyman who owned a baseball team and another by a former prizefighter. These proposals had the backing of Charles Ebbets, who lobbied on their behalf and canvassed for support among Brooklyn's semi-pro teams. None of these bills went, figuratively speaking, beyond first base.[34]

A similar fate befell another bill introduced on a cold January day in 1909 by Assemblyman Patrick McGrath, a lawyer and a staunch supporter of Sunday baseball. This proposed legislation would allow amateur games in New York City between 3:30 and 6:30 p.m. on Sundays if no admission was charged and no child under the age of sixteen was admitted. Playing another hand, McGrath offered a second bill empowering local legislatures to regulate Sunday performances and sporting events. These seemingly tame measures failed to get out of committee and joined the growing pile of legislative initiatives bound for the dustbin.[35]

Reformers were constantly thwarted by the asymmetrical structure of politics in the state. Between 1901 and 1919, the Republicans controlled the senate, except for the four years between 1911 and 1914. By contrast, the Democrats held a majority in the assembly for only three years: 1911, 1913, and 1914. Furthermore, Republican governors, with the exception of Dix, Sulzer, Martin Glynn (briefly), and Al Smith, ruled the executive branch for over three decades. The predominance of Republicans in the corridors of power meant that the various ministerial associations and Sabbatarian groups could count on their political connections to hold the line on Sunday observance.

The persistence of Republican domination in Albany can be attributed in large part to the disproportionate number of seats held by upstate legislators. Whereas the five boroughs of New York City contained roughly half the state's population between 1910 and 1920, upstate controlled three more senate seats and roughly 79 percent of the assembly seats. Ensconced in their comfortable majority, the Republicans willingly rebuffed any suggestion of reapportionment, which had previously taken place in 1894, and subsequently in 1907, at a time when the state's population was quickly growing, especially in urban areas. Moderate reapportionment would not come about again until 1916.

In the hierarchical world of New York State politics, everything conformed to majority rule. The legislative session lasted only four months, from January to the start of May at the latest. Within that short span of time, hundreds of bills would be put forward for consideration. To handle this multitude of proposed legislation, tight control over the process was dictated by the Rules Committee, which determined the agenda for the legislative session, and the Speaker of the Committee on Ways and Means, who could decide which bills would be brought to the floor for a vote. Since the Republicans dominated both committees, bills to reform the Sunday laws could be expected to have a short life.

Republicans in the assembly and senate were backed by a host of lobbyists concerned with maintaining Sunday observance. After the Reverend J. W. Huff, secretary of the Law and Order Union of New York State, became pastor of the First Baptist Church in Waterford, near Albany, he vowed to establish the Union on a firmer and more active basis in the eastern part of the state. This involved keeping in close touch with member churches and channeling information relating to the Union's lobbying interests. As the Albany representative of the Law and Order Union, he pledged to keep a close eye on all legislation pertaining to its interests.[36]

The chief lobbying organization for those favoring Sunday restrictions was undoubtedly the New York Civic League. The League had a broad agenda, including activities like gambling, temperance, divorce, and Sabbath violations. Speakers from the Civic League, such as the Reverend O. R. Mills, traveled around the state meeting with church groups and sympathetic civic organizations to garner support for such issues.

Keeping to his busy schedule, Reverend Mills was busy traveling and speaking to various church groups during the spring of 1911. Meeting with one such group, he outlined the various initiatives of the league and explained what measures had been achieved on a broad range of matters. The routes taken by Sabbatarian lobbyists, predictably, covered those areas where support for Sunday observance and other moral issues were the strongest.

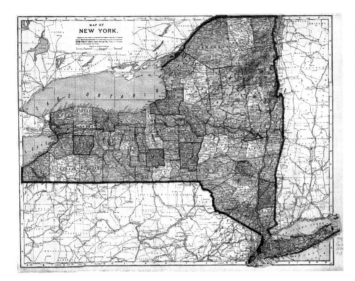

New York State in 1899 had a much-dispersed population residing in many towns and villages at the expense of larger urban regions. *Courtesy of Cornell University Libraries*

Located near the Gowanus Canal in the Park Slope region of Brooklyn, the field, known originally as the 5th Avenue Grounds, was sometimes home of the Brooklyn Baseball Club from 1883 until the team moved to Ebbets Field in 1913. *National Baseball Hall of Fame Library, Cooperstown, NY*

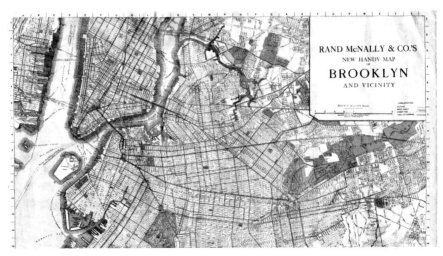

Brooklyn had become one of the largest cities in the United States before it was incorporated as a borough into Greater New York in 1898. The borough quickly spread southward and eastward thereafter. *Courtesy of Cornell University Libraries*

RIGHT: The region west of Binghamton, known in 1890 as Lestershire, was later renamed Johnson City after George F. Johnson, the owner and guiding light of the Endicott-Johnson Shoe Company. *Courtesy of Cornell University Libraries*

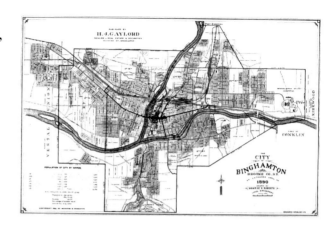

LEFT: Known as the Salt City due to the mining of salt by the large Salina Solar Coarse Salt Company, Syracuse was the home to a number of important industries. Star Park, home to the Syracuse Stars Baseball Club, at one time was situated at the corner of West Taylor Street and South Salina Street in the city's downtown district. *Courtesy of Cornell University Libraries*

BELOW: Percy Field was originally used by Cornell University athletic teams in the late nineteenth and early twentieth centuries. It was also used by Ithaca's amateur and semi-pro baseball teams. *Courtesy of The History Center in Tompkins County, Ithaca, NY, Sports Photo Collection*

ABOVE: There were several locations of Star Park (Star Park 1, Star Park 2) that were home to the Syracuse minor league baseball club from 1885 to 1899, and from 1902 to 1904. *Courtesy of Onondaga Historical Association Museum & Research Center, Syracuse, NY*

LEFT: John T. Brush was owner of the New York Giants from 1890 until his death in 1912. Prior to this time he was a successful businessman with clothing stores in Albany, Troy, and Lockport, New York. He initially became involved in baseball as a means of promoting his stores. *National Baseball Hall of Fame Library, Cooperstown, NY*

Ban Johnson (right) attending a game at Chicago's Comiskey Park. He was the driving force behind the creation of the American League, and served as president of the league until 1927. *National Baseball Hall of Fame Library, Cooperstown, NY*

The $750,000 cost of building Ebbets Field forced Charles Ebbets to include his contractors, the McKeever Brothers, as partners. In March 1912, they broke ground for a new stadium. *National Baseball Hall of Fame Library, Cooperstown, NY*

Game between the Brooklyn Dodgers and the Chicago Cubs at Washington Park in 1912. The field had a seating capacity of 18,000. *National Baseball Hall of Fame Library, Cooperstown, NY*

"Greatest Game on Earth." *Courtesy of the National Baseball Hall of Fame Library, Cooperstown, NY*

"Yes, Let Him In," *Rochester Democrat and Chronicle,* **March 18, 1918.** *From* Comments and Editorials on Sunday Baseball, *courtesy of the National Baseball Hall of Fame Library, Cooperstown, NY*

"All Work and No Play," *The Evening World*, **July 19, 1917.** *From* Comments and Editorials on Sunday Baseball, *courtesy of the National Baseball Hall of Fame Library, Cooperstown, NY*

"Baseball Players in Jail," *New York Evening Sun.* *From* Comments and Editorials on Sunday Baseball, *courtesy of the National Baseball Hall of Fame Library, Cooperstown, NY*

"With and Without Sunday Baseball," *Rochester Democrat and Chronicle.*
From Comments and Editorials on Sunday Baseball, *courtesy of the National Baseball Hall of Fame Library, Cooperstown, NY*

"Is This True Americanism?" *The Globe and Commercial Advertiser*, **March 18, 1918.** *From* Comments and Editorials on Sunday Baseball, *courtesy of the National Baseball Hall of Fame Library, Cooperstown, NY*

"Gambling: Baseball on the Cross," *Collyer's Eye*, **September 15, 1923.** *Courtesy of the National Baseball Hall of Fame Library, Cooperstown, NY*

Orange County was one hotbed of activism, as were other rural counties along the southern tier and in central and eastern New York. In an age prior to mass communication, lobbying was carried out on a personal basis with speakers directly addressing large audiences. With a dearth of leisure activities, such events attracted much attention.[37]

On April 28, 1911, another field secretary for the Civic League, the Reverend C. B. Miller, met with religious groups in Middletown to apprise them on what the current legislature was doing with respect to a whole range of legislation on moral topics. Earlier that month he had appeared before the Troy Methodist Conference to argue that professional baseball interests had raised $250,000 to back the Sullivan Sunday baseball bill, introduced by Tim Sullivan, the powerful Tammany boss of the notorious Bowery on the Lower East Side included in the state's twelfth senatorial district. He noted that gamblers were behind a number of such pieces of legislation being proposed and warned the clergy to keep an eye on their senators and assemblymen to make sure they were not swayed from their moral duty. Reverend Miller stated that public support had been instrumental in the defeat of another bill, sponsored by Assemblyman McGrath, by which the League had ensured victory by inundating religious groups with 100,000 letters, telegrams, and circulars opposing the measure.[38]

Lobbying also took place in church pulpits with sermons preached on a regular basis in myriad religious organizations. It was generally acknowledged that one of the most important channels through which public opinion could be galvanized was rural churches. While the church had lost ground in many places, it could still be a potent force in advocating for Sunday observance when congregations were given moral direction. Sermon topics, listed in the local press, frequently revolved around Sabbath issues. The Reverend George E. Wright, for instance, preached a sermon at the Pine Bush Methodist Church in Orange County on "The Christian Sabbath and Its Observance." Parishioners at the Circleville Presbyterian Church (also in Orange County) heard a Sunday lecture on the topic "Shall We Give up the Sabbath?" The spiritual needs of the Sabbath were part of a sermon on the physical and spiritual uplift and progress of man preached one Sunday in Middletown. Reverend Miller, again, presented from the pulpit an analysis of the great moral battles pending in the legislature to a packed house at the First Congregational Church in Middletown on May 29, 1911.[39]

The Sunday observance theme was often woven into messages relating to temperance and other perceived moral ills of the age. The Hon. Oliver W. Steward, a supposed charismatic speaker and representative of the National Temperance Society, was particularly adept at piecing together a number of common themes, Sabbath desecration included, into a call against the pervasive evil of drink and its perpetrator, the saloon. The Sunday closing issue, which since the passing of the much-abused Raines Law in 1896 effectively gave legal sanction for hotels above a certain size to sell alcoholic drinks, essentially married together temperance and Sunday law matters.[40]

The emergence of the Prohibition Party in New York dealt not only with the drink trade but also the enforcement of state laws and ordinances that helped the Sabbatarian cause. Essentially a law and order party, there was a strong nativist element within the Prohibitionist movement that favored, for instance, the employment of "American" labor in preference to alien workers whenever possible. Never an electorally significant political organization, they were only able to garner 3.6 percent of the votes for governor in 1914. Curiously, their gubernatorial candidate was none other than William Sulzer, who attempted to rise from the ashes after his impeachment the previous year as the standard bearer for two small parties, the other being the American Party.

Temperance-related organizations frequently considered Sunday observance to be an important part of their overall strategy. The New York Methodist Conference, meeting in New York City, raised a consensual voice of protest against open saloons on Sunday, which they thought catered to the more debased elements in society. The conference directed a subcommittee to launch a protest to the committee on excise in the legislature, which happened to include many of the same people on whom they counted to hold firm on Sunday reform legislation.[41]

Having instilled the message of Sunday observance in Ithaca, the WCTU acted as a pressure group in local and state politics. Nearly every community in Tompkins County had branches of the WCTU, which repeatedly petitioned the mayor of Ithaca "to exercise to the fullest extent his power as chief executive of the city in enforcement of the city ordinance and county and state laws regarding Sabbath closing and Sabbath observance." On the occasion of Sabbath Observance Day, the same organization was again active around the state, planning afternoon teas, promoting activities, and arranging talks on the importance of this subject.[42]

Popular evangelists further enhanced lobbying efforts. One such person was the Reverend Ernest Crabill, a former NYSL player turned evangelical preacher. Based in Lestershire, he was undoubtedly involved in the Sunday baseball and temperance battles in the Binghamton region. While Reverend Crabill was perambulating around Central New York lecturing his audiences on the need for abstinence from alcohol and other moral evils, another more famous ballplayer-turned-preacher, Billy Sunday, was doing the same thing on a much larger scale. By far the most notable evangelist of his era, the ubiquitous Sunday could be counted on to draw huge crowds to his camp meetings and rallies. While his primary pitch was against the evils of "demon rum"—"John Barleycorn," as he referred to it in his folksy way—Sunday's list of topics ranged from Sabbath desecration to the moral dangers brought on by rich, idle women. The aptly named Sunday, whose earlier career in the major leagues gave him a measure of credibility when speaking about baseball on the Lord's Day, often used baseball analogies in his hectoring lectures.[43]

According to his writings in a popular literary magazine, Sunday felt the national game had no objectionable features. He did think, however, that one day a week was not too much to give up to higher things, which could not be done sitting in baseball bleachers on a Sunday afternoon. The American Sabbath, to Sunday, was the country's greatest strength against the invasions of the cosmopolitan idea of a holiday. At a rally in front of twenty-four hundred people in Manhattan, Sunday proclaimed that New York was not cold to God, but he was probably not thinking of Sabbath-day baseball at the time.[44]

In the short term at least, Sunday's revivals had a pronounced effect. As a result of one such visit to Paterson, New Jersey, the police chief announced that in the future every baseball game and other sporting amusements would be banned on Sundays. Fortunately Paterson was not home to a professional team that season and the ultra-conservative sentiment on this issue soon dissipated after the temporary religious fervor wore off.[45]

The hypocrisies and contradictions generated by Sunday baseball were not entirely lost on church congregations. It was reported that a majority of members in one prominent church had come out in favor of Sabbath-day baseball. Many people were well aware of the fact that no one interfered with members of wealth and social standing if they chose to play golf, tennis, or go for leisurely drives in their automobiles on the Sabbath, while baseball was forbidden to working-class lads for whom Sunday was their one day of leisure. The question of Sunday recreation was difficult for the churches, faced with standing pat or having the courage to take a more liberal view against a well-organized lobby that kept an eye on bills passing through the legislature.[46]

In the face of such formidable opposition, legislators in Albany went to great lengths to devise bills that would engender broad support. A bill introduced by Senator T. Harvey Ferris called for a licensing system whereby Sunday games would be bound by tight restrictions as to the length of games and the conditions under which they could be played so as to appease religious sensibilities. Ferris's bill was a response to the cry of fans in central and southern New York the previous summer, whose enjoyment of professional baseball had been interrupted. A number of clergy and advocates of Sabbath restrictions back home in Oneida County saw this measure as a wedge to fully legalize commercialized baseball and launched a vigorous opposition. Not that this harmed Ferris politically. The Democratic state senator was reelected to office after his first term.[47]

With the Democrats in control of the state assembly, McGrath introduced another bill, like the one he had presented two years before, designed to legalize amateur baseball from 3 to 6 p.m. on Sundays. The Reverend Julius Lincoln from rural Chautauqua County spoke in opposition, claiming that by having Sunday as a day of sports and amusements, the movement to make Saturday a half holiday would suffer. Even though the Democrats held a twenty-two-vote majority in the assembly, the bill was voted down sixty-five to seventy-three after a bitter debate.[48]

With the backing of court decisions allowing for Sunday games, there was support for a bill sponsored by majority leader Robert P. Bush of Chemung County that would countenance non–fee paying baseball. Assemblyman John A. Goodwin of Westchester was particularly scathing about what he termed "ecclesiastic lobbyists" and "Sky Pilots who disgrace their cloth." In spite of the fact that the majority of his constituents favored a more open Sunday, or so he claimed, Goodwin was forced to vote against the Bush bill due to intense clerical pressure and the threatened loss of popular support. In voicing their opposition to the measure, assemblymen Fred Hammond and James Connell of Onondaga County cited a general principle of the inviolability of breaking the Sabbath. The bill was defeated by a margin similar to the vote on the McGrath bill.[49]

Early in the 1912 legislative session, various bills (including one that would grant women suffrage) were again presented. Assemblyman Bush once more introduced two baseball bills: one was the usual local option bill, and the other prohibited jacking up the price on baseball tickets. Bush had presented a local option bill in the previous session that had been passed by the assembly but, in spite of expectations, never got much further. Though Democrats maintained some degree of control over the legislature, the 1912 assembly session apart, Sunday law reform failed to make much headway. In the aftermath of the tragic Triangle Shirtwaist Company fire in New York City on March 25, 1911, in which 146 girls and young women (mostly immigrant teenagers) died in the city's worst industrial disaster, an investigating commission was formed to probe into the state's deplorable factory conditions. Their findings produced a flood of regulatory proposals that occupied the attention of politicians in Albany during the 1912, 1913, and 1914 legislative sessions, and consequently took precedence over proposed changes to the Sabbath laws. By 1915, New York had the most advanced labor and industrial laws in the country.[50]

Local option continued to be a popular theme among reformers. Ironically, it was an argument used by temperance advocates as a means of enabling largely rural upstate districts to remain dry, and on this score it was effective. By 1916, 498 of New York's 933 towns were no-license communities, mostly in the rural counties, with a 43 percent decline in the number of licensed saloons. On the Sunday baseball issue, however, this support was lacking. Such contradictions did not faze opponents of Sabbath reform, and with the Republicans again in control of the assembly by a two-to-one majority, local option for Sunday baseball soon became a dormant issue in Albany.

Two years later the same question emerged again when Republican assemblyman S. Peter Quick of Broome County stated that he was preparing a local option bill that would be the platform on which he would seek reelection. The bill, he said, would allow towns outside of Greater New York to be governed by their own laws regarding Sunday baseball. Quick's bill was one of three such measures that would allow games in second- and third-class towns and cities, meaning those below 250,000 in population, but would exclude first-class cities (New York City) and thus the three metropolitan major league teams. The Quick bill received a hearing with arguments made on both sides. Laboring men in Binghamton and Auburn presented petitions in favor of Sunday baseball, yet in spite of all this activity, the Quick baseball bill went the way of all such previous measures.[51]

While advocates for Sunday law reform scratched their collective heads as to ways they could appease the opposition, the upholders of the blue laws refused to budge. The game of politics is predicated on the principle of reasonableness, which involves compromise and negotiation. The question arises as to what then did the Sabbath upholders have to negotiate? As the years progressed, opponents of Sunday baseball were playing with an increasingly weaker hand save for one trump card, the penal law. Backed into a corner, the Sabbatarian element knew that compromise measures, such as local option, would pull the rug from under them. Like many conservatives fearing the loss of power, their only alternative appeared to be to stand firm and hope for the best.

With the exception of a few die-hards, the proponents of Sabbath observance were not entirely negative in approaching the Sunday baseball issue. Suggestions had been put forward in a number of venues favoring a half-day holiday on Saturday (or some other day of the week) that would compensate for the restrictions placed on Sunday activities. These suggestions did not take into account business interests and the revenue that would be lost to local firms. A proposal in Ithaca, which did not have a professional team, to continue the usual Wednesday afternoon half-day holiday during July and August for the benefit of the City Baseball League, was met with stiff resistance by the retail grocers. The grocers claimed that because they handled many perishable goods in the summer, closing on Wednesday afternoons would result in material loss.[52]

Consequently, there were fears that the abandonment of the half-day holiday would probably end league baseball in Ithaca. This sparked activists on both sides of the question to petition the Board of Aldermen. The success of those favoring a summer half-day holiday was contingent upon certain merchants closing their stores on a weekday afternoon. At a meeting of local businessmen it was decided to declare a half-day holiday during August. Despite a counter petition circulated among certain church congregations, the City League moved ahead in scheduling Wednesday afternoon games. In larger communities with more complex local economies, the half-day holiday issue was dead before it started.[53]

The Turning of the Tide

Though ministerial associations and other Sabbatarian groups maintained a headlock on Sunday reform legislation in Albany, by the middle of the decade a steady stream of articles flowed across the pages of newspapers and magazines calling for an open Sabbath. Much ado was made by those holding to Sunday observance even in the face of contrary evidence. One such account entitled "New York's Demoralizing Sunday" noted that many churches in the metropolis were closed for the summer, leaving New York's millions "a day devoted to the feverish pursuit of a relaxation they do not find." While prosperous churchgoers could escape to the golf courses and to the fresh air of the countryside, the masses experienced "a day of heat and suffocation in the city or of crowding and discomfort in the so-called pleasure resorts of the people," referring to limited spaces in parks, seaside areas, and congested neighborhoods.[54]

The emerging consciousness of what actually constituted a blue law Sunday, as opposed to what it was meant to be, marked the distinction between social class and religion. Social class was not just about deference, hierarchies, and control but also about having choices and the ability to distance oneself from others. Having the means to escape to the countryside in one's motorcar, or go to a concert, as opposed to being stuck in overcrowded conditions with limited opportunities and without the freedom to watch or participate in games and sports on Sunday, was as much of a class issue as any of a number of indicators of social inequality. Changing attitudes regarding

Sunday activities were not necessarily a rebuff to the prevailing acceptance of religion and moral authority, as much as a desire to establish a level playing field of fairness, which would allow the working classes the opportunity to enjoy the fruits of the day, as did their counterparts higher up the social scale. A question posed in a letter to the *New York Times* wondered why there could be theater and dancing on Sundays and not baseball, especially since the majority of people in the city would rather go to a ball game. That was the issue in a nutshell.[55]

As the decade progressed, the tide of reform swept across towns and cities around the state. Former mayor of Auburn Thomas H. O'Neill proposed a new Sunshine League, "to promote the health and happiness of the people of the state by encouraging and fostering outdoor sports . . ." Sunday baseball was included in the league's activities with the idea that it would operate statewide. Imaginative though this thought may have been, it never came to much. It did, however, reflect the shift toward the acceptance of reform in Auburn reinforced by the fact that the people of that city favored Sunday baseball. When officials of the Empire State Baseball League gathered in Syracuse in the spring of 1913, Auburn was one of six Central New York clubs selected to play in the league. Other teams included Oswego, Watertown, Fulton, Geneva, and Rome. Sunday baseball had been an issue in the previous city elections in Auburn in which the Democrats outvoted the Republicans by a comfortable majority.[56]

Despite the fact that the bulk of Protestant churches in the state stood firm on the side of Sunday observance, reformers could count on the relative indifference, if not compliance, of the Roman Catholic clergy. As an immigrant church, the influence of priests and bishops with regard to Sunday activities increased in proportion to the number of the new arrivals pouring into the state. Bishop Patrick A. Ludden of Syracuse openly favored Sunday baseball as a decent and healthy amusement for those who were cooped up in an office or shop all week. His influence and support did carry the caveat that order needed to be preserved at games.[57]

A more practical gesture in the direction of Sunday baseball was taken by a Catholic priest in Buffalo who changed the hour for mass to accommodate his parishioners who wished to attend a Sunday game. He believed that religion and recreation were not incompatible and that God was in the sunshine as well as in the church. "Absence of effort was not rest; a mind quite idle is a mind distressed. Rest consists in change," said the priest. Sounding the note of personal liberty, he further stated that folks should be allowed to rest in their own way so long as they did not interfere with others. This attitude now prevailed in America. Baseball did not replace church, but the cultivation of outdoor sports at the expense of indoor pastimes was a good thing.[58]

The question of Sunday baseball was on the agenda in 1913 at the annual Conference of New York mayors at Binghamton, where there was some disagreement on the issue. Consequently, the mayors decided to poll city fathers from around the state to determine whether a majority wanted the Sunday laws against baseball retained or repealed. With thirty-two of the fifty mayors responding, twenty-seven favored permitting Sunday baseball. The conference then contacted Governor Sulzer and asked that the proposition be put before a special session of the legislature, recommending a change in the law. Having caved in to the demands of the Binghamton Anti-Sunday Baseball Committee the previous spring, Sulzer, after meeting with representatives of the conference, expressed approval of and sympathy with their formulated proposal to let municipalities permit or forbid Sunday baseball according to local preference. Within two months, however, Sulzer was preoccupied with impeachment charges, and there is no evidence he followed up on the mayors' proposal.[59]

When the mayors met again two years hence, the consensus of opinion was to make local option more inclusive. Mayor Roslyn M. Cox of Middletown, president of the Conference of Mayors, and William Capes, secretary of the Conference, outlined a proposed home rule for cities. A resolution to amend the state constitution had been submitted the previous month at a gathering of mayors in Troy and was approved. It stated that the total number of bills introduced into the legislature since 1910 was 13,508. Of this number, 2,776 were special bills, meaning that they dealt only with particular issues in certain regions. Of the special city bills, 1,353 were defeated in the legislature, and 1,423 were passed. The total number of bills that became law came to 4,260. The gathering thought that the weight of legislation, in spite of the fact that many special bills were approved without debate, effectively clogged up the legislative process. Likewise, state representatives were asked to vote on local matters for which they had no knowledge, or interest. Therefore, logic and necessity, as far as the mayors were concerned, dictated that local cities were best able to decide their own affairs.[60]

By mid-decade changes were also taking place within the legislature. The influence of Tammany Hall had been gradually on the wane for several decades, causing a split in the Democratic Party between upstate and downstate factions. Ever jealous of power concentrated in the metropolis, upstate Democrats, especially those from the more rural counties, had gone along with Republicans to hold the line on reapportionment. On the other hand, the quickly changing demographics of the state were forcing the issue. The Democratic Party, when last in power, had set up a constitutional convention to redistrict Senate and Assembly seats to secure Greater New York additional members. With New York City Democrats holding important leadership positions within the party, a shift in the geographic balance of power appeared inevitable.[61]

Moreover, the Republican Party, which lost the governor's race in 1912 by 200,000 votes, could take little comfort in the fact that their electoral strength had dipped somewhat. While the total Republican enrollment in 1911 was 334,294, it declined in 1912 to 330,860; a falling off of 3,434. This decline continued in regions of fast population growth. Republican Party enrollment in the rural parts of Albany, Clinton, Cortland, Franklin, Fulton, Jefferson, Livingston, Monroe, Ontario, Orange, Oswego, Putnam, Schenectady, Suffolk, Seneca, Tompkins, Wayne, Westchester, and Yates counties remained in excess of the Democrats. Conversely, the counties of New York, Queens, Rensselaer, Richmond, and Kings, where population expansion was the greatest, were solidly in the Democratic column.[62]

After much haggling, reapportionment led to a moderate shift in political power. Little changed in the Senate, which was already close to parity. In the Assembly, however, upstate districts declined from 119 to 84, whereas those in Greater New York, inclusive of Long Island, virtually doubled. While the balance of power still remained upstate, albeit tenuously, the state legislature could no longer be considered, in the words of Al Smith, "constitutionally Republican." The stage was now set for a new chapter in the Sunday baseball saga, as the more vocal segments of public opinion became increasingly impatient at the intransigence of those manning the walls against the growing pressure for Sunday law reform.

5

Local Option, the War,
and the Modification of the
Sunday Baseball Law,
1917–1919

While the Sunday baseball issue was playing out in the legislature, Charlie Ebbets was biding his time. During this period Ebbets had purchased a piece of property just east of Prospect Park in a scrubby area of Flatbush, appropriately called Pigtown, to build a new ballpark (it opened in 1913) that bore his name. His Dodgers, which had always been a mediocre team at best, won the National League pennant in 1916 under the direction of an able and colorful manager, Wilbert Robinson. Having achieved some degree of financial solvency and with a stadium containing twenty-four thousand grandstand seats, Ebbets was more eager than ever to fill them whenever possible.

The rub of course was Sunday games. Knowing the police stood firm against professional baseball on the Sabbath while taking a more casual position regarding semi-pro and amateur games, Ebbets decided to take advantage of this opportunity. His efforts, however, to schedule Sunday matches between the Dodgers and semi-pro or amateur clubs in the borough were to no avail. A game against the Brooklyn Elks Lodge in May 1913 was cancelled by order of Police Commissioner Rhinelander Waldo even though it was a benefit event for the Brooklyn Press Club, which had lost its home due to a fire. The following year the police again called off a game against a semi-pro team at the old Parkway Driving Club grounds, which came to be known as Daubert's Field. The police warned Ebbets that if the game went ahead both teams would be subject to arrest.[1]

In October, following Brooklyn's defeat in the 1916 World Series at the hands of the Boston Red Sox, Ebbets decided to survey the patrons at his ballpark as to their views on Sunday baseball. To that end he ordered uniformed attendants to circulate petitions among the crowd, which they were at liberty to sign or not sign as the case may be. A *Baseball Magazine* editorial applauded this move on the basis that it might reveal once and for all that opposition to Sunday baseball stemmed from a "loud-mouthed minority." Included in this category were saloon keepers, who thought that Sunday games would compromise their trade by having their customers spend their money and time at the ballpark. The results of the survey are not known, but perhaps it gave the Dodgers owner reason to press ahead.[2]

Clearly, Ebbets was primed to take a lead in the push for Sunday baseball reform. Initially the focus of his efforts was upstate where he picked up a cause that had been pressing itself on minor league magnates for the previous ten years without success. Ebbets jumped on the local option question by promoting a huge petition addressed to the legislature asking for the passage of a bill that would permit each municipality to vote on the issue. Though unsuccessful, local option would rise again with greater vigor, aided by World War I.[3]

War, Patriotism, and Baseball's Internal Conflicts

On April 6, 1917, the United States entered the Great War against the German Empire and her allies, ostensibly "to save democracy." The war, which put nearly five million U.S. troops in uniform, a million of whom saw action on the Western Front, was greeted by many Americans with patriotic fervor. Even before the start of the war, there was evidence of a resurgence of interest in patriotism and military preparedness in schools, colleges, and among the general public, in light of growing "radicalism" at home and the war in Europe. Prior to World War I, the United States became embroiled in a war with Mexico following a revolution in 1911 in which one dictator (Francisco Madero) overthrew another dictator (Porfirio Díaz), who was then assassinated by a third would-be dictator (Victoriano Huerta). Sensing a challenge to American economic interests, and contemptuous of such uncivilized political behavior in a neighboring country, President Woodrow Wilson sent U.S. troops into Mexico to establish order and "teach Latin Americans to elect good men."

The American interventions into Mexico in 1914, and again in 1916, were indications of national virility. This was abetted by Muscular Christianity, which had been an underlying theme propagated by various religious organizations and was becoming more muscular in response to President Wilson's proclamation for national readiness. Churches and youth groups also picked up the beat of the war drums and hammered out a similar message of physical fitness and martial spirit.

Organized baseball joined in the flag-waving with great relish, and many people thought the national pastime had never before been so equated with nationalism. Robert Elias, in his book *The Empire Strikes Out*, chronicled the close association between baseball and America's militaristic adventures abroad. By the end of the war, 55 percent of players under contract to American league clubs and 64 percent of those reserved to National League teams, according to some estimates, had served in the armed forces.[4]

A closer examination of American society, however, belies the fact that the country was united in the war effort. It would not be out of place to say that the state was at war with the nation, or at least certain elements within the nation. As journalist and social critic Ralph Bourne put it, "if the State's chief function is war, then the State must suck out of the nation a large part of its energy for its purely sterile purposes of defense and aggression." In other words, the power of the state is achieved at the expense of the people, thus enabling it to stifle dissent and nonconformity.[5]

Beneath the surface there were a multitude of internal conflicts that divided the nation according to class, race, gender, religion, and ethnicity. The intensity of these conflicts was largely offset by the internal forces of blind nationalism and the external power of the state, but they persisted nevertheless. Baseball was not immune from the conflicts that divided the country. The war brought to a climax underlying issues that had gnawed at the infrastructure of organized baseball for decades, such as salary disputes, the exploitation of the game's employees, and incompetent management. These matters would be played out in dramatic fashion during the war years.

With the smell of war in the air, Capt. T. L. Huston of the Yankees put forward a proposal early in 1917, approved by Ban Johnson, to set up training camps in the South for the purpose of putting players through daily drill under the watchful eye of a trained military officer. Such a plan, Huston surmised, would set a fine example for American youth by impressing upon them the need for military preparedness. American League owners quickly adopted this proposal, and training stations, emphasizing military instruction and drill, were soon integrated into spring training. Huston's plan also included extending military training throughout the season, with mandatory attendance at an army base camp after the World Series. Some National League teams, particularly the Dodgers, were less enthusiastic and voted not to join in the fun of military drill—for reasons of interference with baseball preparations, not out of any lack of patriotism.[6]

With the opening of the regular season, Maj. Gen. Leonard Wood threw out the first ball at the Polo Grounds before reviewing a military drill by Yankees players. Echoing the words of a future president during another world war, General Wood stated that the highest military authorities believed that baseball should be continued as usual since the game maintained mental balance, instilled patriotism, and aroused manly instincts, which were necessary if the nation were to stand up for its rights.[7]

The spirit of militarism and patriotic fervor also extended into the minor leagues. Tom Hickey, president of the American Association, proposed a plan to organize all the eligible patrons in each city where the association had a team into military units and get them on to the field an hour before the game for field maneuvers under the direction of drill sergeants. It is easy to imagine the lack of enthusiasm with which this idea would have been greeted. Hickey, however, was undeterred. The spectacle of players and fans drilling together would enable them to get better acquainted, so he thought. Stretching his imagination further, Hickey saw that in every baseball city at least a battalion of players and fans could be organized, while in the larger cities whole regiments could march together.[8]

Fanciful though this idea may have been, the incorporation of baseball into military operations was in keeping with the established idea of citizen soldiers. In spite of the defeat of the General Staff's Universal Training bill due to opposition from the secretary of war, a campaign of preparedness, orchestrated by the military, spread across the country. The idea of a citizenry trained for national defense had been around since the time of the American Revolution, and many felt that a universally trained civilian corps best reflected the democratic principles upon which the republic was based.[9]

Almost immediately the focus of the baseball hierarchy was directed to the war effort. Looking ahead, Ban Johnson announced that in case the war continued until the following spring there would be no attempt to open the 1918 season. Believing that most American League players were eligible for conscription, he publicly acclaimed it was the duty of every young and able-bodied man to serve his country in every way he could. Johnson also gave assurances that no American League magnate "would offer any obstacle to a player's performance of their duty." These were fine sentiments which belied the fact that the primary concern of the baseball establishment was to protect their interests, and while support of the war was considered patriotic and good public relations, keeping the game going and holding on to their assets (meaning players) was of overriding importance.[10]

Inadvertently, the war offered another possible avenue to Sunday baseball. About a month after hostilities began both leagues announced they were planning to play Sunday games and, as a patriotic gesture, they would donate receipts to the army. The Yankees decided to make the first move by scheduling a game against the St. Louis Browns at the Polo Grounds for some time in June. Mayor John Purroy Mitchel gave his support to this plan and agreed to be the custodian of the receipts so as to give respectability to this token of magnanimity.[11]

A *Sporting News* editorial gave strong endorsement to this decision. Taking a not-so-subtle dig at the antireform elements in state legislatures, the paper remarked, "we insist that the self-constituted authorities of Kaiserland shall not prevent their people to pursue happiness and enjoy peace, but the authorities of our Eastern states are meanwhile quite obdurate when freeborn American citizens supposed to exercise their pursuits and enjoyment under the Constitution and Declaration of Independence seek to assert their guaranteed privileges." Continuing in a more mawkish vein, readers were told that "if the games are not played, the soldiers and sailors will go to France, denied the comforts that were to have been provided. And as they go to fight for liberty, what memories must they have of the land that sends them, which denies its own people even the liberty of seeing a ball game on Sunday, the first day of the week."[12]

In keeping with this sentiment, and predicated on the club's earlier announcement, the Yankees did their bit for the war effort when nearly twenty-five thousand fans jammed the stands to hear a band play patriotic airs before the first regular league game ever played at the Polo Grounds on a Sunday. By all accounts it was a festive occasion. The stadium was decked out with national colors and dozens of flags, including the French tricolor and the Union Jack. A band played "The Star-Spangled Banner" and George M. Cohan's new song "Over There." Col. Jacob Ruppert, Yankees president, was the master of ceremonies. A distinguished assembly of top military brass was present along with a number of troops, accompanied by their mothers, sisters, and sweethearts. Despite the outcome of the game, in which the Browns beat the Yanks 2–1, the big winner was the First Reserve Regiment of New York, due to be shipped overseas, who were in receipt of the funds provided by ticket admissions, totaling over $10,000.[13]

By midsummer nearly everyone was drinking the effervescent cocktail of patriotism. Billy Sunday, long an opponent of Sabbath-day baseball, argued that no greater mistake could be made than to discontinue baseball because of the war. The great industry of baseball, he said, was one of the worthiest enterprises, and the war should not undermine the game in any way. "Baseball is a war game," added Clark Griffith, owner of the Washington Senators, perhaps making some kind of abstruse comparison. The *New York Times* noted that a number of Australian baseball players, who had been introduced to the game during Albert G. Spalding's world goodwill tour in 1888, had "answered the call of their country" and were now serving with the Allies on various war fronts. Moreover, delegations of soldiers and sailors waiting to go overseas were treated to a Sunday concert and baseball game held at the Polo Grounds between the Giants and the Cincinnati Reds on August 19. The game was for the benefit of the 69th New York Infantry with two thousand uniformed members of the Irish regiment on hand. Unfortunately, the game ended on a sour note when a police detective assigned to watch the game made a report, which resulted in arrests.[14]

Baseball magnates continued to be notable cheerleaders on the patriotic bandwagon. Known as a hard, penny-pinching businessman, Charlie Comiskey, owner of the Chicago White Sox, was nearly reduced to tears by the sight of young men preparing for war. "I could not stand there and watch those boys marching without choking up," he effused. "After watching such drill by organizations of fine American manhood, one is bound to be a better citizen. He is bound to be impressed with the thought that these boys are a means of boosting world peace as well as participants in the World War." Carrying his sentimental feelings a step further, Comiskey proposed that a military day become a feature of the American League season every year.[15]

Not content just to promote military training on the diamond, Captain Huston joined himself, and was soon on a troop ship leaving for France with a regiment of army engineers. Before departing, he called on Ban Johnson to bid farewell. Johnson asked if there was anything special that could be done to please Huston's boys. The answer was that everything had been provided for and it was their greatest sorrow to say goodbye to baseball since the love for the grand old game came next after their country and families. Huston returned home after the war and continued to play an important role in major league baseball.[16]

For some of those players who joined the armed services, willingly or otherwise, baseball was not necessarily postponed, since the military conveniently established teams at various camps. Charles Weeghman, president of the Chicago Cubs, was impressed by the sight of teams of young men playing baseball at the Great Lakes Naval Station. One enthusiast made the improbable suggestion to Clark Griffith that he might finance sending two major league baseball teams to France to play exhibition games for thousands of American soldiers behind the lines. Not surprisingly, the idea was dropped. A more plausible suggestion held that major league players be organized to play exhibitions for the benefit of soldiers in the South after the regular season, but it never happened.[17]

As an aside, the flu pandemic that swept around the world between June 1918 and December 1919, killing between 50 million and 100 million people, was detected in its early stages at the Fort Riley, Kansas, army base. From there it quickly spread across the country. Although the disease, which afflicted mostly the young and able, caused the death of thousands of soldiers on military installations and at the front, it had little impact on professional baseball.

Earlier, during the summer of 1917, baseball owners repeatedly talked up the importance of baseball as part of the war effort. "I can see no justification for the views of Alarmists," wrote Garry Herrmann, chairman of the National Commission, "nor do I believe that baseball will or should cease to be a permanent feature of American life."[18]

Disputes over Salaries

Events over the preceding months, however, challenged Herrmann's optimism and gave him cause for alarm. Prior to the start of the 1917 season major league owners, sensing the inevitability of war, sought to reduce the number of players under contract, which could save both leagues about $264,000. This added fuel to the existing fire of discontent. From the beginning of 1916, rumors circulated about a possible strike by the fledgling Players Fraternity on behalf of a number of disgruntled ballplayers.[19]

The threatened strike became a reality when Dave Fultz, president of the fraternity, called for industrial action on February 20, the initial date for the start of spring training. The dispute was multi-causal but centered primarily on the spike in salaries resulting from the baseball war with the Federal League. Formed in 1913, the Federal League challenged the American and National League clubs during the 1914 and 1915 seasons by luring players with the promise of higher salaries and freedom from the restrictive reserve clause. The impact of the Federal League, which set up teams in already existing Major League cities, was to drive up operating expenses through competition for player's services. With the anticipated expiration of war contracts at the end of 1917, the American and National League bosses were determined to reduce expenditures to what they considered parity.[20]

There were also other issues such as traveling expenses to training camps, affecting both the major and minor leagues, which had been a sore spot for years. Unable to convince the owners to negotiate, Fultz made overtures to Samuel Gompers of the American Federation of Labor about possible affiliation. Initially tempted, Gompers, having wisely assessed the tenuous position of the fraternity, declined. His suspicions were realized when the magnates threatened to close down training camps to any unsigned player, thus squelching strike plans.[21]

In the aftermath of the strike threat the overwhelming response by the club owners was one of disdain and a desire to equate industrial action with radicalism. John Tener, president of the National League, remarked that such actions appeared "to border almost on conspiracy." Terms such as "fire-eaters," "anarchists," and "weak-kneed pacifists," were directed by owners against players sympathetic to the fraternity. Connie Mack, manager of the Philadelphia Athletics, said he would welcome a strike as it would bring matters to a crisis and prove that the players had not been imposed upon. He estimated that minor league salaries were 50 percent too high and were in need of adjustment.[22]

The Baseball Players Fraternity soon collapsed, leaving a legacy of suspicion and hostility. Newspaper reports criticized the players for their ingratitude in wanting better pay. As one article noted, baseball would be a greater game, "if the players would take a little more interest in baseball and a little less in what they were going to get out of it." Other sources condemned both sides, noting that the fans were the real losers in such disputes.[23]

By the autumn of 1917 there was growing concern that the 1918 season would be in jeopardy if the war continued. This was despite signals from high officials in Washington that "the continuance of the national game should be encouraged." In addition to large operating expenses, the owners were burdened with crippling war taxes that caused further pecuniary hardship. When the American and National League bosses met independently in December to chart a course for the coming year, cost cutting was very much on their minds.

The course that the National Commission proposed was the insertion of a clause in each player's contract making some provision that if the season ended early, salaries would be downgraded accordingly. The owners no doubt anticipated that such a move would cause an outcry from the players—not that they cared about player reaction. Fiscal prudence they felt was in the best interests of the game.[24]

The inevitable outcry by the players led to agitation for a holdout that was greeted with little sympathy by the *Sporting News*. The paper claimed that a hundred or more major league players were "trying to back their employers up against a wall on the salary proposition." In fact there was a wide differentiation in pay between top stars, such as Ty Cobb of the Detroit Tigers and Hal Chase of the Cincinnati Reds, and the many good but less exalted players earning less than $4,000 a season. At a time when some bosses seriously considered closing their gates, ball players, in the eyes of the press, were no longer deserving of the public's sympathy.[25]

Financial problems confronting major league clubs paled before those of the minor leagues. With the close of the 1917 season, many of the lower level minor league teams were ready to close down shop permanently. At least five leagues had already done so, while others had taken drastic measures such as cutting their seasons short. A couple of circuits adopted a scheme of encapsulating two pennant races into a single season. As more and more young men were called into military service, even the relatively healthy leagues, such as the Pacific Coast League and the International League, were feeling the pinch of lost attendance, not to mention the conscription of some of their players.[26]

Conscription and the War against Slackers

The threat of holdouts and strikes exacerbated the hardships affecting baseball. With the passage of the Selective Service Act, the ranks of the military swelled while teams were systematically depleted of players. In the face of new regulations and expanding eligibility requirements for the draft, the question was raised as to what would be the owners' response. Reacting to the suggestion that the richer, more fortunate clubs aid the less favored teams, the magnates opted for a free enterprise approach, meaning that each team should fend for itself. If baseball's bosses refused to take concerted action in the face of an obvious crisis, the question remained: Would the draft take matters out of their hands?[27]

Subsequent events answered this question in the affirmative. From the start of the war, a policy of enforced patriotism was instigated from the national level downwards aimed at rooting out dissenters, radicals, and slackers. Federal and state legislation, used to silence critics of the war, was buttressed by government and private organizations, such as the American Defense Society, the National Security League, and the American Protective League, along with dozens of local vigilante groups. Roundups of slackers, many of whom took refuge in large cities (particularly New York), along with people having inconvenient political views, routinely occurred, in defiance of basic constitutional rights and civil liberties.

While a number of players, reluctantly or enthusiastically, were pulled into military service, others sought exemptions to avoid conscription. There is no evidence that any ballplayer actively opposed the war on political grounds; however, more than a few players broke their contracts and jumped to more lucrative jobs in the shipyards and steel plants. Joe Jackson of the White Sox (who would later be implicated in the 1919 Black Sox scandal), in spite of being classified as fit for the draft, signed on with a shipbuilding company and spent the duration of the war playing baseball. Al Mamaux of the Brooklyn Dodgers followed suit. Comiskey was so disgusted by Jackson's lack of patriotism that he tried to sell him to another club after the war. Not finding anyone prepared to meet his price, Comiskey decided, largely to his benefit, to keep him.[28]

Predictably, the owners threw their support on this matter behind the government. Ban Johnson criticized the shipbuilding and steel corporation industrialists, who effectively lured valuable resources (players) from another essential industry (baseball). This perpetuated a great wrong, so he thought, against the national pastime, against the patriotic players who went to war, and against the government whose intention it was to make all able-bodied men available for military service. Johnson vowed to take steps to protect the good name of baseball from being associated with slackers by turning over to the War Department the names of those who had violated their contracts. This perceived shirking of one's patriotic duty by the slackers sat hard with Johnson who, at the close of the war, urged American League owners at their annual meeting to blacklist all ballplayers who were unwilling to serve their country. Faced with more pressing problems, this proposal was never carried to fruition.[29]

Matters changed drastically with the issuing of Gen. Enoch Herbert Crowder's "work or fight" order in May 1918, which determined that all able-bodied men of eligible age be required to "join the colors," or engage in necessary war work. Slackers in vital industries could now be seen as contributors to the war effort, although the government implemented controls with some success to eliminate the practice some companies had to recruit ballplayers at bank president's salaries and camouflage them as workers so they could play ball on company teams.[30]

The order to work or fight raised the question of whether baseball should be put in the same category as theaters, opera, and other amusements, or if it should be considered an essential war industry. There were two arguments against the continuation of the baseball season. First, there was the need to keep working men in useful employment during the daylight hours when games were played. Second, due to a few highly publicized cases of ballplayers escaping military service, there was a general sense in some quarters that ballplayers as a class had shirked their duty to their country in a time of crisis. Club owners made the argument to President Wilson that baseball was an essential industry that should be permitted normal operation while the war in Europe continued. Their points carried some weight but with the loss of key players and a critical cohort of fans gone to war, the ranks of all professional clubs were seriously weakened. The editors of the *Sporting News* felt the war should not be an excuse for giving up all pleasures and diversions, but with the country fully on a war footing and people suffering, theirs was a minority opinion.[31]

In classifying baseball as a nonproductive occupation, the welfare of baseball fell into the hands of Secretary of War Newton D. Baker, whose decision opened the door for local draft boards to induct players. This, as many feared, would adversely affect the rest of the 1918 season. The *Sporting News* again pointed to the large crowds of twenty to thirty thousand people attending games in New York to show that the fans wanted the season to continue. "Millions of our patriotic citizens are deeply interested in the squarest and cleanest sport in the world," so echoed President Wilson, who "knows what baseball means to Americans who seek relaxation from the worries of the war."[32]

Dysfunctional Management

For some time, matters affecting major league clubs had been in a state of disarray. With the flight of players into war industries, or the armed services, the owners were faced with the real possibility that professional baseball would be closed down for the remainder of the 1918 season, and perhaps beyond. Indecision, procrastination, and open hostility between the two leagues and within baseball's governing body led to widespread bickering and politicking among the commissioners and between the owners. Columnist Hugh Fullerton observed that the National Commission had been a joke for years. He referred to the falling out between two of the commissioners, Ban Johnson and Garry Herrmann, the refusal of John Tener to serve on the commission, and the breaking off of diplomatic relations between the two leagues as examples of this dysfunction. Known in baseball circles as a czar, Johnson had come under fire from owners in his own league for being too tyrannical.[33]

The *Sporting News*, usually a dependable advocate of the owner's interests, pointed to the sorry plight of the game due to a lack of harmony between magnates of both major leagues. Organized baseball, so it was noted, "was practically disorganized at a time when it should have been united and fighting for its inalienable right." Some even suggested that a full season without baseball might not be a bad thing since the game would ultimately rebound in a manner, which would be more "business-like, sensible, and built around the principle of fairness."[34]

After much bickering and a number of delays, the owners decided to close the season on August 20 and stage the World Series immediately thereafter. Johnson, who backed the plan, believed it would result in a large saving to clubs in both leagues as the attendance, according to reports, appeared to be dropping despite a reprieve by the War Department allowing the season to continue until September 1. Herrmann stated that clubs should play through Labor Day and then have a short World Series for the pennant winners.[35]

Less than two weeks before the close of the season, the owners were mute about whether there would be a World Series or not. Herrmann wanted to wait on the outcomes of the Cleveland and Boston games, which were neck-to-neck in the American League pennant race, before deciding whether the Labor Day games of September 2 would be played. Many ballplayers were perturbed about the thought of going into the army and were not keen to perpetuate the season by playing beyond Labor Day. The Brooklyn club was scheduled to play two games on that date, since the previous day was a Sunday when no games were allowed. As it turned out, the season ended on Labor Day.[36]

The World Series began on September 5 and was over six days later. Conflict between players and the National Commission erupted during the fifth game over a demand by the players that the second, third, and fourth place clubs be cut out of a share of the receipts. Cubs and Red Sox players refused to play while feverish negotiations with Herrmann, representing the commission, continued. Harry Hooper finally agreed to instruct his teammates to take the field after a long holdup, with the proviso that the public was informed of what had transpired.[37]

Even though the fans may have felt shortchanged, and the players left in limbo, the owners did quite well. Not only did they cut the season short, but they managed to avoid paying the players their salaries. This was done by releasing all of them and giving only ten days' notice, as stated in the small print of their contracts. Normally the release of players would have made them free agents, but the magnates entered into a gentlemen's agreement not to tamper with each other's men. Hence the owners saved about $200,000 in payroll while retaining a monopoly over their players. According to the *New York Times*, when "the petted and pampered stars of the diamond" learned that they had lost a full month's salary, they were "very likely to make a noise which will be heard from coast to coast."[38]

Noise was indeed heard. Some players sued over the loss of their salaries. Ebbets was far from pleased when his star first baseman, Jake Daubert, went to court to claim the balance of his salary, as was Clark Griffith when one of his players sued the Washington club for $1,400. At least one press report, caught up in the irrational frenzy of the times, referred to these "ungrateful players" as Bolsheviks.

With the war drawing to a close, the future of baseball remained uncertain. While expressing optimism that the game would revive, a writer for *Baseball Magazine* noted that the present state of the game was "very hazy, very chaotic." Ban Johnson was quoted as saying that he would oppose any resumption of the game before the 1920 season, so the sport could undergo a major housecleaning and readjustment. Speaking at a dinner given in his honor, Colonel Huston—after paying tribute to American troops—remarked, "Now we have peace, let us also have peace in baseball." He went on to say, "There seems no reason why this great game always should be in a turbulent condition. Baseball seems to go through one upheaval after another."[39]

The one point that united the magnates was that baseball would continue a policy of retrenchment. At their annual winter meetings, both leagues agreed to cut salaries, which would save the clubs more than $200,000. They would chop one month off the season, reducing the number of games played from 154 to 140, and thus pay players for five months' work instead of the usual six months. Having forfeited a month's wages during the 1918 season, the players almost certainly would have been outraged at their 1919 contracts. After the National League imposed a salary cap on each club of $11,000 a month for its entire payroll, some predicted the players would force a big strike before or during the 1919 season.[40]

Without a union to stand up for them, however, there was little they could do except hold out for more pay, which many did. At least one owner, Harry Frazee of the Red Sox, warned his players that the club would refuse to pay spring training expenses for any holdouts. Considering the demands of the Players Fraternity two years before, the circumstances of baseball's employees with respect to their employers had just about returned full circle. Arguably, had the war continued, the national game would have become one of its victims, at least for the immediate future.[41]

By the time the baseball season had reached its premature conclusion in the autumn of 1918, the mood of the country had changed dramatically. The various expressions of moral reform had now been sidetracked by a flood tide of patriotic fervor that swept across every city, town, and region with the same force by which it flowed through baseball itself. The disdain for Sabbath desecrators, saloonkeepers, gamblers, and other targets of the upholders of moral respectability was transferred to a hatred of Germans, slackers, radicals, and alien influences and fed by an unprecedented propaganda campaign, which was both blunt and vivid. Information about the war, appearing in the local press, was interspersed with articles on topics of parochial concern, such as gasoline observance on Sunday, local efforts to raise war bonds, and assaults on social norms—for instance, the impropriety of unescorted young women on the streets late at night.

The war—in elevating the status of the soldier, and by association the patriotic masses of laboring people—gave these groups greater social visibility. While there was public antipathy toward avaricious owners and prima donna players, organized baseball was never more popular. The voices championing the cause of the laboring classes to enjoy their one free day at the ballpark, and the frequent assertion that Sunday games provided wholesome recreation, received more serious attention. The barriers that seemed so impregnable just two years before now faded before the growing possibility of legal Sunday baseball in New York.

The Fight for Sunday Baseball in 1917

As the war progressed there was much activity on the Sunday baseball front. The flood of proposals put before the legislature to legalize Sabbath games in New York continued in earnest, backed by the momentum of increased pressure from minor league owners, whose schedules were already disrupted by the war. The *Sporting Life* saw no reason why Sunday baseball should not be permitted, but, as usual, this was a premature opinion.[42]

While bills to legalize Sunday baseball continued to stall in the legislature, action in favor of prohibition was proceeding nicely. Since the turn of the century temperance advocates had been pushing for the passage of a local options bill that would modify the excise law and repeal the hated Raines Law, which permitted the sale of alcoholic beverages on Sunday only in licensed hotels. That opportunity finally arrived in February 1917 when the legislature passed the Hill-Wheeler bill, providing for a local option vote on the manufacture and sale of liquor in counties, towns, and cities with a population over fifty thousand. The bill, which contained a referendum clause, had previously been carried in the senate with little debate along strict party lines by a vote of thirty-five to thirteen. Following assembly approval, the bill landed on the desk of Republican governor Charles S. Whitman, who signed the measure into law. Although the supporters of this legislation were the same people who generally opposed Sunday baseball reform, Sabbath reformers were hopeful insofar as the bill provided a convenient framework for modification of the blue laws.[43]

Meanwhile, police interference with Sunday games continued. Charles J. Harvey, former secretary of the State Boxing Commission, was arraigned in Harlem court with four other men on a charge of violating the Sunday law by indulging in a game of baseball. The arrest followed a complaint from the New York Sabbath Society regarding a game between the Lincoln Giants and the Brooklyn Eagles. The court heard testimony that a table was placed at the entrance to the ground where bills in various denominations were deposited and scorecards received.[44]

When the case came to court nearly a month later, Judge Francis X. McQuade, a staunch reformer and avid baseball supporter, dismissed the men and then lectured Mr. Powell Crighton, the attorney for the "Sabbath Society," on the advantages of Sunday baseball, especially for the working man who labored six days a week. The *Sporting News* took this opportunity to issue one of its frequent harangues against the New York legislature for ignoring "the plea of rational citizens of the state for a removal of the ban on Sunday baseball." "While the salons of Albany continued their bigoted stand," the paper warned that the advocates of Sunday baseball were gaining recruits.[45]

With the Fourth of July a couple of days away, Ebbets decided to follow the example of the Yankees and stage a Sunday game in Brooklyn. In a contest marked by military drill along with a concert of patriotic music, Wilbert Robinson's wayward Dodgers downed Philadelphia 3–2 in the first regularly scheduled National League Sunday baseball game played in the borough since 1906. According to the *Sporting News,* no one was scandalized by this game, put on before fifteen thousand fans, a crowd similar to any weekday match. Apparently overlooked was the report of unruly behavior by the crowd, which turned its hostility toward umpire Bill Klem. For the Dodgers owner and their manager, however, this was of secondary concern.[46]

After the game, Ebbets and Robinson were arrested for violating the ban on Sunday baseball. According to Ebbets, the admission money paid was to hear a pregame concert with receipts going to a charity connected with war work. Magistrate Alexander Geismar held that the question of admission money did not affect the issue. He reasoned that the assembling of a vast throng to see a professional game might constitute a violation of the law whether the game was played or not.[47]

Fearing that the law was against him, Ebbets presented his side of the case. He noted, disingenuously, that games played on Sunday at Ebbets Field were for the comfort of soldiers and sailors "who are to fight for the cause of freedom against German autocracy." Continuing his line of thought, Ebbets equated the judges and sheriffs, "who feel the souls of millions have been saved by stopping Sunday baseball, for the Kaiser, we reckon, will rejoice at any move that will lessen the comfort and curb the spirit of the American soldier boy. And how he must laugh," exclaimed Ebbets, "when he was told that we of America are fighting for liberty," yet did not even have the right to witness a ball game on Sunday because it was against the law. One supposes that the kaiser had other things on his mind.[48]

Ebbets's troubles were matched by those of Max Rosner, a cigar manufacturer and baseball entrepreneur. He owned a semi-pro team, the Brooklyn Bushwicks, known as the Cypress Hills Club. To get around the law, Rosner sold pencils, programs, and cushions for grandstand seats at twenty-five cents each, bleacher seats for ten cents. Every Monday during the season he was dragged into court where the magistrate, obviously a Bushwicks fan, would suspend the sentence until the end of the season at which time a small fine was levied. Not surprisingly, Rosner worked hard to get the blue laws changed. At one time he loaned Ebbets money to cover expenses for his hard-strapped Dodgers in exchange for an exhibition game. Much to Ebbets's annoyance, the Bushwicks defeated the major league club and then denied them the opportunity for a return match.[49]

Again, the *Sporting News* set forth a flood of scathing remarks directed not just at the Sabbatarians but also against the prohibitionists whom they characterized as compounding the very problem they were trying to solve. The editorial calculated that "the anti-Sunday baseball fanatics" in New

York had overplayed their hand in stopping benefit games that were to have been played for a comfort fund for the army and navy. "Old women in pants and petticoats chuckled with glee when the authorities dragged the baseball men into court and stopped Sunday games." In urging the state legislature to take action in Albany, the editorial surmised that legislators would be bombarded with petitions signed by thousands of "right thinking people" demanding that the laws against Sunday amusements be modified.[50]

Such petitions were already on their way. Following Ebbets's arrest, the representatives of several relief organizations went to Albany to urge Governor Whitman to modify the law prohibiting baseball games on Sunday when an admission fee was charged. One of the petitioners, James Douglas Campbell of the Militia of Mercy, believed the governor would sign a bill repealing the statute if the legislature passed such a measure in the coming session. Understandably, Governor Whitman didn't commit himself. While advocates for Sunday baseball who supported funds for charitable purposes might have felt they had a strong ally in the governor, there was every reason to believe he would disappoint them. On two previous occasions Governor Whitman had vetoed Sunday reform bills without giving any specific reason. Moreover, there is no evidence he cared that much about baseball, and as a previous district attorney of New York City, upholding the existing law was of primary concern.[51]

The trial of Ebbets and Robinson for violation of the blue laws was put before the Court of General Sessions on August 29. Over the previous month, Ebbets had been canvassing the neighborhood of the ballpark and expected to have at least fifty witnesses to appear in court to refute the charges. In the end, the only witness to appear for the defense was James D. Campbell (the same man who the previous month had gone to Albany to lobby the governor for reform). He testified that the proceeds of the entertainment that took place at Ebbets Field on the day in question were for the benefit of his charity, the Militia of Mercy. However, his efforts were of no consequence. Both owner and manager were found guilty of breaking the law by permitting their team to play a Sunday game. The bench warned both men they must not do it again. Even so, the judge proved to be sympathetic, indicating that neither Ebbets nor Robinson would be punished for their offense. The judge did not think the moral damage was as serious as the Sabbath observance people had tried to claim, but he felt he had he had no other recourse but to enter a guilty verdict. From Ebbets's perspective, the decision would put an end to Sunday ball in Brooklyn until a more amenable law was on the books.[52]

Livid at what he saw as legal nuisance, Ebbets directed his pent-up anger against the sheriff of Brooklyn, Edward Riegelmann, whom he saw as the instigator of police harassment. He was personally affronted by the sheriff's actions in enforcing the laws, hinting that his motives were politically inspired to gain support from middle-class, churchgoing voters for the upcoming election. Ebbets reiterated that it was the object of the club to play games with Sunday concerts for worthy war charities in compliance with the law, which permitted exhibitions for charitable purposes.[53]

For some time Ebbets had felt that the law discriminated against professional major league baseball on the East Coast. Putting pen to paper in an article for *Baseball Magazine*, he wrote that some laws were a matter of custom and that people were used to doing things in a particular way. He also commented that changes in the law did not come about easily and that he was willing to work with friend and foe alike to institute agreeable results. Ebbets felt the Brooklyn team's offer to play Sunday games and donate receipts to charitable organizations was a positive step in this direction. But he lamented, such efforts had been derailed by the Law and Order Society with its cozy association with politicians in Albany. Glancing around the borough, Ebbets wondered at the anomaly of allowing Negro teams to play on Sunday, where admission was charged, and permitting all paid amusements on Coney Island to remain open while disallowing white baseball. Such was his case for local option by which the blue laws would be decided by the majority in any community.[54]

Ebbets raised an interesting point about the inconsistency of enforcing the Sunday laws against teams consisting entirely of white players, and allowing games for African Americans. While blacks had been driven out of organized baseball in 1890, there is little or no evidence of any black players ever being arrested in New York for playing Sunday ball. The reason, apart from a dearth of reports of such cases, was embedded in the structure of de facto segregation. Marginalized and invisible, African Americans were largely ignored unless they came in contact with white society and thus transgressed racial and social boundaries. Law enforcement officials therefore thought it prudent not to risk racial confrontation with blacks by needlessly enforcing violations of the penal laws, about which many of them were less than enthusiastic. Besides, the concerns of evangelicals, who were the driving force behind much police activity, centered more on disciplining the largely immigrant working classes and promoting Sunday observance as a means of maintaining order within a more visible white society than in going outside those racial boundaries.

Meanwhile, arrests for Sabbath games continued. The aforementioned August 19 match between the New York Giants and the Cincinnati Reds resulted in the arrest of managers Christy Mathewson and John McGraw, which indicated that Brooklyn was not alone in its frustrated efforts to play Sunday charity games. Mathewson's arrest may have come as a surprise to some since the straightlaced "Christian gentleman," as he was called, was opposed to playing on Sunday and allegedly had made a promise to his mother as a young man to keep the Sabbath. The war and the spirit of the times appear to have softened his stance, which brought him in line with the reform attitude of the baseball hierarchy.

When the two managers appeared in court, Detective John McGovern of the Fifth Avenue Police Station in Brooklyn, who was assigned to watch the game, told Edgar V. Frothingham, the magistrate, that it was a regular season game on the National League schedule in violation of Section 2145 of the New York penal code. When the case came to court a week later, Judge McQuade, a magistrate with an entirely different outlook, was not impressed. In rendering an opinion on the case, he lectured Powell Crighton, agent for the Sabbath Society of New York. Rather than penalizing the two managers, McQuade believed they ought to receive a public vote of the highest commendation for lending their services gratis to a patriotic cause. The *Sporting News* added its two cents, noting that Mr. Crighton and his ministerial backers might better use their time hunting down white slavers and sedition talkers than bothering with Sunday baseball, especially when played for such noble objectives.[55]

There was further evidence in Brooklyn of judicial disgust involving Sunday baseball cases. After throwing out a case against fifteen young men arrested and charged with violating the Sunday law, despite that there was no disturbance, Judge Henry Miller in the Jamaica Magistrates Court offered a reproachful opinion: "It is beyond my understanding why persons are permitted to go to a moving-picture show, pay admission, and be in a place where the doors are kept closed and there is poor ventilation, and why they are not allowed to see a baseball game where they will be out in the open and clear air and see good, clean sport."[56]

Taking a safer course, the Yankees consented to stage an exhibition game out of state in Bridgeport to aid the Connecticut State Tuberculosis Association. Since Sunday was the only day the Yankees could play a charity game, and Bridgeport was the only Connecticut town where local ordinances would permit a Sunday game, a match was scheduled there. Accordingly, the Eastern League cancelled its regularly scheduled Sunday game so the Yankees could help raise a couple thousand dollars for the association, and display their talents for the local fans.[57]

At the close of the season, following the Chicago White Sox's World Series victory, the Sunday baseball question took a momentary hiatus. The only relevant news involved a fine of $100 leveled by Ebbets on Dodgers star Rube Marquard for pitching an exhibition Sunday match in Manhattan against Ebbets's wishes. Marquard and the Philadelphia Phillies' star pitcher, Chief Bender, had formed a professional team to do some barnstorming. Brooklyn right fielder, Casey Stengel, signed on to play in the same game but backed off when Ebbets made his displeasure known.[58]

Attention soon turned to the upcoming elections in November. Most of the candidates sought to sidestep the issue of Sunday baseball, given the volatility of New York politics. The war years marked the high point of socialist popularity in the state even though the party was still very much a minority. In 1912 the socialists claimed 11 percent of the municipal vote in New York City, rising to 22 percent in 1917. Socialists in other cities around the state garnered a similar percentage of votes, particularly in Buffalo and Schenectady where socialist candidates got 30 percent and 24 percent of the ballots, respectively, even though none of them were elected. The promise of their electoral success, coupled with the toxic political air generated by wartime propaganda and police crackdowns, caused internal fissures within Tammany Hall and the downstate Republicans. Such political volatility meant the moment was not ripe for addressing controversial matters such as Sunday baseball.

In spite of the improbabilities on the political front, Ebbets was optimistic about the chances for Sunday baseball in New York for the 1918 season. He was heartened by the results of a circular he had sent candidates for the upcoming election regarding professional baseball on Sunday. He had received positive responses from New York mayor John Purroy Mitchel, from Al Smith, and from the leaders of both parties. Officials of the Brooklyn Club, which was leading the fight for reform, estimated that 90 percent of people in New York favored Sunday baseball with proper restrictions such as good conduct and noninterference with church times. Ebbets received additional support from J. A. Livingston, chairman of the Executive Committee of the Republican Party in Kings County, who said he had no objection to playing baseball on any day of the week. Other Brooklyn Republicans reported they would favor repeal of the Sunday baseball law, or would work to put forth a bill to legalize games on the Sabbath.[59]

At the same time, Jacob Ruppert, co-owner of the Yankees with Huston, joined forces with Ebbets in sounding out candidates of all parties on the Sunday baseball question. As with those in Brooklyn, office seekers in Manhattan and the Bronx gave bipartisan backing to eliminating the blue laws regarding baseball. In a letter to Ebbets, Ruppert "pointed out that the obsolete law under which the prohibition is now enforced was enacted in response to the sentiment of a primitive community, differing vastly from that of the present age."[60]

While returns from the New York mayoral election were coming in, the *Sporting News* predicted that the next mayor would have to work for a more liberal interpretation of the Sunday baseball law. The issues in the election had been colored by the war, laced with strong anti-German, anti-radical, and pro-Americanism rhetoric on one side, along with attacks, voiced by those on the left, on social ills brought on by capitalism. The paper, true to form, identified the key issue as not so much about Americanism as about permitting citizens of the nation to enjoy baseball games to the fullest on Sunday.[61]

Within a week following the elections, Ebbets was busy sending a circular to all the clergymen in Brooklyn explaining the position of the club regarding Sunday baseball and asking their views on the subject. Quoting his letter from Ruppert, he noted that people were living in a far different community from the one that existed when the original 1787 statute was passed. Ebbets considered the legal prohibition of Sabbath-day baseball to be irrelevant and noted that the issue was now how to conduct Sunday games so as not to interfere with the repose of the community and religious activities. He further reminded the clergy that between forty thousand and fifty thousand of the borough's residents had signed a petition requesting the legalization of Sunday ball.

As 1917 drew to a close, Ebbets and other downstate proponents of Sunday baseball law reform could look ahead to 1918 as the year they had long been waiting for. "Thus it seems that there is really some hope that the scales will have fallen from the eyes of law makers of the Empire State— or to put it another way that they will have the courage to turn deaf ears to a blatant minority of fanatics and give the people they are presumed to represent what is prayed for," so editorialized the *Sporting News*. Taking a more visionary stance, the paper saw that the fight was developing along broader lines than anything previously imagined when the menace of Kaiserism first loomed. Out of the war, so it was thought, would emerge a new religion and a new view of morality. "Big things being made up of a host of little things," and one of the big things, in the estimable opinion of "the bible of baseball," was the privilege "to see a ball game in New York on Sunday," which "has a part in the whole."[62]

1918 and the Final Push for Reform

At the start of the new year the National Commission, sensing that Sabbath reform could be imminent, drew up two schedules, one of which would include Sunday games in New York and Brooklyn in case the New York legislature passed a bill lifting the present ban. Considering the build-up of pressure for reform, the Giants and Yankees owners—perhaps surprisingly—took a disinterested position by assuming that if the public wanted Sunday ball they would be happy to furnish it. With the exception of Ebbets, organized baseball took no active part in the campaign, perhaps sensing that their cause would not be furthered by "stirring the pot." Needless to say, baseball's bosses expected that the bill would be passed.

Meanwhile the Brooklyn owner continued to take a proactive stance, which essentially brought the matter full circle. Those who had followed the battle over the blue laws throughout the years were keenly aware that the agitation for the Sunday baseball issue started in Brooklyn. Some members of the legislature observed that Sunday baseball was played in Brooklyn in the 1880s, when the borough's professional team was in the American Association. At that time, they reasoned, the various Sabbath observance committees made no determined fight against Sunday baseball before Brooklyn became a National League team. Of course, Sabbath keeping was a more pronounced social norm at that time.[63]

Fittingly, and perhaps ironically, state senator Robert Lawson of Brooklyn carried on the fight in the legislature. After consulting with senate leader Elon Brown, he submitted his Sunday baseball bill to a conference of Republican senators in Albany. Lawson noted that the bill had gained many new supporters within the past few days, including former president and ex–New York governor Theodore Roosevelt, who had long been a proponent of the active life and perhaps saw the open Sunday as a means to that end. Those favoring Sunday baseball argued that prohibition of such games was undemocratic, while using the often repeated and admittedly questionable argument that sport on the Sabbath would keep young men from loafing, gambling, and other forms of mischief.[64]

At the conclusion of a lengthy hearing attended by people from all over the state, the codes committee reported out the Lawson bill, its first important hurdle. With the Republicans in firm control of both the assembly and the senate, there was every reason to believe that the measure had little chance of success on the floor of either house. As with practically every other piece of controversial legislation, the war entered into the battle. Canon Chase of New York City argued that while the war was on "there is not room for squabble over Sunday baseball." Proponents of the measure contended that the sport would develop young men physically and fit them for service. Opponents of the bill saw it as an attempt to commercialize the Sabbath, as the courts had already ruled that amateur ball was permissible where admission was not charged. Hence the debate raged on.[65]

Perhaps sensing defeat, supporters of the Lawson bill wisely amended it so that the legality of Sunday games would depend entirely on the decision of local, rather than state governing bodies. Thus, if the authorities in a town where the religious element was strong did not want baseball on the Sabbath, they could prevent it. Judge McQuade, who presided over the case against team managers McGraw and Mathewson the previous August and had taken a special interest in the Sunday baseball question, spent much time in Albany at his own expense urging the passage of the bill. While the Democrats supported the bill almost to a man, some felt that with the backing of a handful of "sensible Republicans" the measure might be nonpartisan enough to squeak through.[66]

Meanwhile, throughout the months of March and April, lawmakers in Albany were besieged with letters, comments, and clippings of newspaper editorials from local politicians, clergymen, newspaper reporters, and the great army of fans around New York and elsewhere, all endorsing Sunday baseball. Most frequently voiced were the usual complaints that Sabbath observance deprived working men and boys of the joys of watching baseball, the hypocrisy of allowing some amusements to flourish on Sunday while denying others, and the benefits, physical and moral, derived from participating in Sunday sports. Ebbets and McQuade, in particular, were singled out for praise based on their advocacy efforts on behalf of Sunday games. Not a small point, as suggested by some, was the war tax, which would be levied on Sunday ball and would enrich the war effort.

Some mayors pointed out that where Sunday baseball existed there were no ill effects. As with all social and moral controversies, there was frequent evocation of the principles embedded in the Constitution, the spirit of democracy, and the appealing idea of freedom within the boundaries of order. While a number of letters were directed specifically to Governor Whitman, it was doubtful that he was at all moved, being predisposed on the matter.

It is interesting that with all the controversy over Sunday baseball, no one cared to ask what the players thought of the matter. The club owners, in speaking for baseball interests, characteristically assumed that the players were fellow passengers on board the Sunday baseball express train. From the players' standpoint, the love of the game was greatly overshadowed by the need to earn a living. This put them squarely within the labor struggles of the industrial age. As hired workers, the players were constantly reminded of the pecuniary attitudes of the owners, whose penny-pinching schemes often reached absurd heights. Since professional ballplayers worked seven days a week, suffered the pain of injuries as the season wore on, and were constantly traveling during the course of a long schedule, it was highly likely, as a *New York Times* editorial suggested, that nearly all the players were vigorous supporters of the prohibitions placed on Sunday baseball. The case of amateur players was different insofar as baseball for them was a form of recreation, not a moneymaking enterprise. Since the courts had previously exempted amateur baseball from the legal restrictions imposed on Sunday baseball, that side of the question was immaterial.[67]

As the Lawson bill worked its way through the Senate, it appeared that a new political alignment was taking place. The Democrats, of course, had been solidly behind the bill, and now they were gaining support from downstate Republicans. When the bill providing for local option came to a vote it passed the senate by a majority of twenty-six to twenty with every Republican south of the Harlem River, save only two senators—A. W. Burlingame Jr. and C. C. Lockwood of Kings County—in support. This meant that twenty-two of the twenty-six votes for local option came from senators representing the metropolitan boroughs. Since there was only one upstate Democratic senator, the Republican opposition upstate was nearly unanimous.[68]

During the following week, the assembly took up the Lawson bill. Only a few days remained to get the bill passed and have Governor Whitman sign it before the legislature adjourned. This gave an advantage to the diehards who could use a variety of delaying tactics. "If the bill is stuck in committee or beaten on the floor of the lower house," the *Sporting News* noted, "there will be a cry of rage from the public extending from the Statue of

Liberty to Niagara Falls." Behind the scenes there were reports that Thaddeus Sweet, the powerful assembly speaker, was using delaying tactics to hold up the bill because the governor wanted to have it sidetracked. In a similar vein, the rules committee received a petition from sixty-seven upstate Republicans who believed it was against the best interests of the state, and especially of the Republican Party at that time, to pass any measure legalizing Sunday baseball. While ignoring the avalanche of public sentiment and without taking a formal vote, the rules committee decided not to report out the Lawson bill, which virtually meant the death of a measure that many people around the state had thought would be a cinch to pass.[69]

With the demise of the Lawson bill, New York's three major league teams finally lost all patience with the legislative process and decided to take matters into their own hands. As early as February, they had proposed playing Sunday games in Newark. This plan was based on the theory that the legislature would not pass a law permitting Sunday baseball in the metropolis. Now that this had come to pass, the owners declared that their fans would be able to watch regular league games at the old Federal League Park across the river in Harrison, New Jersey, just thirty minutes from Broadway. That playing major league games in Harrison would interfere with the International League schedule by ignoring the territorial rights of the Newark and Jersey City clubs was of small consequence to the New York teams. The two major leagues had agreed to pay a rental fee of $10,000 a year for the use of the park as part of the settlement made with the defunct Federal League, and they were not prepared to let territorial niceties get in the way.[70]

Such high-handedness may have been of little concern to the major league clubs, but it was a more serious matter for New Jersey's minor league teams that were struggling to stay alive. Territorial rights were a prerequisite for ensuring fan loyalties and bringing customers through the gates. This would all be put in jeopardy if the New York clubs snapped up the lucrative Sunday market. The Yankees did in fact schedule a Sunday game at Harrison against the Red Sox in early May. It was then left to the league presidents to decide if further games would be allowed. The National Agreement between the major and minor leagues stipulated that "no games shall be played within five miles of the protected territory without the consent of the club occupying the territory." John Tener, president of the National League, said that the commission would not withhold protection from the new International League, provided a settlement of the Newark situation was reached.[71]

Simultaneously, the International and New York State Leagues were up in the air about a decision as to their plans for the coming 1918 season. This procrastination aroused resentment not only of players but of club owners in other leagues who could have found use for players looking for work. Serious criticism was also raised over the actions of the International League in sending out contracts to players at nominal salary figures for the purpose of holding claim to them, even if the season was canceled. Meanwhile, magnates in both leagues were peddling their players for large sums so that the best talent could be disposed of for cash.[72]

Over the previous year the owners of the International League gradually came to realize that the only thing that could save the organization from going out of business would be a bill permitting Sunday games in Rochester and Buffalo. For several months the league fought to stay alive. In April team officials met to round out an eight-club circuit. The chief stumbling block was Newark, which was in financial trouble and where the president of the franchise, no doubt taken aback by the invasion plans of the New York clubs, didn't seem to care what was going on. Buffalo was another club with economic woes. Happily, financial support came from affluent businessmen who stepped in at the last moment to save the team from bankruptcy. Wealthy persons also arrived to rescue Newark, which was considered "a fine baseball city and a good Sunday town in normal times." With minor league baseball saved in Newark, the territorial ambitions of New York's major league clubs were put to rest. In the end the reconstituted International League survived with teams in Binghamton, Buffalo, Jersey City, Newark, Rochester, Syracuse, and Toronto.[73]

While the owners of New York's professional teams sat on their hands waiting for a change in the political climate, officials in other eastern localities were moving ahead with Sunday baseball. An ordinance permitting games and sports on Sunday was passed by the city council in Baltimore and signed by the mayor, following a series of failed efforts dating back to 1911.

Lifting the lid on Sunday baseball in Washington, D. C., not only enhanced the revenue of the Senators and visiting American League clubs, but allowing Sunday games in the nation's capital encouraged reform efforts elsewhere. After securing professional baseball in Washington, the local blue law proponents began a campaign to pressure Congress to make the Lord's Day a holiday in the District of Columbia.[74]

By the beginning of 1919 three states—New York, Rhode Island, and Pennsylvania—had introduced anti–blue law legislation that would, among other things, open the door for Sunday baseball. The Walker-Malone bill (named after Tammany politician and future New York mayor Jimmy Walker and Albany senator John G. Malone) was introduced into the New York legislature. In content, it was virtually an exact replica of the Lawson bill. Once again the *Sporting News* remarked that Sunday baseball looked like a sure thing for New York fans, but this time with just cause. Al Smith, the working-class Irish kid from the streets of the Lower East Side, had been elected governor, and there was no question where he stood on Sabbath issues.[75]

Although both branches of the legislature were in Republican hands, McQuade, a tireless proponent of Sunday baseball, had enlisted the support of many influential lawmakers representing both parties to get behind the new measure. McQuade was far from a disinterested party in the matter since control of the New York Giants, held by the estate of John T. Brush, was in the process of being sold to a group that included himself, broker Charles A. Stoneham, and manager John J. McGraw for the sum of $1 million.[76]

While the passage of the Walker-Malone Sunday reform bill appeared all but certain as the 1919 legislative session opened, the opponents of such a measure remained on the offensive. A petition protesting professional baseball where admission was charged was sent to the New York Civic League from various churches in Kingston. The petition portrayed the greed of baseball corporations, the motion picture trust, and liquor trafficking as a conspiracy to undermine the Christian Sabbath. While the Civic League held out little hope that Governor Smith would be sympathetic—judging by his voting record on moral issues over the previous twelve years—all they could do was maintain pressure on the legislature, both directly and indirectly. In a public letter, Rennetts C. Miller, the district superintendent of the Civic League, commended Republican senators from Ulster County (where Kingston is located) for their past support for moral reform, with the expectation that they would vote correctly on the current Sabbath bill.[77]

Shortly thereafter, thousands of Presbyterians gathered at a two-day conference in New York City to raise funds for a campaign to deal with various social problems. Consequently, men and women in the church were asked to carry on the fight with enthusiasm in support of the victory campaign to raise $38 million to pay to run the church and their various campaigns. Presbyterian clergy repeatedly observed that only the church, as the authority on morals, ethics, and religion, could provide the leadership that was required in the modern world.[78]

Such a grandiose claim reinforced what others had been saying for some time: that the moral reform element had drifted into the realm of unreality. Like the tale of the Dutch boy who sought to plug a leaky dyke with his finger only to see more leaks spring forth, those who opposed the desecration of the Sabbath were besieged by a complexity of moral affronts, fanned by a plethora of entertainments and the desire for leisure pursuits. The war had been the single most important catalyst for change. Whereas, on one hand, the Wartime Prohibition Act hastened the march toward a drink-free New York—the crowning achievement for the "dry lobby" and the temperance crusaders, the war had the opposite effect in curbing efforts to maintain the dignity of the Puritan Sabbath.

As the 1919 New York legislative session shifted into gear, Albany was besieged with supporters calling for Sunday baseball. Acting New York mayor Robert L. Moran, Judge Cornelius F. Collins of the Court of Special Sessions, and United States Marshall Thomas McCarthy led a delegation to the state capital that included twenty-five women to actively lobby and to speak on behalf of the Walker-Malone bill at the public hearing. The *New York Times* remarked that this was the first time that women had taken an active interest in the baseball question.[79]

The straw that broke the camel's back regarding Sunday baseball came from military men who spoke out in favor of the Walker-Malone bill before the state legislature. Two officers who saw action in France were united in declaring that the factor contributing most to the high morale among the

American Expeditionary Forces was baseball. "You are not giving the boys a square deal if you deny them the recreations that must be theirs, which they can best get by Sunday baseball," declared Lt. Charles Brice Muir. "I ask you," he said, "to pass a bill in memory of the men who will never get back to the diamond, the men who have made the great home run." Such sentimental comments equated Sunday baseball with doing the right thing for American heroes, which was enough to overcome most moral arguments for the moment.[80]

A month later the Walker-Malone bill passed the Senate by a vote of twenty-eight to twenty-one, with six Republican senators joining with the Democrats to ensure a majority. Three days later the assembly gave its approval by a vote of eighty-two to sixty, following a two-hour debate. The passage of the bill permitting baseball on the Sabbath between 2 and 6 p.m. by local option was by a larger majority than expected. Governor Al Smith, in approving the legislation, invoked the principle of fairness. He felt that a minority should not be permitted to impose its will on the majority. Conversely, where the majority of the community, represented by its local legislative body, opposed Sunday baseball, then such amusements would be prohibited in that locality. He thought that in no way did watching a game deteriorate the moral fiber of the general public. Hardly had the ink from Smith's signature dried on the bill when the New York City Board of Aldermen enacted a previously prepared ordinance permitting Sunday games in the city.[81]

The first action taken by officials in both leagues after the city's local ordinance went into effect was to adjust their respective schedules. One alternative was to advance Monday's games to Sunday; the other was to move up games from the end of the season. League officials seemed to favor the latter plan. The team owners had already resolved the question of Sunday doubleheaders. This decision was a "no-brainer" since neither league, in the unlikely event that two games could be played in four hours, was interested in playing more than one game on that day. The heads of the two leagues, ever mindful of the need not to offend religious sensibilities and to maintain a balance of interests, took this position primarily so as not to interfere with other religious activities. Finally, the National and American Leagues agreed to divide the Sunday dates at the Polo Grounds so that each circuit would have eleven Sundays.[82]

Sunday baseball became a reality for the first time on May 4, 1919, when record-breaking crowds poured into the Polo Grounds and Ebbets Field to witness the first legal Sunday games in the history of the state. A crowd of thirty-five thousand fans saw the Giants defeat the Phillies, while across the river nearly the same number saw the Dodgers beat Boston. There was no reported evidence of any disorderly conduct or rowdiness. In summarizing this historic event the *New York Times* observed, "The legalizing of the national game on Sunday in this city has hit popular fancy hard, and the public's answer yesterday leaves slight room for doubt, even in the minds of those who have bitterly opposed the innovation, that the sport can be conducted without interfering with the quiet, peaceful pursuit of the Sabbath."[83]

6

The Aftermath, 1920–1924

The legalization of Sunday baseball in New York did not bring the matter to closure. If anything, the issue became more heated as the ministerial backers of the blue laws sought to regroup in their effort to turn back the clock on Sunday games. Local option provided a segue to transfer the Sunday question from state to local environments, particularly ones where the New York Civic League and the ministerial groups were especially strong.

The Sunday Battle Continues

Whereas it was widely expected that cities across the state would at once take advantage of local option to field teams for Sabbath baseball, the rush to play Sunday games, though geographically widespread, gathered momentum only gradually over time and was resisted in isolated spots. Within days after the Walker-Malone bill passed, the *Kingston Daily Freeman* published a letter from a representative of the New York Civic League stating that Christian and moral forces in the state were blind to the impending danger. The *Freeman* noted that the class who supported the baseball referendum was the same element who bitterly fought against temperance two years before. Given the widescale public indifference surrounding opposition to local option, the diehard upholders of the Sabbath used inflated rhetoric, seeing Sunday games as a threat to civilization. In fact, the Walker-Malone bill amounted to only a moderate challenge to traditional folkways. In the words of Rennetts C. Miller, deputy superintendent of the New York Civic League, "Can New York State afford to go to the Bolshevik extreme of laxity about the rights of people and open the way for the overthrow of our long cherished moral standards and institutions like the Sabbath that have been mighty bulwarks of our national life?" "God pity democracy and the world," so Miller continued, "if this great pillar is removed."[1]

The fight against imagined Bolsheviks and Sunday desecrators persisted in Kingston. A political battle ensued when local teams that had played uninterruptedly for free on Sundays decided to petition the common council to allow an admission fee to be charged. Immediately the local churches sprang into action. A large meeting at the Kingston Methodist Church gave consideration to the pros and cons (mostly the cons) of the matter. One speaker, Dr. George Grinton, commented that he was not opposed to Sunday baseball but thought it unnecessary since it was not intended to gratify the masses but to line the pockets of the owners. In response to a motion favoring Sunday games, the aldermen voted to table the matter after receiving communications from the Federated Parent-Teachers Association (PTA), chapters of the Daughters of the American Revolution (DAR), and the women's auxiliary of the YMCA opposing this violation of the Sabbath.[2]

A month later the aldermen in Kingston once more took up this issue. Again a large delegation from the leading Protestant churches attended a public meeting and made it known that they were opposed to commercialized Sunday baseball in any form. Written protests also came from the YMCA, the "Monday Club," the local Union of Christian Endeavor, the Reformed Church, and the Albany Street Baptist Church.[3]

Two weeks hence, following a lengthy debate, the aldermen of Kingston defeated a resolution to legalize games on the Sabbath by a vote of seven to six. According to the Reverend A. K. Fuller, a Baptist minister, the question was not whether baseball should be played, but when. He noted that only a minority favored the motion, including those "who would like to make a profit out of Sunday baseball, a few citizens." He also included in this group a number of "what we call 'the hoodlum element,' those who were not old enough to have the right conception of things, and what we might call the sporting element of the city."[4]

The Sunday baseball question resurfaced during a local election campaign the following autumn, but none of the candidates were eager to take sides. The Democratic candidate for mayor, Mr. E. Metzger, decried a letter from a taxpayer accusing him of supporting Sunday baseball and deferred the matter to the common council, claiming that if elected it would be beyond his jurisdiction. The Republican candidate for alderman, William A. Van Valkenburgh, took a more populist position, calling for a referendum on all moral, civic, and welfare issues so as to let his constituents (comprising what he probably estimated to be the moral majority) decide such matters.[5]

For all practical purposes, Sunday baseball in Kingston soon became a dead issue. It would seem that games on the Sabbath, especially those that did not charge admission, became increasingly more common, with little fuss, to the point of being tolerated. From 1921 to 1927 Kingston had a semi-pro team that played seventy-five games a season, with occasional exhibitions against major league clubs. Two years after the legalization of Sunday ball in the state, the *Kingston Daily Freeman* reported that a large crowd had gathered at the fairgrounds to watch the reopening of Sunday baseball in the city.[6]

Meanwhile, towns and cities around the state were adapting themselves to playing games on Sunday. Not surprisingly, professional clubs jumped on the bandwagon immediately. The major leagues aside, the greatest beneficiaries of changes to the Sunday law were the minor leagues, which had been struggling for years to keep afloat. Semi-pro teams, operating with impunity around the state for some time, got a new lease on life. New leagues, such as one formed in Binghamton in 1920, looked to benefit from a more open Sunday. The proposed league included eight central New York teams from Elmira, Montour Falls, Oneonta, Owego, Cortland, Endicott-Johnson, Groton, and Binghamton. With baseball drawing large crowds in all these towns, club owners saw no reason why the new league should not succeed.[7]

Gradually towns and villages repealed or altered their local ordinances in favor of Sunday ball. Long Lake, a small town nestled in the Adirondacks, had by the turn of the century become a magnet for summer visitors who brought with them a desire for baseball games as well as other recreational pursuits. Inevitably, the town council ruled on April 20, 1920, that Sunday baseball would be allowed after two o'clock in the afternoon, the earliest starting time sanctioned by law.[8]

A similar resolution, submitted by the Board of Trustees, called for a special village election in Rockville Center, Long Island, to permit Sunday games. The quick passage of this resolution and the prospect of open week-end baseball led immediately to the formation of the Rockville Center League. Existing leagues and teams, as well as individuals eager to play and manage organized baseball clubs across Long Island, did not hesitate to take advantage of the elimination of Sunday restrictions.[9]

One such enthusiast, the Reverend Charles Nelson, a Long Island preacher, announced that he planned to organize a team among the young men of his congregation to play games every Saturday and Sunday after-noon. He equated rest on the Sabbath with recreation and believed that through baseball the church would be able to reach out to some who would otherwise not hear the gospel.[10]

Such was not the opinion of the general assembly of the Presbyterian Church, comprising many organized religious bodies determined to carry on the fight for a holy Sabbath. At their annual meeting in St. Louis, the assem-bly issued an unqualified condemnation of the desecration of the Sabbath, highlighted specifically by the legalization of Sunday baseball and motion pictures. The report issued by a select committee of the assembly declared that Republican and Democratic leaders in New York had joined hands in yielding to powerful commercial forces declaring for local option, oblivious to the voice of public opinion. The general assembly gave approval to a res-olution reiterating emphatic disapproval of all Sabbath Day sports and other secular activities and recommending a campaign to bring about a Christian Sabbath.[11]

The campaign launched by the Presbyterians to "Save the Sabbath of America" was part of a determined crusade to close dance halls, movie the-aters, and baseball parks on Sundays. Part of this initiative sought to create a program of education to advise churches on legal problems related to

Sunday issues and to develop effective strategies against all secular uses of the Sabbath day, including sports. Likewise, the initiative called for every Presbyterian Church and synod to organize working committees involved with Sabbath observance, to take direct action in their communities, and to assume the role of political action committees.

To the defenders of the Puritan moral order, Sunday desecration was associated with new horrors, such as Bolshevism and communism, along with the more familiar horrors of anarchism, socialism, all shades of radicalism, and the International Workers of the World. The lack of respect for Sunday laws gave the perception of weakening the civil safeguards that upheld the American Christian Sabbath. The failure of public officials to enforce the existing laws seemed to the Presbyterians, and to like-minded religious groups, to have emboldened the advocates of anarchy to strike down long-standing institutions and the whole structure of law and order in the country. Thus the unholy alliance of radicals and greedy magnates (together strange bedfellows) was now seen as a specter haunting America.

Gambling and Internecine Conflicts

While the Presbyterians were stewing over insurgent radicals and the apparent collapse of a civilized moral and social order, the baseball bosses were moving on to other matters. As the 1919 World Series drew to a close, reports from sundry sources questioned whether the games had been on the level. As the conspiracy between gamblers and eight of the Chicago White Sox players unraveled over the following year, it became clear that baseball's failure to keep the game clean had plunged the sport into its most serious crisis. As dark clouds gathered over baseball, Garry Herrmann, president of the World Series champion Cincinnati Reds and chairman of the National Commission, promised to do everything in his power to stop gambling at baseball parks the following season. Such sentiments were echoed by owners in both leagues.[12]

Even before the appointment of Judge Kenesaw Mountain Landis as baseball's first commissioner on November 12, 1920, with virtual dictatorial control over affairs of the game, drastic action had been taken by both the American and National Leagues to stamp out gambling. During the spring of that year frequent newspaper reports chronicled efforts to eliminate ballpark betting. "The war against gambling at baseball games, which began in New York was taken up by the National League," noted the *New York Times*, in reporting that five men were arrested for gambling at a Giants-Braves game and hauled before a magistrate.[13]

Teams often hired detective agencies to patrol ballparks, leading to a spike in the number of arrests for betting on games. One case involved six men taken in tow by the police at the Polo Grounds on suspicion of gambling. As with many instances in which men and boys were arrested for playing Sunday baseball, the magistrate discharged the men for want of evidence.[14]

Efforts to stamp out baseball gambling were marred by continuous infighting among the magnates, by open battles between Landis and Ban Johnson, and by Landis's controversial, and often arbitrary, judicial decisions, which resulted from his absolute legal authority over the game. In March 1921 the new commissioner banned Gene Paulette, the former St. Louis Browns and Philadelphia Phillies infielder, from the game for associating with gamblers. Less than a month later he overruled an application for reinstatement by George Dumont, who abandoned the Toledo club to play on the semi-pro Tamson Tractor team of Janesville, Wisconsin. When shortly thereafter a similar case involving the Yankees regular third baseman Frank "Home Run" Baker came before the Judge, Landis declared him eligible to return to pro-ball. Baker had gone on the voluntary retired list following the death of his wife and during that time played on a semi-pro team near his home.[15]

Landis then reverted to the draconian side of his nature and disbarred Benny Kauff of the Giants from professional baseball. Kauff had been arrested for being party to an auto-stealing racket. Despite the fact that the case against him was sub judice, a point that Landis recognized, the commissioner held to his decision, citing section two, article four of the Major-Minor league rules making a player who was under indictment for a felony ineligible. Eight months later after Kauff was acquitted of any wrongdoing, his attorney, Emil Fuchs, who later became the controversial owner of the Boston Braves, had nothing but scathing remarks regarding the new czar of baseball.[16]

The following year Ban Johnson, a persistent opponent of baseball gambling, brought to the attention of the American League owners a report detailing the pervasive activities of unscrupulous operators of baseball pools, which robbed fans of thousands of dollars. On the advice of the magnates, Johnson, as a matter of protocol, turned the results of his two-year investigation over to Landis. The data so impressed the commissioner that he took over the investigation with a determination to "wage war" against what he termed "the slimiest crooks I have ever encountered." To a proud man like Johnson, whose dislike of Landis was well-known, the snatching away of his investigation was clearly a slap in the face.[17]

Landis's high-handed arbitrariness was further demonstrated when he blacklisted Phil Douglas, who had been a valued member of John McGraw's World Championship New York Giants team of 1921. Douglas, a difficult man, was given to the ballplayer's common failing of constant inebriation. He had worn out the patience of a number of managers and was frequently the object of one of McGraw's tongue-lashings. Late in the season, in a muddled state caused no doubt from too much drink and deeply annoyed with his manager, Douglas penned a letter to one of his former teammates, Leslie Mann, in which he wrote: "I want to leave here. I don't want to see this guy [McGraw] win the pennant." Mann reluctantly turned the letter over to St. Louis manager Branch Rickey, and from there it made its way to Landis's office. Called out on the carpet by the commissioner, Douglas admitted writing the incriminating words. Ignoring all the circumstances of the case, Douglas's admission of authorship was all Landis needed to evict the Giants pitcher permanently from organized baseball.[18]

Festering resentments against Landis from among baseball officials—especially Johnson and his loyal coterie of American League owners—came to a head at the annual meetings of both leagues in December 1923. Apparently, tensions had become exacerbated by a demand by the commissioner that he be allowed to assert full control over the umpires. Behind the scenes there were rumors of secret meetings and grumblings about how the commissioner's office was being run. Landis was also aware of circulating reports that some of the magnates were willing to pay him his salary for another four years if they could get rid of him. Wasting no time, Landis called a special meeting of the owners from both leagues and surprised them by announcing his willingness to resign his office and income if they were not satisfied with his job performance. By calling their bluff, Landis threw the owners into a state of disarray. National League president John Heydler, a loyal supporter of the commissioner, and other senior circuit club owners met separately with Landis and quickly gave him a vote of confidence. The American League officials were more divided. Inevitably, Landis and Johnson exchanged heated words. Observers noted the judge's forceful and vehement attack on the American League president and his followers. A diplomatic and compelling speech by Yankees owner Colonel Ruppert largely dissolved the opposition, leaving Johnson and his faithful ally Phil Ball, owner of the St. Louis Browns, seething alone.[19]

Strengthened by the near-full support of the owners, Landis was confronted with yet another opportunity to assert the arbitrary power of his office. A scandal erupted later in the 1924 season that again pitted Landis against Johnson. With only a few games left, the Giants were in a close battle with the Dodgers for the National League pennant. Apparently, before the first game of a doubleheader with Philadelphia, Giants outfielder Jimmy O'Connell approached Phillies shortstop Heine Sand with an offer of $500 if he and his teammates would take it easy, and in effect throw the game. Appalled by such a brazen proposal, Sand reported the bribe to his manager, Art Fletcher, who passed this information up the chain until it reached Landis's ears. Summoned to the commissioner's office, O'Connell admitted his guilt but stated that he was following the instructions of Giants coach Cozy Dolan, who was McGraw's right hand man. At the same time, O'Connell implicated three of the team's star players—Frankie Frisch, Ross Youngs, and George Kelly—as having previous knowledge of the bribe, implying also that the team's management knew about the matter as well.[20]

Somewhat naive, O'Connell maintained that as an employee of the Giants he was only doing what he thought management wanted, and later said that "if Dolan would tell all, I would be cleared." When called before the judge, Dolan exhibited a convenient loss of memory about the entire incident. These explanations did not impress the commissioner who, three days before the start of the World Series, banned both men for life, while exonerating the others O'Connell had implicated. Frisch's comment that "there is always a lot of kidding going around" with respect to stories of gambling seemingly did not faze nor amuse Judge Landis.[21]

Reacting to the commissioner's decision, Ban Johnson, whose hatred of McGraw rivaled that of Landis, called for a federal investigation and demanded that either Brooklyn be awarded the pennant, or that the World Series be canceled. Johnson was also critical of Landis for closing the door on the investigation while questions, such as who put up the $500 to begin with, remained unanswered. Barney Dreyfuss of the Pirates, another of McGraw's implacable enemies, gave his support to Johnson. Landis, of course, brushed these proposals aside, but he could not have been happy that Congressman Sol Bloom of New York backed Johnson's call for a statute to regulate organized baseball as interstate commerce. Coming up short again in his head-to-head duel with the commissioner, Johnson expressed his pique by absenting himself altogether from the World Series.[22]

Matters came to a head during the winter of 1926–1927 when an investigation against two of baseball's star players, Ty Cobb and Tris Speaker, for game fixing gave Landis the leverage he needed to ease Johnson (whose health was declining anyway) out of baseball. Despite continued efforts to suppress ballpark betting, the gambling problem was never resolved. Even after the Cobb/Speaker matter it was no secret that notorious gamblers, wagering huge sums of money, could be found at games in various parts of the country. Yet, the culture of professional baseball was changing, and, casting aside its tarnished image, the game was riding high both financially and in popularity.[23]

Sunday Baseball Opponents' Last Stand

Whatever strength the opponents of Sunday ball possessed within and beyond New York State, it was sufficient to raise the issue of federal legislation dealing with Sabbath observance. With a permanent lobby in Washington, supporters of the blue laws were well placed to pester Congress continually on the matter. One local newspaper editorial from a nominally conservative region of western New York opposed the idea of a federal blue law, which would have banned all public activity across the nation on Sundays, save for church functions. The editorial, reflecting local sentiment, stated that while there was a decided feeling in the country against many Sunday pursuits, the religious zealots had gone too far in seeking to restore the Puritan Sabbath. The editorial deemed it pointless to make any change in the present Sunday arrangements, cautioning the zealots to be more responsible to the demonstrated needs of the people. President Calvin Coolidge would have agreed. An ardent conservative and enthusiastic baseball fan, he had earned a reputation for common sense on public issues. Addressing the subject several years later in his typically modest manner, President Coolidge surmised that "Washingtonians, like the fair minded people of all our cities, are almost unanimously against the blue laws."[24]

No one better epitomized the changing moral climate in the state than Christy "Matty" Mathewson. For the better part of his life as one of baseball's greatest players, he was opposed to Sunday ball, and as the star pitcher on the New York Giants he had refused to pitch on the Sabbath. Over the years, however, Matty's perceptions on the question shifted from the moral to the pragmatic and personal choice. Whether a person chooses to play on Sunday or not should be his own individual decision, he noted. The central question, he said, was whether Sunday baseball was good or bad for the community. "If playing games on Sunday makes for orderliness and keeps young men out of harm during the day of rest, who otherwise would be getting into trouble or taking their pleasure," then he thought it would be a good thing. He claimed to have investigated communities where baseball was played on Sunday and found that the police blotters showed a marked decrease in the number of arrests for public disorder and petty crime on the Sabbath. His conclusion was that Sunday baseball must therefore be an influence for the good. As to the circulating rumors that John G. Downs, an assemblyman from Suffolk County, had introduced a measure to amend the penal code making Sunday ball illegal, Matty thought it was not fair that a gentleman from Cutchogue should impose a moral prohibition on larger cities around the state.[25]

Fair or not, Assemblyman Downs and a number of his Republican colleagues made a strong effort to repeal the laws legalizing Sunday baseball in the next session of the legislature. The *Sunday Grit*, an outspoken opponent of the blue laws, reported that the Lord's Day Alliance was even more aggressive than the Anti-Tobacco League in pushing its agenda. A bill placed before the New York State legislature, according to the paper, would prohibit every kind of Sabbath activity except churchgoing. The measure was easily defeated, but the alliance promised that a similar bill would be introduced in the next session of the legislature. Just how much strength the foes of Sunday baseball in the legislature possessed by the middle of the decade is questionable. While unsuccessful in New York, the Lord's Day Alliance was more successful in killing legislation in Pennsylvania and Ohio that would have allowed certain outdoor activities. The persistence of well-heeled and nationally based Sabbatarian groups, along with powerful statewide organizations, held back reform efforts in places like Massachusetts and Pennsylvania for some time. Professional baseball was not allowed in those states until 1929 and 1934 respectively.[26]

Many of the men who championed the cause of repeal two years before had passed from office, as had some of the opponents, opening the way for new legislators who were ready to fight the good fight all over again. However, things had changed. Baseball had over the previous year (1919) enjoyed a spurt of popularity, as witnessed by a boost in attendance in nearly every city and village around the state where Sunday ball was allowed. In the mean-time "plans are being made to make baseball an everyday sport," including Sunday. If the Sunday game were to continue, in the words of one editorial, it would provide the state and local communities with much revenue.[27]

Not to be caught off guard, the representatives of various sporting inter-ests, particularly boxing and baseball, were alert to any attempt to rescind the prevailing legal interpretation of the Sunday laws. These interests possessed two arguments. The first was that since the present revision of the penal code was put through by a Republican legislature in the interests of the public, it would be difficult to backtrack, having agreed to local option already. Since politicians frequently alter their positions, this was hardly a compelling argu-ment. Furthermore, if the clock were to be turned back, many reformers believed it would be many years before another liberal interpretation of the law would be possible. The second (and stronger) argument was financial. Since the passage of the Walker-Malone bill, the fortunes of Sunday baseball had been closely tied to the boxing bill, which had been objected to for other reasons. Many saw the possibility of levying a tax on tickets for both sports, thus providing welcome revenue to local municipalities.[28]

That is exactly what happened. As a result of conferences between local Republican leaders and governor-elect Nathan Miller—who had recently defeated Al Smith—a decision was reached not to interfere with Sunday baseball. Instead, the Republican caucuses agreed to tax professional Sunday games based on a percentage of ticket prices and were adamant that the tax should come out of the pockets of club owners and not patrons. The Sunday baseball law vested legal authority for games with local authorities, which had the power to levy taxes. An ordinance passed by the New York City Board of Aldermen, stipulating that the charge for Sunday games could not be greater than for those played on any other day of the week, meant that base-ball's bosses could not use Sabbath-day games to gouge the public. While some upstate Republicans still favored repeal of both boxing and Sunday baseball laws, they were soon persuaded otherwise by their colleagues.

The last word in the Sunday baseball drama is left to Charlie Ebbets. At the start of the 1924 season, the Rev. Frederick M. Gordon, executive sec-retary of the Brooklyn section of the Federation of Churches, and Claude Coile of the Moral Reform Committee, representing the Protestant Churches in Brooklyn, called on Ebbets to protest the Dodgers' opening their home season against the Phillies on Easter Sunday. In a lengthy discussion, Ebbets pointed out that the same thing had happened in 1922. He patiently outlined the problems of scheduling games around Easter, stating further that the issue was out of his hands and that a change in the schedule would have to be approved by all league clubs, a virtual impossibility. As a consolation, Ebbets informed the two clergymen, diplomatically, that he would try to see that games in the future would not be scheduled on Easter. That would never happen. A year later, almost to the day, Charlie Ebbets died. Not the least among his many achievements was the role he played in legalizing Sunday baseball in New York.[29]

Epilogue

During a spirited debate surrounding the passage of the Walker-Malone bill, Ida B. Sammis, a Republican assemblywoman from Suffolk County, declared that the bill was contrary to the divine law on which all law is founded, saying, "You can't have local option on the Ten Commandments." Perhaps unwittingly, she had put her finger on the crux of the entire debate over Sunday observance.[1]

The dichotomy between moral absolutes and pluralism has a long and deep-seated history in American life. Puritanism, which cast a shadow over subsequent centuries, particularly in the Northeast, effectively combined both these elements, albeit in an uneasy truce. Inevitably the Puritan model of order would be repeatedly challenged by the atomizing forces of secularization. Such was the fate of the Puritan Sabbath.

In many respects the battle over Sunday baseball resembled today's clashes over abortion, school prayer, and same-sex marriage. The existence of well-organized lobbies to promote the cause of religious groups, the jeremiads over supposed moral decline, and grassroots populism are nothing new and are as much a part of social life today as they were at the turn of the twentieth century.

Inevitably, however, Sunday observance, with respect to baseball, was a lost cause. In spite of traditional folkways that determined that Sunday would be a day of rest, particularly in the rural areas of the state, strict adherence to the blue laws was never a reality and was frequently compromised in the decades following the Civil War. Over time, the social norms that reinforced conformity to Sabbath observance weakened to the point where defiance became widely accepted, and often condoned. The best that reform opponents could do was to engage in selective obstruction, while ignoring the fact that Sunday games were often played with impunity fully within the public gaze.

Even before the turn of the century, numerous Protestant clergymen noticed the emergence of secular trends and affronts to their comfortable world view. Challenges to the Sunday laws in the courts led to a series of decisions, particularly the opinion of Justice Gaynor, that Sunday baseball was not a crime unless a fee was charged for admission. The focus of attention then turned more singularly toward prohibiting professional games on Sunday, while magistrates, often under pressure, directed the police to obstruct Sunday baseball in any region where ministerial groups were particularly active.

Opponents of Sunday baseball in New York were more effective on the legislative front, given the powerful and well-financed lobbies that represented their interests and their cozy connections with legislative representatives and power brokers within the Republican Party. In the end a combination of factors, particularly World War I, the continued immigration of peoples who were either hostile or indifferent to the Puritan Sabbath, the spirit of reform stimulated by progressivism, and the multiplication of diversions and leisure activities, proved to be the tipping points in bringing about Sunday law reform.

Even so, the changes to the penal code with respect to Sunday baseball could, at best, be considered only a partial victory for reform. Sensitivity to public opinion, which on the whole favored incremental changes in the law, and a desire to appease the Protestant religious establishment led to the local option compromise in which Sunday games would be restricted to specific hours on the day and that local ordinances, not state law, would be the determining factor of legality. Unlike Prohibition, which sought to uniformly eliminate the drink trade (with disastrous results), the Sunday baseball question in New York was raised to the higher ground of inclusiveness and fairness, which accorded more closely with America's "better angels," to borrow a phrase from Abraham Lincoln.

At the same time nothing is static, and in the long run the worst fears of the Sabbatarian element have come to pass. The forces of commercialism and popular culture proved to be so powerful that almost all of the blue laws lost their hold over time and were swept away. While Sunday in New York, as everywhere else, has become like any other day, save for the absence of weekday labor, some of us often have a nostalgic yearning for the quiet and peaceful ambience of a Puritan Sunday, when the repose of the community stood as a welcome respite from the noise, commotion, and the tedium of work.

As is always the case, some things are gained and others are lost. The world my father grew up in is radically different from the world I live in today. His may have, in retrospect, seemed a more simple and peaceful time but it was, comparatively speaking, a hard life riddled with religious divisions, racial and ethnic hatreds, labor troubles, and class conflicts. Beneath the surface, Sunday baseball was a class issue in which some opponents of Sabbath games believed it would be dangerous to allow a group of workers to congregate lest civil unrest occur. The hypocrisy that surrounded Sunday sports made the pastimes of the respectable classes acceptable and the enjoyments of the laboring poor prohibited. When local option passed in New York, it was hailed by many as a victory for the working class.[2]

Whether the quality of life for New Yorkers over the past century has changed for better or worse is beside the point. It is always the job of the historian to capture the world we have lost and reveal its intricacies, thus illuminating our own world. In a time gone by, during a tumultuous period in the history of the United States, the battle over Sunday baseball in New York symbolized one of the defining moral issues of the day, and it is therefore an important story.

Appendix:
New York State Ball Clubs to 1989

ALBANY

1879 International Association
1880 International Association
1881 Eastern Association
1885 New York State League
1886 Hudson River League
1888 International Association
1890 New York State League
1891 Eastern League
1892–1893 Eastern League
1894–1895 New York State League
1896 Eastern League
1899–1916 New York State League
1920–1932 Eastern League
1933–1936 International League
1937 New York-Penn League
1938–1959 Eastern League
1983–1989 Eastern League

AMSTERDAM

1894–1896 New York State League
1902–1908 New York State League
1938–1942 Can-Am League
1946–1951 Can-Am League

AUBURN

1877 League Alliance
1878 National Association
1888 Central New York League
1888–1889 New York State League
1897–1899 New York State League
1906–1908 Empire State League
1910 Central New York League
1938 Can-Am League
1940 Can-Am League
1946–1951 Border League
1958–1980 New York-Penn League
1982–1988 New York-Penn League

BATAVIA

1939–1953 PONY League
1957–1959 New York-Penn League
1961–1987 New York-Penn League

BATH

1890 Western New York League

BINGHAMTON

1877 League Alliance

BINGHAMTON (*continued*)
1878 International Association
1884–1885 New York State League
1886–1887 International League
1888 Central League
1892–1894 Eastern League
1895 New York State League
1899–1917 New York State League
1918–1919 International League
1923–1937 New York-Penn League
1938–1963 Eastern League
1964–1966 New York-Penn League
1967–1968 Eastern League

BROOKLYN
1872–1875 National Association
1877 League Alliance
1881 Eastern Association
1883 Inter-State Association
1884–1890 American Association
1890 Player's League
1890–1957 National League
1907 Atlantic League
1908 Union League
1913 United States League
1914–1915 Federal League

BUFFALO
1877 League Alliance
1878 International Association
1879–1885 National League
1886–1887 International League
1888 International Association
1889–1890 International League
1890 Player's League
1891 Eastern Association
1892–1898 Eastern League
1899 Western League
1900 American League
1901–1911 Eastern League
1912–1970 International League
1979–1984 Eastern League
1985–1989 American Association

CANANDAIGUA
1888–1889 New York State League
1897–1898 New York State League
1905 Empire State League

CANISTEO
1890 Western New York League

CANTON
1900 Northern New York League

CATSKILL
1903 Hudson River

CHATAUQUA
1898 Iron and Oil League

COBLESKILL
1890 New York State League

CORNING
1951–1956 PONY League
1957–1960 New York-Penn League
1968–1969 New York-Penn League

CORTLAND
1886 Central New York League
1897–1898 New York State League
1899–1901 New York State League
1905 Empire State League
1910 Central New York League

DUNKIRK
1890 New York-Penn League
1898 Iron and Oil League

ELMIRA
1888 Central League
1889 New York State League
1891 New York-Penn League
1892 Eastern League
1895 New York State League
1900 Atlantic League
       New York State League

ELMIRA (*continued*)
1908–1917 New York State League
1923–1937 New York-Penn League
1938–1955 Eastern League
1957–1961 New York-Penn League
1962–1972 Eastern League
1973–1986 New York-Penn League

FULTON
1905–1908 Empire State League

GENEVA
1897 New York State League
1905–1908 Empire State League
1910 Central New York League
1930 Central New York League
1947–1951 Border League
1958–1973 New York-Penn League
1977–1988 New York-Penn League

GLENS FALLS
1906 Hudson River League
1980–1988 Eastern League

GLOVERSVILLE
1890 New York State League
1895 New York State League
1902–1908 New York State League
1926–1927 New York-Penn League
1937–1942* Can-Am League
1946–1951* Can-Am League
*with Johnstown and Amsterdam

GREEN POINT
1870–1872 National Association

HAVERSTRAW
1888 Hudson River League

HORNELL
1878 International Association
1890 Western New York League
1914–1915 Inter-State League

1942–1946 PONY League
1957 New York-Penn League

HUDSON
1885 Hudson River League
1903–1906 Hudson River League

ILION
1901–1904 New York State League
1905 Empire State League

JAMESTOWN
1890–1891 New York-Penn League
1906* Inter-State League
1914–1915 Inter-State League
1939–1956 PONY League
1957 New York-Penn League
1961–1973 New York-Penn League
1977–1989 New York-Penn League
*with Oil City, Pa.

JOHNSTOWN
1890 New York State League
1895–1896 New York State League
1898 New York State League
1902–1908 New York State League
1909 Eastern Association
1926–1927 New York-Penn League
1938–1942 Can-Am League
1946–1951 Can-Am League

KINGSTON
1886 Hudson River League
1903–1905 Hudson River League
1906 Hudson River League
1909 Eastern Association
1913 New York-New Jersey League
1947 North Atlantic League
1948–1950 Colonial League
1951 Can-Am League

LITTLE FALLS
1977–1988 New York-Penn League

LIVINGSTON
1877 League Alliance

LOCKPORT
1942–1950 PONY League
1951 Middle Atlantic League

LOWVILLE
1886 Central New York League

LYONS
1897–1898 New York State League
1905 Empire State League
1907–1908 Empire State League

MALONE
1887 Northeastern League
1900 Northern New York League
1902 Northern New York League

MASPETH
1886 Eastern League

MIDDLETOWN
1909 Eastern Association
1913 New York-New Jersey League
1914 Atlantic League

NEWARK
1973–1979 New York-Penn League
1983–1987 New York-Penn League

NEWBURGH
1886 Hudson River League
1903–1907 Hudson River League
1909 Eastern Association
1913 New York-New Jersey League
1914 Atlantic League
1946 North Atlantic League

NEW YORK
1871–1875 National Association
1876 National League
1881 Eastern Championship
    Association
1881–1882 Eastern Association
1883–1887 American Association
1890 Player's League
1896 Atlantic League
1883–1957 National League
1903–1989 American League
1962–1989 National League

NIAGARA FALLS
1908 International League
1939–1940 PONY League
1946–1947 Middle Atlantic League
1950–1951 Middle Atlantic League
1970–1979 New York-Penn League
1982–1985 New York-Penn League

NORWICH
1886 Central New York League

NYACK
1946–1948 North Atlantic League

OGDENSBURG
1908 Empire State League
1936–1940* Can-Am League
1946–1951 Border League
* with Ottawa, Ont.

OLEAN
1890–1891 New York-Penn League
1905–1908 Inter-State League
1914–1916 Inter-State League
1939–1956 PONY League
1957–1959 New York-Penn League
1961–1962 New York-Penn League

ONEIDA
1886 Central New York League
1889 New York State League
1905 Empire State League
1908 Empire State League
1910 Central New York League

ONEONTA
1890 New York State League
1924 New York-Penn League
1940–1942 Can-Am League
1946–1951 Can-Am League
1966–1989 New York-Penn League

OSSINING
1903 Hudson River League

OSWEGO
1885 New York State League
1886–1887 International League
1888 International Association
1898–1900 New York State League
1905–1908 Empire State League
1910 Central New York League
1936–1940 Can-Am League

PALMYRA
1897–1898 New York State League
1905 Empire State League

PEEKSKILL
1903 Hudson River League
1905 Hudson River League
1905 Atlantic League
1946–1950 North Atlantic League

PENN YANN
1888 New York State League
1906 Empire State League

PLATTSBURGH
1902 Northern New York League
1905 Northern League

PORT CHESTER
1947–1948 Colonial League

POTSDAM
1902 Northern New York League

POUGHKEEPSIE
1886 Hudson River League
1903–1907 Hudson River League
1909 Eastern Association
1913 New York-New Jersey League
1914 Atlantic League
1947–1950 Colonial League

ROCHESTER
1877 International Association
1879 International Association
1885 New York State League
1886–1887 International League
1888–1889 International
    Association
1890 American Association
1891 Eastern Association
1892 Eastern Association
1895–1911 Eastern League
1912–1989 International League

ROME
1898–1901 New York State League
1905 Empire State League
1909 New York State League
1910 Central New York League
1937–1942 Can-Am League
1946–1951 Can-Am League

SARATOGA SPRINGS
1886 Hudson River League
1906 Hudson River League

SAUGERTIES
1903–1905 Hudson River League

SCHENECTADY
1895–1896 New York State League
1899–1904 New York State League
1909 Eastern Association
1946–1950 Can-Am League
1951–1957 Eastern League

SENECA FALLS
1888–1889 New York State League
1905–1907 Empire State League

SYRACUSE
1877 League Alliance
1878 International Association
1879 National League
1885 New York State League
1886–1887 International League
1888–1889 International Association
1890 American Association
1891–1892 Eastern Association
1894–1901 Eastern League
1906 Empire State League
1902–1917 New York State League
1918 New International League
1920–1927 International League
1928–1929 New York-Penn League
1934–1955 International League
1956–1957 Eastern League
1961–1989 International League

TROY
1871–1872 National Association
1877 League Alliance
1879–1882 National League
1886 Hudson River League
1888 International Association
1890 New York State League
1891 Eastern Association
1892–1894 Eastern League
1895–1896 New York State League
1899–1916 New York State League

UTICA
1878 International Association
1879 National Association
1880 International Association
1885 New York State League
1886–1887 International League
1888 International Association
1890 New York State League
1892 Eastern League
1898–1917 New York State League
1924 New York-Penn League
1939–1942 Can-Am League
1943–1950 Eastern League
1977–1989 New York-Penn League

WALDEN
1946 North Atlantic League

WATERLOO
1888 New York State League

WATERTOWN
1886 Central New York League
1908 Empire State League
1936 Can-Am League
1946–1951 Border League
1983–1988 New York-Penn League

WAVERLY
1901 New York State League

WELLSVILLE
1890 Western New York League
1914–1916 Inter-State League
1942–1956 PONY League
1957–1961 New York-Penn League
1963–1965 New York-Penn League

YONKERS
1894 Eastern League
1905 Hudson River League

Source: John Pardon and Jerry Jackson, "New York State Ball Clubs." In *The Empire State of Base Ball: A Look at the Game in Upstate New York* (© 1989 by Northeastern N.Y. Chapter of the SABR). Used by permission of the Society for American Baseball Research.

Notes

Introduction

1 David M. Ellis, James A. Frost, Harold C. Syrett, and Harry J. Carman, *A Short History of New York State* (Ithaca, NY: Cornell University Press, 1957), 449.
2 "Moral and Social Issues Around the State," *Ithaca Weekly News*, December 5, 1900.
3 "Ambassador des Planches Gives Results of His Study of the Italian Immigrants to This Country and Their Possible Future," *New York Times*, May 31, 1908; "To Scan the Coming Man," *Ithaca Weekly Journal*, August 30, 1906.
4 "Growing up in Ithaca in the 1890s," in *What They Wrote, 19th Century Documents from Tompkins County, New York*, ed. Carol Kammen (Ithaca, NY: Cornell University Libraries, 1978), 145.
5 Robert H. Wiebe, *The Search for Order, 1877–1920* (New York: Hill and Wang, 1967), 155.
6 David Hackett Fischer, *Albion's Seed: Four British Folkways in America* (New York: Oxford University Press, 1989), 189.

1. The Battle Lines: Blue Laws, Religion, and the Evolution of Baseball

1 Bruce C. Daniels, *Puritans at Play: Leisure and Recreation in Colonial New England* (New York: St. Martin's, 1995), 167; Fischer, *Albion's Seed*, 148.
2 Edmund S. Morgan, *The Puritan Family: Religion and Domestic Relations in Seventeenth-Century New England* (New York: Harper & Row, 1966), 149; "Blue Laws," *New York Times*, December 27, 1908; State of New York, Legislative Document #50, *Preliminary Report of the Joint Legislative Committee on Sabbath Law* (Albany, NY: Williams Press, 1952), 11–12.

179

3   *Laws of the State of New York Passed at the One Hundred and Forty-Second Session of the Legislature*, volume I, chapter 260, Collected Laws of the Legislative Session, (Albany, NY: J.B. Lyon Company, State Printers, 1919), 865.

4   *Laws of the State of New York Passed at the One Hundred and Fourth Session of the Legislature*, volume III, chapter 676, An Act to Establish the Penal Code, (Albany, NY: Weed, Parsons, and Company, 1881), 64, 65.

5   Abram Herbert Lewis, *Sunday Legislation: Its History to the Present Time and Its Results* (New York: D. Appleton, 1902), 240–41.

6   Editorial, "New York At Nashville," *New York Times*, July 14, 1897.

7   William A. Blakely, *American State Papers Bearing on Sunday Legislation: Legislative, Executive, Judicial* (New York: Da Capo Press, 1970), 597; Lewis, *Sunday Legislation*, 218, 221, 231–33, 244, 247–48; Warren L. Johns, *Dateline Sunday, USA* (Mountain View, CA: Pacific Press, 1967), 64.

8   Alexis McCrossen, *Holy Day, Holiday: The American Sunday* (Ithaca, NY: Cornell University Press, 2000), 43–44.

9   "Sabbath Evening," *Ohio Repository*, October 12, 1815.

10 "Letter to the Pastors, Church Sessions, and Congregations under the Care of the Synod of Philadelphia," *Adams Sentinel and General Advertiser*, May 15, 1837.

11 "The Sabbath Convention," *Tioga Eagle*, June 26, 1844; "The Lord's Day Address," *Star and Republican Banner*, March 12, 1847; "Meeting in Behalf of the Christian Sabbath," *New York Times*, March 18, 1858.

12 Milton M. Klein, ed., *The Empire State: A History of New York* (Ithaca, NY: Cornell University Press, 2001), 331; Paul E. Johnson, *A Shopkeeper's Millennium: Society and Revivals in Rochester, New York, 1815–1837* (New York: Hill and Wang, 1978), 102–3.

13 Johnson, *Shopkeeper's Millennium*, 38.

14 Ibid., 84–85; Klein, *Empire State*, 332–33.

15 Andrew C. Rieser, *The Chautauqua Movement: Protestants, Progressives, and the Culture of Modern Liberalism, 1874–1920* (New York: Columbia University Press, 2003), 26–29.

16 "Sale of Liquor on the Sabbath," *Syracuse Herald Journal*, November 26, 1866; Temperance Movement/Sunday Closing Law file, Onondaga Historical Society, Syracuse, NY; Harmon Kingsbury, *The Sabbath: A Brief History of Laws, Petitions, Remonstrances and Reports, with Facts and Arguments, Relating to the Christian Sabbath* (New York: Jonathan Leavitt, 1840), 252.

17 "More Stringent Observance of Sunday Closing Urged by W.C.T.U.," *Ithaca Weekly Journal*, January 20, 1916.

18 Paul Boyer, *Urban Masses and Moral Order in America, 1820–1920* (Cambridge, MA: Harvard University Press, 1978), 112–15.

19 "Sunday Observance," *New York World*, July 9, 1890; "Cardinal Gibbons Endorses Baseball," *Base Ball Guide*, 171; Baseball and Religion File, A. Bartlett Giamatti Library.

20 Harold Seymour, *Baseball: The Early Years* (New York: Oxford University Press, 1960), 295.

21 George M. Marsden, *Fundamentalism and American Culture: The Shaping of Twentieth-Century Evangelicalism, 1870–1925* (New York: Oxford University Press, 1980), 13.

22 *History of the State of New York*, ed. Alexander C. Flick, vol. 9, *Mind and Spirit* (New York: Columbia University Press, 1937), 158.

23 "Sunday Saloons, New York Clergymen Favor Opening Them Part of the Day," *Olean Democrat*, March 15, 1895.

24 McCrossen, *Holy Day, Holiday*, 97.

25 John Thorn, *Baseball in the Garden of Eden: The Secret History of the Early Game* (New York: Simon & Schuster, 2011), 30–32; Dean A. Sullivan, ed., *Early Innings: A Documentary History of Baseball, 1825–1908* (Lincoln: University of Nebraska Press, 1995), 2; Warren Goldstein, *Playing for Keeps: A History of Early Baseball* (Ithaca, NY: Cornell University Press, 1989), 17; George B. Kirsch, *Baseball in Blue & Gray: The National Pastime During the Civil War* (Princeton, NJ: Princeton University Press, 2003), 60–61.

26 Goldstein, *Playing for Keeps*, 31; "Historical Crotchets," *New York History* 70, no. 3 (July 1989): 309.

27 Jim Mandelaro and Scott Pitoniak, *Silver Seasons: The Story of the Rochester Red Wings* (Syracuse, NY: Syracuse University Press, 1996), 2–3.

28 Charlie Tiano, *More Balls than Strikes: 120 Years of Baseball in New York's Hudson Valley* (Saugerties, NY: Hope Farm Press, 1995), 13–14.

29 Harold Seymour, *Baseball: The People's Game* (New York: Oxford University Press, 1990), 191.

30 "Exhibitions to Ladies," *New York Clipper*, May 10, 1878; "Bloomer Girls Baseball," *Ithaca Weekly News*, July 23, 1902; Gai Ingham Berlage, "From Bloomer Girls' Baseball to Women's Softball: A Cultural Journey Resulting in Women's Exclusion from Baseball," in *The Cooperstown Symposium on Baseball and American Culture, 1999*, ed. Peter M. Rutkoff (Jefferson, NC: McFarland, 2000), 249, 251–52; "Female Ballplayers Stoned," *New York Clipper*, September 6, 1879.

31 Carol Kammen, *Ithaca, New York: A Brief History* (Charleston, SC: History Press, 2008), 55; newspaper clippings, Baseball file, Onondaga Historical Association Collections; "Golden Days of Ilion Baseball," *Observer-Dispatch*, March 17, 1957; Thorn, *Baseball in Garden of Eden*, 130–31.

32 Seymour, *Baseball: Early Years*, 45.

33 Goldstein, *Playing for Keeps*, 84–85; Thorn, *Baseball in Garden of Eden*, 124–25; Seymour, *Baseball: Early Years*.

34 Goldstein, *Playing for Keeps*, 88.

35 Gate money refers to the admission fees collected from customers at the gate or turnstiles at a ballpark, which were then distributed among the players. This was different from paying the players a salary. "Alaska vs. Americus," *New York Clipper*, April 21, 1877.

36 "Baseball Was Started Here 50 Years Ago," *Syracuse Herald Journal*, June 23, 1917; "Pro Baseball Was Started Here in 1874," *Syracuse Post Standard*, September 18, 1929.

37 Ron Gershbacher, "74 Years of Syracuse Baseball," (unpublished paper), Baseball File, Onondaga Historical Association Collections.

38 Baseball Clippings file, Onondaga Historical Association Collections.

39 Jimmy Daley, "Sixty Years of Baseball in Syracuse," *Syracuse Journal*, February 22, 1937–March 16, 1937; "Interest Is Rising In Indoor Ball," *Syracuse Post Standard*, December 17, 1899.

40   "Baseball Outlook Continues Bright," *Ithaca Weekly News*, July 19, 1906.
41   "Ithaca Ball Team Made Good Record," *Ithaca Weekly Journal*, September 13, 1906.
42   "Enthusiastic Meeting-Indications the Team Will be Well Supported," *Cortland Evening Standard*, April 2, 1901; "Baseball Interests-Stock Nearly All Sold-Officers to be Elected at Next Meeting," *Cortland Evening Standard*, April 6, 1901.
43   "Troy Turns the Tables," *Cortland Evening Standard*, June 5, 1901; "Cortland Ballplayers Make Stupid Plays," *Cortland Evening Standard*, June 21, 1901; "Ball Season is Over," *Cortland Evening Standard*, July 11, 1901; "Moral and Social Issues Around the State," *Ithaca Weekly News*, July 10, 1901; "Moral and Social Issues Around the State, *Ithaca Weekly News*, July 17, 1901.
44   "Sunday Baseball—New York State League," *Ithaca Weekly News*, July 24, 1901.
45   Seymour, *Baseball: Early Years*, 90.
46   "The League Meeting," *New York Clipper*, August 17, 1878.
47   *New York Clipper*, October 11, 1879; *New York Clipper*, November 1, 1879.
48   Seymour, *Baseball: Early Years*, 104–10.
49   "Sunday Baseball—National League," *Sporting News*, October 25, 1886.
50   Seymour, *Baseball: Early Years*, 139.
51   Ibid., 228–29.
52   Steven A. Riess, *Touching Base: Professional Baseball and American Culture in the Progressive Era* rev. ed. (Urbana: University of Illinois Press, 1999), 140.
53   "Will Join in Jubilee," *Syracuse Evening Herald*, September 27, 1897.
54   "Bluff on Cleveland Sunday Baseball," *Sporting News*, April 10, 1897.

2. The Emergence of the Sunday Baseball Issue in the Nineteenth Century

1   Ellen M. Snyder-Grenier, *Brooklyn!: An Illustrated History* (Philadelphia: Temple University Press, 1996), 221.
2   "Baseball Playing on Sunday," *New York Clipper*, April 29, 1876; George B. Kirsch, *Baseball and Cricket: The Creation of American Team Sports, 1838–72* (Urbana: University of Illinois Press, 2007), 113.
3   "Sunday Arrests," *New York Times*, May 13, 1878; "The Desecration of the Sabbath," *Brooklyn Daily Eagle*, August 24, 1878.
4   Kirsch, *Baseball and Cricket*, 113.
5   "Making a Day of Rest," *New York Times*, December 11, 1882; "Base Ball Playing and the Sunday Laws," *Brooklyn Daily Eagle*, June 29, 1884.
6   James M. DiClerico and Barry J. Pavelec, *The Jersey Game: The History of Modern Baseball from its Birth to the Big Leagues in the Garden State* (New Brunswick, NJ: Rutgers University Press, 1991), 50.
7   Thorn, *Baseball in Garden of Eden*, 116.
8   Snyder-Grenier, *Brooklyn!*, 225–26; Riess, *Touching Base*, 107.
9   Charlie Bevis, *Sunday Baseball: The Major Leagues' Struggle to Play Baseball on the Lord's Day, 1876–1934* (Jefferson, NC: McFarland, 2003), 53–55.
10   "Sunday Baseball Games," *New York Times*, September 1, 1884; "Sunday's Baseball Games," *New York Times*, August, 30, 1886.

11 Riess, *Touching Base*, 139; "Baseball on Sunday," *New York Times*, September 6, 1886.

12 "Sunday Baseball Playing Stopped," *Brooklyn Daily Eagle*, April 11, 1887.

13 "Baseball Notes," *Brooklyn Daily Eagle*, May 10, 1896; "Amateur Baseball on Sunday," *Brooklyn Daily Eagle*, July 2, 1896; "Gossip of the Diamond," *Brooklyn Daily Eagle*, March 14, 1900.

14 "Varuna Committees," *Brooklyn Daily Eagle*, January 31, 1894; "Another Semi-Pro Game Allowed," *Brooklyn Daily Eagle*, October 30, 1897; "Bay Ridge Outing," *Brooklyn Daily Eagle*, July 27, 1899; "Colored Athletes at Ridgewood," *Brooklyn Daily Eagle*, August 2, 1890.

15 "Thousands of Sunday School Children Having a Day's Outing," *Brooklyn Daily Eagle*, June 18, 1898; "By a Game of Ball, Matters Have Been Brought to a Crisis in the Diocesan Union," *Brooklyn Daily Eagle*, April 6, 1891.

16 "Brooklyn Fosters Outdoor Sports," *Brooklyn Daily Eagle*, June 10, 1900.

17 Bevis, *Sunday Baseball*, 51–52; "Baseball, Can it be Played on Sunday at the Island," *Brooklyn Daily Eagle*, May 16, 1885.

18 "Blue Laws at Rockaway," *Brooklyn Daily Eagle*, July 24, 1895; "Quiet Day at the Island," *Brooklyn Daily Eagle*, July 2, 1900.

19 "Ball Games on Sunday," *Brooklyn Daily Eagle*, April 30, 1894.

20 "Organization Formed in the Village of Jamaica to Battle for the Strict Observance of the Sabbath," *Brooklyn Daily Eagle*, June 16, 1879.

21 "Sunday Observance Association," *Brooklyn Daily Eagle*, June 3, 1889; "Sabbath Breaking at Ridgewood," *Brooklyn Daily Eagle*, October 4, 1889.

22 "Ball Playing on the Sabbath," *Brooklyn Daily Eagle*, June 13, 1889; "Shepard Talks at the Sunday Observance Association Meeting," *Brooklyn Daily Eagle*, May 20, 1889.

23 "Sabbath Alliance Meeting," *Brooklyn Daily Eagle*, December 1, 1900; "Women's Sabbath Alliance," *Brooklyn Daily Eagle*, December 8, 1900; "Women Begin a Crusade against Sunday Golf," *Brooklyn Daily Eagle*, May 31, 1900.

24 "Radical Views on Sabbath Breaking," *Brooklyn Daily Eagle*, March 28, 1888.

25 "Sunday Ball Playing," *Brooklyn Daily Eagle*, May 7, 1888.

26 "Loss of Christian Sabbath Would Be a Dire Calamity to the English Speaking People," *Brooklyn Daily Eagle*, September 25, 1899.

27 Carl N. Degler, *Out of Our Past: The Forces That Shaped Modern America* (New York: Harper & Row, 1984), 370.

28 "Sabbath Breaking," *Brooklyn Daily Eagle*, October 12, 1885; "Reverend Dr. Ford Speaks Against Sunday Amusements at Middle Reformed Church," *Brooklyn Daily Eagle*, February 15, 1886.

29 "Criticism of an Assemblyman by the Reverend Jesse W. Brooks," *Brooklyn Daily Eagle*, February 22, 1892; "Sabbath Desecration," *Brooklyn Daily Eagle*, July 26, 1886.

30 "Sports on Sunday," *Sporting News*, January 17, 1891; Editorial, "Sunday Papers," *New York Times*, April 25, 1886.

31 "Civic League, Albany, NY, A Non-Sectarian and Non-Sectional Organization," *New York Times*, March 15, 1895.

32 "Ball Players Take a Rest on the Sabbath," *Brooklyn Daily Eagle*, August 4, 1890; "Amateur Baseball on Sunday," *Brooklyn Daily Eagle*, July 2, 1896; "Another

Baseball Game," *Brooklyn Daily Eagle*, October 30, 1897; "Sunday Semi-
Professional Baseball. Bryant and Stratton Baseball Club," *Brooklyn Daily Eagle*,
April 14, 1897.

33   "Brooklyn's Legal Dilemma," *New York Times*, September 4, 1894; "Judge
Gaynor on the Boys' Side," *Brooklyn Daily Eagle*, August 9, 1894; "May Play
Ball on Sunday," *New York Times*, August 12, 1894; "Opposition to Games in
Brooklyn," *Sporting News*, January 9, 1897.

34   Michael A. Lerner, *Dry Manhattan: Prohibition in New York City* (Cambridge,
MA: Harvard University Press, 2007), 14.

35   Roger I. Abrams, *The Dark Side of the Diamond: Gambling, Violence, Drugs,
and Alcoholism in the National Pastime* (Burlington, MA: Rounder Books,
2007), 122; David Quentin Voigt, *American Baseball, Volume I: From
Gentleman's Sport to the Commissioner System* (Norman: University of
Oklahoma University Press, 1966), 53–54.

36   Frank Graham Jr., *A Farewell to Heroes* (New York: Viking, 1981), 7.

37   "Fraud on the Ball-Field," *New York Clipper*, October 25, 1873.

38   "Baseball Notes," *New York Clipper*, September 13, 1879; "How Gamblers Do
Not Win," *New York Clipper*, May 12, 1883.

39   Scott Fiesthumel, "D. Dishler, Utica's Most Interesting Operator," *Life and Times
of Utica*, January 17, 2002; Scott Fiesthumel, "The Utica Newspapers Expose
Dishler's Gambling Activities," *Life and Times of Utica*, January 17, 2002.

40   Rico Longoria, "Baseball's Gambling Scandals," *ESPN Classic* (July 31, 2001),
http://espn.go.com/classic/s/2001/0730/1233060.html

41   "Arrest Baseball Bettors," *New York Times*, April 17, 1909; "After the Gamblers,"
Sporting Life, April 24, 1909.

42   "First Fixed Game," *New York Clipper*, Baseball Gambling file, A. Bartlett
Giamatti Library.

43   Abrams, *Dark Side of Diamond*, 25; Benjamin G. Rader, *Baseball: A History of
America's Game* (Urbana: University of Illinois Press, 1992), 40, 72.

44   "Against Sunday Baseball," *Brooklyn Daily Eagle*, July 13, 1901.

45   "Anti-Gambling Bills Expected to Pass," *Ithaca Weekly Journal*, April 30, 1908.

46   "The Abuse of Umpires," *New York Clipper*, June 7, 1879; "Assaulted an
Umpire," *Sporting News*, July 7, 1906.

47   "A Disorderly Scene," *New York Clipper*, August 11, 1883.

48   "Umpiring in Baseball," *New York Clipper*, August 18, 1883.

49   "Lawlessness on the Sabbath," *Brooklyn Daily Eagle*, May 14, 1888; "Decline of
Baseball," *New York Times*, September 23, 1900.

50   "Hoodlums in Syracuse," *Syracuse Post-Standard*, September 9, 1902.

51   "'Iron Man' Arrested By Order of Mayor," *New York Times*, July 25, 1906.

52   "Quotes and Comments: The American Game in Auburn," *Syracuse Post-
Standard*, May 23, 1905; "Riot on Central Train," *New York Times*, February 9,
1906; Jim Reisler, ed., *Guys, Dolls, and Curveballs: Damon Runyon on Baseball*
(New York: Carroll & Graf Publishers, 2005), 89; "Ball Players Bailed," *Ithaca
Daily Journal*, February 9, 1906.

53   "Umpires Admonished," *Cortland Standard*, May 21, 1909; "Ban Johnson Goes
After Rowdies in American League," *Sporting News*, July 6, 1916.

54   "Little Betting on Baseball," *Middletown Daily Times-Press*, July 23, 1917.

55   "Various Observations," *Olean Weekly Democrat*, May 28, 1891; "The Need of the Brooklyn Club," *Sporting Life*, November 25, 1916.

56   "Trying to Stop Sunday Games," *Sporting News*, August 4, 1888. The *Sporting News* erroneously identified the president of the International League in 1888 as a Mr. Cushman. According to reliable sources in the International League Office, the president of the league at that time was E. Strachen Cox. However, in 1888 there was a Mr. Charlie Cushman who was the manager of the Toronto Canucks of the International League.

57   "Whistler Continues His Search for Stars," *Sunday Syracuse Herald*, February 19, 1899.

58   "May Play at Pier," *Sunday Herald of Syracuse*, February 21, 1897.

59   "Voice of the Pulpit," *Evening Herald of Syracuse*, May 24, 1897.

60   "Barbers Take Exception," *Evening Herald of Syracuse*, May 26, 1897.

61   "Invading Army, Hordes of Foreigners Responsible for the Cry of Personal Liberty," *Syracuse Standard*, May 17, 1897.

62   "A Large Petition," *Sunday Syracuse Herald*, May 16, 1897.

63   "Opposing Sunday Ball," *Evening Herald of Syracuse*, May 31, 1897.

64   "Sunday Baseball in Auburn," *Sunday Syracuse Herald*, May 30, 1897.

65   "Law Violated for Spite," *Evening Herald of Syracuse*, July 13, 1897.

66   Scott Fiesthumel, "Sunday Baseball Games Led to Arrests in Utica and Rome," *Life and Times of Utica*, May 9, 2002.

67   "No Cause for Action in the Sunday Ball Playing Case," *Utica Daily Press*, July 4, 1891. It is interesting to note that some years later Chief of Police Dagwell was brought to court charged with failing to perform his duties of office. Specifically, he was cited for refusing to enforce the penal code against disorderly brothels and to uphold a host of other local statutes and ordinances in Utica. He was found guilty and reduced in rank to a patrolman. After Prohibition went into effect in 1920, he was back in court charged with the unlawful seizure of whisky and neglect of duty. "Gossip of the Trial," *Saturday Globe*, March 19, 1896; "Unlawful Seizure of Whisky Against Policeman," *Utica Herald Dispatch*, April 16, 1920.

68   "The Base Ball Game," *Utica Daily Press*, July 4, 1891.

69   "Couldn't Call It A Game So Judge Killed Case," *Brooklyn Daily Eagle*, June 29, 1911, Sunday Baseball File, A. Bartlett Giamatti Hall of Fame Library Collections.

70   Mandelaro and Pitoniak, *Silver Seasons*, 10.

71   "Arrested Again," *Rochester Democrat and Chronicle*, June 24, 1890.

72   Mandelaro and Pitoniak, *Silver Seasons*, 10.

73   Riess, *Touching Base*, 139.

74   "May Play at Pier," *Sunday Herald of Syracuse*, February 21, 1897; "No Sunday Games in the Empire State," *Sporting News*, April 10, 1897; "Hits from the Diamond," *Evening Herald of Syracuse*, June 11, 1897; Mandelaro and Pitoniak, *Silver Seasons*, 11.

75   "Sunday Baseball in New York State," *Sporting News*, December 4, 1897.

76   "Leaders are Dubious About Sunday Ball," *Syracuse Post Standard*, November 28, 1899, Baseball Clippings file, Onondaga Historical Association Collections.

77   "Sunday Observance," *Olean Evening Herald*, June 14, 1884; "Vox Populi,"
      Evening Observer (Dunkirk), April 21, 1883; George Gipe, "They Tried to Throw
      the Rascals Out," *Sports Illustrated*, May 20, 1974, E7.

3. The Sunday Question: Commercialized Baseball, Evasions, and the Courts, 1900–1909

1   G. Edward White, *Creating the National Pastime: Baseball Transforms Itself,
      1903–1953* (Princeton, NJ: Princeton University Press, 1996), 80–83; Seymour,
      Baseball: The Golden Age, 420; Harold Seymour Papers, Box 44, Olin Graduate
      Library, Cornell University, Ithaca, NY. According to Dr. Seymour, it is
      interesting that the Supreme Court in New Mexico ruled in 1913 that baseball did
      not belong in the same class as horse racing, cock fighting, or card playing. "It is
      a sport or athletic exercise."
2   Mark Lamster, *Spalding's World Tour: The Epic Adventure that Took Baseball
      Around the Globe—And Made It America's Game* (New York: Public Affairs,
      2006), 62–63.
3   "The Baseball Season," *New York Times*, October 8, 1905.
4   "Cornell Will Not Adopt New Rules," *Ithaca Weekly News*, March 27, 1901.
5   "Laws in Schenectady: Union College Baseball, 1870–1900," paper presented by
      Denis Brennan at the 24th Cooperstown Symposium on Baseball and American
      Culture, Cooperstown, NY, May 30, 2012.
6   "President Eliot on College Sports," *New York World*, November 3, 1903; "The
      Greatest Athletic Organization in the World, Public Schools Athletic League,"
      New York Times, April 14, 1907.
7   "Campaign Against 'Pros' in College," *New York Times*, March 12, 1914.
8   "Summer Baseball Problem Discussed," *New York Times*, April 4, 1909.
9   "Sport Out of Favor," *New York Times*, January 6, 1902; Johan Huizinga, *Homo
      Ludens: A Study of the Play-Element in Culture* (Boston: Beacon Press, 1950),
      51.
10   "Baseball Trust Origin," *New York Times*, January 13, 1902.
11   "No Peace in Baseball," *New York Times*, January 14, 1902.
12   Riess, *Touching Base*, 74; "Freedman is on Top," *New York Daily Tribune*,
      December 17, 1901; Frank Graham, *The New York Giants* (Carbondale and
      Edwardsville: Southern Illinois University Press, 2002), 25, 26.
13   "Baseball Men in Town," *New York Times*, January 7, 1902; "No Baseball Trust,"
      New York Times, September 26, 1901; "Freedman's Retirement," *Syracuse
      Evening Herald*, September 30, 1902.
14   "Baseball as a Business, Baseball as Pleasure," *Atlanta Constitution*, August 30,
      1908.
15   "Asks Probe of Baseball Trust," *Evening Record*, March 12, 1912; "Fans
      Disquieted By Attempts of Gallagher To Insert So-Called Baseball Probe," *Olean
      Evening Times*, March 22, 1912; "Baseball Trust May Be Probed," *Atlanta
      Constitution*, May 12, 1912.
16   Louis A. Dougher, "An Evil in Baseball," *Baseball Magazine*, June 1910, 18–19;
      James J. Corbett, "Baseball Owners Have Been Playing Up the Financial Side
      Too Much," *Syracuse Herald*, February 9, 1919.

17 "Money Princes of Baseball," *Syracuse Herald*, September 23, 1913; Charles
    Webb Murphy, "Is Professional Baseball a Trust?" *Baseball Magazine*, July 1919,
    15–22.

18 Albert Theodore Powers, *The Business of Baseball* (Jefferson, NC: McFarland,
    2003), 29.

19 "Fight For Boxing Is On In Earnest," *New York World*, March 2, 1900; "The Fight
    To Save the Horton Law is on Today," *New York World*, March 28, 1900; "Senate
    Passed by a Vote of 26 To 22 The Lewis Bill," *New York World*, March 29, 1900.

20 "Mayor Horton Speaks to Women of the W.C.T.U.," *Ithaca Journal*, June 18,
    1909.

21 "Against Sunday Sports and Activities," *Ithaca Weekly News*, June 18, 1902.

22 "Cortland Ministers Want Law Enforced," *Syracuse Post-Standard*, April 22,
    1905; "Moral and Social Issues Around the State," *Ithaca Weekly News*, July 16,
    1902; "Moral and Social Issues Around the State," *Ithaca Weekly News*, June 19,
    1901.

23 "Preacher Loves Baseball," *New York World*, October 6, 1906, Baseball and
    Religion File, A. Bartlett Giamatti Library.

24 "Students 'Fork Over' to the City Treasury, Indulgence in Sunday Ball Causes
    Shrinkage in Rolls," *Ithaca Daily Journal*, May 17, 1909; David DeKok, *The
    Epidemic: A Collision of Power, Privilege, and Public Health* (Guilford, CT:
    Lyons Press, 2011), 65, 106.

25 "Guy B. Galligher-Reformer," *Syracuse Sunday Herald*, July 14, 1901.

26 "Moral and Social Issues Around the State," *Ithaca Weekly News*, July 16, 1902;
    "Moral and Social Issues Around the State," *Ithaca Weekly News*, May 21, 1902.

27 "Moral and Social Issues Around the State," *Ithaca Weekly News*, January 16,
    1901; "W.C.T.U. Against Sunday Noise," *Ithaca Weekly News*, May 14, 1902;
    "Moral Reform Crusades," *Ithaca Weekly News*, July 23, 1902; "Foreigners Defy
    the Law," *Ithaca Weekly Journal*, April 16, 1908; "Send Them Away," *Ithaca
    Weekly News*, April 26, 1906.

28 William McAdoo, *Guarding a Great City*, Historical Reprint Series (New York:
    Harper & Brothers, 1906), 311.

29 Riess, *Touching Base*, 142; "Ministers Plead for Sabbath Observance," *New York
    Times*, April 18, 1904; "Brooklyn Crown Sees Baseball on Sunday," *New York
    Times*, April 18, 1904. Although he saw no harm in Sunday games, McAdoo said
    that he had to keep ahead of the Law and Order Societies and the Sunday
    Observance Association, who wanted him impeached. Harold Seymour Papers,
    Box 44.

30 "Sunday Games in Manhattan Forbidden," *New York Times*, April 23, 1904.

31 "Sold Score Cards, Sunday Ball in Brooklyn A Big Success," *Sporting News*,
    April 23, 1904.

32 "M'Adoo Orders Test of Sunday Baseball," *New York Times*, April 25, 1904.

33 "Sunday Baseball Cases," *New York Times*, April 28, 1904. There is some dispute
    as to where the Phillies-Dodgers Sunday game was played. Seymour notes that it
    was at Ridgewood Park, but in fact it was played at Washington Park, as noted in
    the *Times*. Harold Seymour Papers, Box 44.

34 "M'Adoo Orders Test of Sunday Baseball," *New York Times*, April 25, 1904;
    "Court Paroles Players," *New York Times*, April 25, 1904.

35   "Sunday Ball Playing," *New York Times*, April 24, 1904. Programs were sold for seventy-five, fifty, and twenty-five cents, which corresponded to grandstand, open stand, or bleacher seats. Harold Seymour Papers, Box 44.

36   "Order Was Obeyed, Police Stop Sunday Ball in Brooklyn," *Sporting News*, July 1, 1905.

37   "Sunday Baseball Scheme," *New York Times*, April 15, 1906. Ebbets claimed that the receipts from the deposit boxes showed very little depreciation and that there was no law violation. The collection box, he said, went well at first but once the National League changed their schedule to get more games into Brooklyn on Sunday, the authorities began to crack down on the scheme. Harold Seymour Papers, Box 44.

38   "Obey Order of Police, No Sunday Baseball for Admission Fee-Arrests in Brooklyn," *New York Times*, June 11, 1906; "Stop Sunday Ball, Police Officials Put Ban on Brooklyn," *Sporting News*, June 16, 1906.

39   "Heavy Handicap, Anthracite Cities Cannot Play Sunday Ball," *Sporting News*, February 28, 1903.

40   "Sunday Baseball Discussed," *New York Times*, January 10, 1904; "Will Try Sunday Ball," *Sporting News*, May 7, 1904; "Editorial," *Sporting News*, May 20, 1905. Harold Seymour Papers, Box 44. In speaking against the New York American League presumed violation of Brooklyn's territorial rights, Ebbets said that according to the agreement between the two major leagues, the Yankees were confined to Manhattan. New York supporters said that American League president Ban Johnson refused this condition at the time.

41   "No Game for Next Sunday, Status of Brooklyn Case," *Sporting News*, April 30, 1904. Harold Seymour Papers, Box 43.

42   "Ministers Plead for Sabbath Observance," *New York Times*, April 18, 1904.

43   Robert Elias, *The Empire Strikes Out* (New York & London: The New Press, 2010), 52; "No Sunday Soldier Games," *New York Times*, June 24, 1910.

44   "Favor Sunday Ball," *New York Times*, May 2, 1904.

45   "The Judge Gaynor Decision," *Syracuse Post-Standard*, May 5, 1904; "Sunday Baseball, No Longer Criminal," *Syracuse Post-Standard*, May 5, 1904.

46   "Will Try Sunday Ball, Brush Says Patrons Want It," *Sporting News*, May 7, 1904; "John T. Brush on Sunday Baseball," *New York Times*, May 22, 1904.

47   "Brooklyn's Baseball War, Clergymen Disappointed by Justice Gaynor's Explanation," *New York Times*, May 9, 1904; "Sunday Baseball–For and Against," *Syracuse Post-Standard*, April 28, 1904.

48   "Sunday Baseball Cases: District Attorney Clarke Will Appeal from Judge Gaynor's Decision," *New York Times*, May 5, 1904.

49   Quotes from notes in the Harold Seymour Papers, Box 43; reportedly taken from *Sporting News*, August 13, 1904; "Editorial," *Sporting News*, July 23, 1914; "Sunday Baseball No Crime," *Brooklyn Daily Eagle*, July 15, 1914. Judge Collins, a strong Tammany Hall man, stated that when he was in the legislature he tried to have the law regarding Sunday baseball changed. There is no evidence that he ever served in the New York State Legislature.

50   "Must Enforce Law Against Sunday Ball," *Syracuse Post-Standard*, July 1, 1904.

51   "Sunday Baseball Illegal," *New York Times*, July 4, 1905.

52   "Gives Opinion on Sunday Ball," *Middletown Times-Press*, July 27, 1910.

53 "Gaynor-Whitman Confab," *New York Times*, December 16, 1909.

54 "Sabbath Observance," *Syracuse Herald*, March 24, 1909; Rabbi Charles Fleischer, "Sunday Baseball, The Crying Need," *Baseball Magazine* 1, no. 4 (August 1908): 19–20.

55 Frederick S. Brooks, "New York's Greatest Amateur Association," *Baseball Magazine* 1, no. 4 (August 1908): 51–55.

56 "The Sunday Laws," *New York Times*, December 4, 1906; "Editorial—Sunday Laws," *New York Times*, June 10, 1907; "Editorial—Sunday Observance," *New York Times*, July 21, 1907; William F. Kirk, "Shall We Have Sunday Baseball?" *Baseball Magazine* 1, no. 3 (July 1908): 47–48; "Editorial—Sunday Ball Playing," *New York Times*, April 4, 1909.

57 "For A Liberal Sunday," *New York Times*, March 30, 1909; C. F. Mathison to August Herrmann, Harold Seymour Papers, Box 44.

58 "Call For A Liberal Sunday," *New York Times*, April 4, 1909.

59 "Open 'Sunday' League Busy," *New York Times*, April 6, 1909; "For Liberal Sunday Laws," *New York Times*, February 18, 1909.

60 "More Liberal Sunday," *New York Times*, January 28, 1908.

4. Local Opposition to Sunday Baseball and the Legislative Initiative, 1910–1916

1 Robert A. Slayton, *Empire Statesman, The Rise and Redemption of Al Smith* (New York: Free Press, 2001), 32.

2 "Charges Made Against Sheriff," *Dunkirk Evening Observer*, June 21, 1910.

3 "Stops Sunday Ball Game," *New York Times*, July 18, 1910; "Elmira Players Acquitted," *Ithaca Journal*, July 22, 1910.

4 "Sunday Ball Game Stopped in Elmira," *New York Times*, July 25, 1910.

5 "Contempt Costs Colonels $300," *Syracuse Post-Standard*, September 13, 1910.

6 "An Even Break," *Syracuse Post-Standard*, September 5, 1910.

7 "To Stop Sunday Ball Games," *New York Times*, July 29, 1912.

8 "Sunday Baseball Trial Farces," *Syracuse Journal*, June 6, 1911, Scott Fiesthumel Archive.

9 "Acquits Players for Sunday Game," *Syracuse Herald*, July 11, 1911; Jimmy Daley, "Six Syracuse Players Arrested for Playing on Sunday in 1911, Then Freed," *Syracuse Post-Standard*, March 9, 1937; "Sunday Ball Despite Law," *New York Times*, July 4, 1910; "League May Start Campaign Here Soon," *Syracuse Post-Standard*, April 4, 1910.

10 "Sunday Ball Despite Law," *New York Times*, July 4, 1910; "League May Start Campaign Here Soon," *Syracuse Post-Standard*, April 4, 1910.

11 "Will Argue Law and Order with 30 Ministers," *Syracuse Herald*, March 30, 1914; "Ban is Placed on Sunday Baseball," *Syracuse Herald*, April 18, 1914.

12 "Stars and Troy Will Play This Afternoon," *Syracuse Herald*, June 7, 1914.

13 "Committee Named to Consider Field Day," *Syracuse Herald*, October 10, 1916; "Roman's Attack on Hyphenates Stirs Ministers," *Syracuse Herald*, October 23, 1916.

14 "Albany Sunday Game Stopped," *New York Times*, July 23, 1910; "Abandon Sunday Baseball," *New York Times*, July 30, 1910.

15 "Dix and Sunday Baseball," *Syracuse Herald*, May 13, 1911.

16 "Dix Man on Sunday Ball," *New York Times*, December 27, 1910; "Won't Regulate Baseball," *New York Times*, October 17, 1911.

17 "Opposes Sunday Baseball," *New York Times*, May 24, 1913.

18 "No Sunday Baseball at Albany," *New York Times*, May 25, 1913; "Baseball by Injunction," *New York Times*, June 1, 1913.

19 "Kingston, N.Y.," *New York Times*, June 15, 1913.

20 "Sunday Ball Safe in Albany," *New York Times*, June 29, 1913.

21 "Sheriff Stops Albany Game," *New York Times*, June 30, 1913.

22 "Approve Sunday Baseball," *New York Times*, July 25, 1913.

23 "Albany Man Says People Desire Sunday Baseball," *Syracuse Herald*, May 13, 1914.

24 "To Continue Sunday Games at Albany Ground," *Syracuse Herald*, May 15, 1914.

25 Gerald Zahavi, *Workers, Managers, and Welfare Capitalism: The Shoeworkers and Tanners of Endicott Johnson 1890–1950* (Urbana: University of Illinois Press, 1988), 2, 25–26.

26 "Sheriff is Warned at Binghamton," *Middletown Daily Times-Press*, May 24, 1913.

27 "Sulzer Raps His Party's Leaders," *Ithaca Daily Journal*, August 13, 1910.

28 "Sulzer Extremely Popular With the People When He Accepted Nomination," *Syracuse Herald*, September 17, 1913; *History of the State of New York*, ed. Alexander C. Flick, vol. 7, *Modern Party Battles* (New York: Columbia University Press, 1935), 194–95.

29 "Opposes Sunday Baseball," *New York Times*, May 24, 1913; "Plan to Run Candidate for Assembly," *Middletown Daily Times-Press*, May 28, 1913.

30 "Fight Sunday Baseball," *New York Times*, June 2, 1913.

31 "Ball Games in Politics," *New York Times*, September 18, 1913.

32 "Clergymen of Hilly City Serve Notice on the Sheriff," *Middletown Daily Times-Press*, May 24, 1913; "Newburgh Local Point of Attack on Sunday Baseball Playing," *Orange County Times-Press*, May 27, 1913.

33 "Newburgh, N.Y.," *New York Times*, June 15, 1913.

34 Riess, *Touching Base*, 144.

35 "Sunday Baseball Bill Introduced," *New York Times*, January 15, 1909.

36 "Huff Takes A Charge," *Ithaca Journal*, July 25, 1910.

37 "Reverend Mills, New York Civic League Speaks At Linden Hall," *Orange County Times-Press*, May 2, 1911.

38 "The Reverend C. R. Miller to Speak on Great Moral Battles For The New York Civic League," *Middletown Daily Times-Press*, April 28, 1911; "Sunday Baseball Law," *Dunkirk Evening Observer*, April 8, 1911; "Fund For Sunday Baseball," *New York Times*, April 8, 1911.

39 "Legislative Action Report–New York Civic League," *Middletown Daily Times-Press*, May 29, 1911; "Sermon on Sunday Observance," *Middletown Daily Times-Press*, September 5, 1916; "Sermon on Sabbath Observance," *Middletown Daily Times-Press*, April 29, 1916; "Church Lawn Donated for Good Recreational Events," *Middletown Daily Times-Press*, April 22, 1915.

40 "Temperance Lecture in Middletown," *Middletown Daily Times-Press*, December 19, 1911.

41 "Methodist Conference Against Osborne Sunday Baseball Bill," *Middletown Daily Times-Press*, March 30, 1911.

42 "Sunday Observance Sermon Preached in Etna," *Ithaca Journal*, April 10, 1913; "More Stringent Observance of Sunday Closing Urged by W.C.T.U.," *Ithaca Journal*, January 20, 1916; "Ellenville," *Kingston Daily Freeman*, April 13, 1916.

43 "Baseball Evangelist Known Here," *Ithaca Journal*, January 11, 1917; "Sunday Gives Devil a Beating," *Republican Press* (Salamanca), November 7, 1913.

44 "Billy Sunday's New York Campaign," *Literary Digest*, no. 54 (June 30, 1917): 1998; "Sunday Sure N.Y. is not Cold to God," *Syracuse Herald*, April 30, 1917.

45 "Calls Baseball Cleanest Sport," January 5, 1909, William Ashley Sunday File, A. Bartlett Giametti Research Center.

46 "Sunday Baseball," *Syracuse Herald*, July 31, 1914.

47 "Sunday Baseball Law," *Dunkirk Evening Observer*, February 10, 1911.

48 "Against Sunday Baseball," *New York Times*, March 15, 1911.

49 "Amateur Sunday Ball Bill Meets Death in Assembly," *Syracuse Post-Standard*, March 15, 1911.

50 "Many Bills at Albany," *Dunkirk Evening Observer*, January 20, 1912; "May Have Sunday Baseball," *New York Times*, July 13, 1911.

51 "Local Option on Sunday Baseball in Proposed Bill," *Middletown Daily Times-Press*, February 7, 1914; "Three Sunday Bills Stir Up Albany," *Syracuse Herald*, February 21, 1914; "Hearing Is Held On The Baseball Bill," *Orange County Times-Press*, March 6, 1914.

52 "No Half Holidays This Year Because of Grocers' Ban," *Ithaca Journal*, June 1, 1916.

53 "Sunday Baseball to be Fought by Churchgoers," *Ithaca Journal*, June 8, 1916; "Five Half Holidays in August Local Merchants Decide," *Ithaca Journal*, June 22, 1916.

54 "New York's Demoralizing Sunday," *Literary Digest*, no. 46 (May 17, 1913): 1129.

55 "A Plea for Sunday Baseball," *New York Times*, May 4, 1914.

56 "Sunday Bill is Object of New League," *Middletown Daily Times-Press*, February 11, 1914; "Empire State Baseball League," *New York Times*, March 1, 1913.

57 "Bishop Ludden's Anniversary Talk," *Syracuse Herald*, May 1, 1911.

58 Elbert Hubbard, "Sunday Baseball–The Nation's Need," *Baseball Magazine* 7, no. 2 (June 1911): 13–14.

59. "Mayors to Vote on Sunday Baseball," *New York Times*, June 15, 1913; "Mayor Wants Sunday Baseball," *New York Times*, July 11, 1913; "Editorial–For Sunday Baseball and Against," *New York Times*, July 16, 1913; "Approve Sunday Baseball," *New York Times*, July 25, 1913.

60 "Home Rule Plan is Explained to People of City," *Ithaca Journal*, July 22, 1915.

61 "Elmira Man May be Next Speaker of the Assembly," *Syracuse Herald*, October 24, 1915.

62 "Editorial–Sunshine for G.O.P.," *Ithaca Journal*, February 20, 1913.

5. Local Option, the War, and the Modification of the Sunday Baseball Law, 1917–1919

1 "Police Prevent Game," *New York Times*, May 12, 1913; "Police Prevent Baseball Game," *New York Times*, April 20, 1914.

2 "Editorials," *Baseball Magazine* (October 1916): 32.

3   "Ebbets Has One Sound Idea," *Sporting News*, June 22, 1916.

4   Bob Lemks, "75 Years Ago Ballplayers Did Their Bit in World War I," in "The Bleacher Bum," *Sports Collectors Digest*, November 26, 1993.

5   Ralph Bourne, "The State," in Howard Zinn and Anthony Arnove, *Voices of a People's History of the United States* (New York: Seven Stories Press, 2004), 301.

6   "The American League and Military Training," *Sporting Life*, February 24, 1917; "Military Training for Ball Players," *New York Times*, February 16, 1917; "No Military Drill for Robby's Team," *New York Times*, March 20, 1917.

7   "New York Opening: Big Military Show," *Sporting News*, April 19, 1917.

8   "Let Fans in on the Drill," *Sporting News*, April 26, 1917.

9   "Citizen Soldiers," *New York Times*, February 25, 1917.

10 "No Baseball Next Year If War Continues," *Ithaca Journal*, May 3, 1917.

11 "Plan Baseball on Sunday," *New York Times*, May 23, 1917.

12 "Commission Makes Baseball History in Special Meeting," *Sporting News*, May 31, 1917.

13 "Music and Drills Better than Ball Playing in First Sunday League Game in New York," *New York Times*, June 18, 1917.

14 William A. Sunday, "A Defense of the Grand Old Game, *Baseball Magazine* 19 no. 3 (July 1917): 361; "Reds and Soldiers Benefitted by Game," *New York Times*, August 20, 1917.

15 "Commy Wants Military Day an Annual Feature in America," *Sporting News*, August 30, 1917.

16 "Cited for Sunday Game in New York," *Sporting News*, August 23, 1917.

17 Charles Weeghman, "Playing Ball for Uncle Sam," *Baseball Magazine* 19, no. 4 (April 1917): 431; "A Bit for the Ball Players," *Sporting News*, September 6, 1917.

18 Garry Herrmann, "Baseball's Immediate Future," *Baseball Magazine* 19, no. 3 (July 1917): 349.

19 "Jim Gilmore Predicts a Strike of Ball Players by April 20," *Frederick News-Post*, February 28, 1916; "Getting Down to War Basis Big Idea With Major League Clubs," *Sporting News*, February 15, 1917.

20 "Feb. 20 is Date Set for Strike by Fraternity," *Syracuse Herald*, January 17, 1917.

21 "Gompers is in Sympathy With the Players Cause, Indicates Charter Will Be Granted Organization," *Washington Post*, January 16, 1917; "No Unsigned Men to go to Camps, Says Tener," *Syracuse Herald*, January 23, 1917.

22 Seymour, *Baseball: The Golden Age*, 240; "Player's Strike Would Clear up Game, Says Mack," *Syracuse Herald*, January 15, 1917.

23 "Baseball Skies Cleared by Action Taken at New York," *Sporting News*, February 22, 1917; "More Money Wanted," *Wakefield Advocate*, May 5, 1917.

24 "War May Curtail Baseball Season," *New York Times*, October 23, 1917; "Magnates to Review Baseball Situation," *Oneonta Daily Star*, December 11, 1917; "Serious Problems for Baseball Body," *New York Times*, December 27, 1917.

25 "Holdout Antics of Players Incite Wrath of Joe Vila," *Sporting News*, February 28, 1918; "Salaries Paid Some Well Known Baseball Stars Came Out Officially Saturday," *Piqua Leader-Dispatch*, August 15, 1917.

26 "Baseball in Minors is Slipping Rapidly," *Lima Daily News*, September 6, 1917.

27 "Are Magnates Still Gambling?," *Sporting News*, April 18, 1918.

28 F. C. Lane, "A Rising Menace to the National Game," *Baseball Magazine* 21, no. 4 (August 1918): 345–47, 372; "Commy Changes Mind About Joe," *Wisconsin State Journal*, January 16, 1919.

29 "Two Big Things for Game by Johnson," *Sporting News*, May 23, 1918; "This 'Honor Roll' is Closed," *Sporting News*, May 16, 1918; "Baseball Slackers May be Put on A.L. Blacklist," *Washington Post*, December 12, 1918.

30 "A Season's Layoff Won't Hurt Game," *Sporting News*, August 8, 1918.

31 "Baseball Really on Trial," *Sporting News*, May 30, 1918; Neil J. Sullivan, *The Diamond in the Bronx* (New York: Oxford University Press, 2001), 21.

32 "Would Uncle Sam Deny All These Fans Their Baseball?," *Sporting News*, July 11, 1918.

33 "Baseball Suffers Heavy Blow With Tener Declaring War," *Syracuse Herald*, July 11, 1918.

34 "Robbins Says Moguls Have Led Baseball Into the Ditch," *Sporting News*, August 1, 1918; "Better No World Series at All Than Under Such a Plan," *Sporting News*, August 8, 1918.

35 "Johnson Favors an Ending August 20," *Sporting News*, August 1, 1918.

36 "Baseball's Finish Nears Farce Stage," *Sporting News*, August 22, 1918; "Commission and Players Squabble," *Dunkirk Evening Observer*, September 10, 1918.

37 "Commission and Players Squabble," *Dunkirk Evening News*, September 10, 1918.

38 Seymour, *Baseball: The Golden Age*, 253; "Salaries to Come Down," *New York Times*, December 22, 1918.

39 F. C. Lane, "Baseball's Future," *Baseball Magazine* 21, no. 5 (September, 1918): 407; "The Situation as to Redemption," *Sporting News*, October 31, 1918; "News Notes in Sport World," *Middletown Daily Times-Press*, February 12, 1919.

40 "Salaries to Come Down," *New York Times*, December 22, 1918; "Ball Players May Have Big Strike in 1919," *Syracuse Herald*, January 16, 1919.

41 "Frazee Delivers Final Ultimatum," *Bridgeport Standard Telegram*, February 25, 1919.

42 "Sunday Baseball in New York," *Sporting Life*, January 13, 1917.

43 "Senate Passes Local Option," *Oneonta Daily Star*, May 10, 1917; "What Hill-Wheeler Option Bill Provides," *Ithaca Journal*, February 1, 1917; "Assembly Passes Local Option, Up to Governor," *Ithaca Journal*, May 10, 1917.

44 "Court Frees Charles J. Harvey," *New York Times*, April 27, 1917.

45 "Voice in the Wilderness," *Sporting News*, May 24, 1917.

46 "In Benefit Game," *New York Times*, July 2, 1917; "A Sunday Game and No One Scandalized," *Sporting News*, July 5, 1917.

47 "Ebbets Held for Trial," *New York Times*, July 7, 1917.

48 "Why Light Up for the Blind," *Sporting News*, July 26, 1917.

49 Seymour, *Baseball: The People's Game*, 264.

50 "When Knocks are Boosts," *Sporting News*, August 2, 1917.

51 "Plea for Sunday Games," *New York Times*, July 31, 1917; "Whitman Enlisted for Sunday Games," *Sporting News*, August 9, 1917.

52   "Ebbets Put on Trial," *New York Times*, August 29, 1917; "No More Sunday Baseball," *New York Times*, September 2, 1917; "Brooklyn Judge Decides Against Efforts to Play Sunday Ball," *Sporting News*, September, 27, 1917.

53   "Beclouding an Issue," *Sporting News*, September 20, 1917.

54   "Ebbets in Court Today," *New York Times*, August 28, 1917; Charles Ebbets, "A Defense of Sunday Baseball," *Baseball Magazine* 19, no. 5 (September 1917): 477, 536.

55   "McGraw and 'Matty' Summoned to Court," *New York Times*, August 21, 1917; "Again a Friend in Court," *Sporting News*, August 30, 1917.

56   "Upholds Sunday Baseball," *New York Times*, September 8, 1917.

57   "Loyalty to the Cause," *Sporting News*, August 16, 1917.

58   "Sunday Ball Live Issue in Brooklyn," *Sporting News*, November 1, 1917.

59   "Sunday Baseball Gains Supporters," *New York Times*, November 1, 1917; "President Ebbets of the Brooklyn Club has Received Additional Support in His Campaign for Sunday Baseball," *New York Times*, November 6, 1917.

60   "Ruppert Bids for Sunday Baseball," *New York Times*, November 3, 1917.

61   "On Record for Sunday Ball," *Sporting News*, November 8, 1917.

62   "Ebbets Appeals to Clergy," *New York Times*, November 30, 1917; "Making Ready for Sunday Ball," *Sporting News*, January 24, 1918.

63   "Fans Fight for Sunday Ball in This State," *Syracuse Herald*, March 1, 1918.

64   Ibid.; "Theodore Roosevelt Endorses Sunday Bill," *New York Times*, April 8, 1918.

65   "Sunday Baseball Bill Reported Out," *New York Times*, March 20, 1918.

66   "New York's Sunday Ball Fight Still On," *Sporting News*, March 28, 1918.

67   "Discussing Sunday Baseball," *New York Times*, March 20, 1918.

68   "Senate for Sunday Games," *New York Times*, April 5, 1918.

69   "This Week Decides Sunday Ball's Fate," *Sporting News*, April 11, 1918; "Oppose Sunday Baseball," *New York Times*, April 11, 1918; "Sunday Baseball Doomed," *New York Times*, April 13, 1918.

70   "New York Fans to Get Sunday Ball," *Sporting News*, May 2, 1918; "Plan Sunday Games in New Jersey," *Sporting News*, February 28, 1918.

71   "Major Leagues Determined to Carry Out Sunday Ball at Harrison," *Syracuse Herald*, May 2, 1918.

72   "Games Every Sunday, Eastern League Plan," *Sporting News*, April 4, 1918.

73   Sunday Baseball League's One Hope," *New York Times*, December 11, 1917; "International League Owners Meet Tonight," *Syracuse Herald*, April 4, 1918; "This Week Decides Sunday Ball's Fate," *Sporting News*, April 11, 1918.

74   "To Permit Sunday Sports," *New York Times*, May 28, 1918; "Independence Day in Washington," *Sporting News*, May 23, 1918.

75   "Sunday Bills Up in Three States," *Sporting News*, February 6, 1919; "It's Not Only Baseball in New York, But on Sunday as Well," *Sporting News*, November 14, 1918.

76   "Control of N.Y. Nationals Sold for $1,000,000," *Olean Evening Herald*, January 14, 1919.

77   "What Sabbath Laws Permit," *Kingston Daily Freeman*, February 11, 1919.

78   "Great Drive on March 23, Presbyterians to Raise $38,000,000," *Orange County Times-Press*, March 18, 1919.

79 "Acting Mayor Will Aid Baseball Bill," *New York Times*, March 3, 1919.
80 "Sunday Baseball Strongly Urged," *New York Times*, March 6, 1919.
81 "Baseball Bill Passes," *New York Times*, April 4, 1919; "Sunday Ball Bill Passed,"
New York Times, April 8, 1919; "Ready to Legalize Sunday Ball Here," *New York
Times*, April 9, 1919; "Amending the Penal Law in Relation to Public Sports on
Sunday," State of New York. Public Papers of Governor Alfred E. Smith, (April
19, 1919), 253.
82 "Bar Sunday Double Bills," *New York Times*, April 16, 1919; "Sunday Baseball
One Step Nearer," *New York Times*, April 30, 1919; "Local Clubs Agree on
Sunday Dates," *New York Times*, May 8, 1919.
83 "Advent of Sunday Baseball Draws 60,000 Persons to the Polo Grounds and
Ebbets Field," *New York Times*, May 5, 1919.

6. The Aftermath, 1920–1924

1 "Sunday Ball Has Won in New York," *Sporting News*, April 10, 1919; "Extension
of Referendum Rule," *Kingston Daily Freeman*, April 9, 1919.
2 "Sunday Movie Public Hearing," *Kingston Daily Freeman*, May 5, 1919;
"Opposes Sunday Baseball and Movies," *Kingston Daily Freeman*, May 6, 1919;
"Sunday Ball Left Up in Air by Aldermen," *Kingston Daily Freeman*, May 7,
1919.
3 "To Settle Sunday Ball June 17," *Kingston Daily Freeman*, June 4, 1919.
4 "Sunday Baseball Defeated By Council, Vote 7 to 6," *Kingston Daily Freeman*,
June 18, 1919.
5 "Metzger's Views on Sunday Ball," *Kingston Daily Freeman*, November 1, 1919;
"Ninth Needs Van Valkenburgh," *Kingston Daily Freeman*, October 29, 1919.
6 "Largest Crowd at Sunday Game," *Kingston Daily Freeman*, May 15, 1922. Lisa
Neilson of Marist College kindly supplied me with information about Kingston
baseball.
7 "New Baseball League," *Oneonta Star*, August 5, 1920.
8 Ted Aber and Stella King, *The History of Hamilton County* (Lake Pleasant, NY:
Great Wilderness Books, 1965), 846.
9 "Sunday Ball Wins at Special Election," *New York Times*, May 19, 1920.
10 "Preacher for Sunday Ball," *New York Times*, May 4, 1919.
11 "Assembly Cheers President's Work," *New York Times*, May 18, 1919.
12 "To War on Gambling," *New York Times*, December 19, 1919.
13 "More Ball Park Arrests," *New York Times*, May 28, 1920.
14 "Six More Arrests Made," *New York Times*, May 29, 1920.
15 Eugene C. Murdock, *Ban Johnson Czar of Baseball* (Westport, CT: Greenwood
Press, 1982), 206; "Landis Denies Appeal," *New York Times*, April 3, 1921;
Landis Declares Baker Eligible to Play With Yanks," *New York Times*, April 22,
1921.
16 White, *Creating The National Pastime*, 113; "Landis Declares Kauff Ineligible,"
New York Times, April 8, 1921; "Call Landis Czar Boycotting Kauff," *New York
Times*, December, 31, 1921.
17 Judge Kenesaw Mountain Landis to August Herrmann, April 26, 1921, Landis
file, A. Bartlett Giamatti Library; "Johnson Condemns Baseball Gambling," *New*

York Times, November, 4, 1922; "Landis Receives Report on Pools," *New York Times*, December 21, 1922; "Landis Continues Fight on Gambling," *New York Times*, April 24,1923.

18 J. G. Taylor Spink, *Judge Landis and Twenty-Five Years of Baseball* (New York: Thomas Y. Crowell, 1947), 109–11; Ed Fitzgerald, "Judge Landis, The Man Who Saved Baseball," *Sport* (June 1950): 56–57.

19 "Landis Threatens to Quit Baseball," *New York Times*, December 26, 1923.

20 Seymour, *Baseball: The Golden Age*, 378; "Ban B. Johnson, Baseball Chief is Dead at 65," *New York Herald Tribune*, March 29, 1931.

21 "Two Giant Players are Ruled Out for Bribery," *Lock Haven Express*, October 2, 1924; "O'Connell's Future Rests With Cozy Dolan's Story," *Chester Times*, January 28, 1925; "Landis in Final Cleanup of Fixers Bars O'Connell and Dolan for Life," *New York World Telegram and Sun*, Landis file, A. Bartlett Giamatti Library.

22 "Thirty-four Years in Baseball—The Story of Ban Johnson's Life," Ban Johnson file, A. Bartlett Giamatti Library; Seymour, *Baseball: The Golden Age*, 379.

23 "No Place in Game for Players Who Associate with Gamblers," *Sporting News*, November 18, 1926.

24 "Sunday Observance," *Dunkirk Evening Observer*, December 11, 1920; "Sunday Ball Saved for Capital People," *Sporting News*, March 25, 1926.

25 "Sunday Baseball as Matty Sees It," *New York Times*, February 1, 1920.

26 "Battle for Sunday Observance," *Sunday Grit*, April 16, 1925.

27 "Listening Post of Sportdom," *Syracuse Herald*, December 6, 1920.

28 "Boxing Commission Willing to Resign, Sunday Baseball to Stay," *New York Times*, December 13, 1920.

29 "Carry Sunday Ball Protest to Ebbets," *New York Times*, April 12, 1924.

Epilogue

1 "Sunday Baseball and Movies Win," *Olean Evening Herald*, April 18, 1919.

2 Richard C. Crepeau, *Baseball: America's Diamond Mind, 1919–1941* (Orlando: University Presses of Florida, 1980), 152–53.

Index

About the Author

Dr. Charles DeMotte is an adjunct professor in the Sociology/Anthropology Department at SUNY Cortland. He received his PhD in history from the University of Kansas in 1977. His previous publications include a book, *The Inner Side of History* (Source Publications, 1997), and articles on a variety of subjects, including baseball and American culture. He resides near Ithaca, New York.